THE SCHENLEY EXPERIMENT

THE SCHENLEY EXPERIMENT

A Social History of Pittsburgh's
First Public High School

JAKE ORESICK

The Pennsylvania State University Press
University Park, Pennsylvania

A KEYSTONE BOOK®

Keystone Books are intended to serve the citizens of Pennsylvania. They are accessible, well-researched explorations into the history, culture, society, and environment of the Keystone State as part of the Middle Atlantic region.

Library of Congress Cataloging-in-Publication Data

Names: Oresick, Jake, 1982– , author.
Title: The Schenley experiment : a social history of Pittsburgh's first public high school / Jake Oresick.
Description: University Park, Pennsylvania : The Pennsylvania State University Press, [2017] | "Keystone Books." | Includes bibliographical references and index.
Summary: "Traces the history of Schenley High, Pittsburgh's first public high school. Includes 150 original interviews examining issues of class, race, ethnicity, and collaboration, and how these reflect on the history of education in Pittsburgh"—Provided by publisher.
Identifiers: LCCN 2016053627 | ISBN 9780271078335 (pbk. : alk. paper)
Subjects: LCSH: Schenley High School (Pittsburgh, Pa.)—History.
Classification: LCC LD7501.P6 O74 2017 | DDC 373.74886—dc23
LC record available at https://lccn.loc.gov/2016053627

The Pennsylvania State University Press is a member of the Association of American University Presses.

It is the policy of The Pennsylvania State University Press to use acid-free paper. Publications on uncoated stock satisfy the minimum requirements of American National Standard for Information Sciences—Permanence of Paper for Printed Library Material, ANSI Z39.48–1992.

This book is printed on paper that contains 30% post-consumer waste.

Additional credits: pages ii–iii, photo by Mark Knobil; page vi, photo from *The Journal* (Schenley High School), 1963.

For my parents,
Stephanie and Peter,
and all they stood
in line for.

10-117

10-120

10-204

0-216

Contents

Acknowledgments

The author is indebted to many, especially the more than 350 present and former Pittsburgh Public Schools stakeholders who contributed their stories to this book. Particular thanks is owed to the following individuals, without whose knowledge, counsel, and resourcefulness this book would be far inferior: Susan (Forgrave) Monroe and every educator who participated; James Hill '11; Jim Burwell '65, and the classes of 1964 and 1965; Annette Werner; Mary Ellen Kirby, and the classes of 1987, 1988, and 1989; Ralph Proctor '56; Leon Boykins '03; and Tina Calabro.

Thanks to the Pennsylvania State University Press, for giving us, the Schenley High School community, a clearer and more powerful voice, and a forum to memorialize our collective story. To the Press's capable staff, and to Kathryn Yahner in particular, the author is ever appreciative of your faith in this project, and your editorial wisdom and patience. Recognition is also due to the Jack Buncher Foundation—whose generous grant helped commission or license many illustrations herein—and to the following institutions that provided research support: the Carnegie Library of Pittsburgh's Pennsylvania Department and William R. Oliver Special Collections Room; the Senator John Heinz History Center's Detre Library & Archives; and the Pittsburgh Public Schools's administrative staff and Law Department.

Grateful thanks to the family and friends who supported this project and its author over the last four years. Special appreciation is owed to the following, for their enduring enthusiasm and indulgence: Edith Flom Schneider; Stephanie Flom; Peter, William, David '03, Mandi, Deanna, Anna, Adelyn, and Will Oresick; Nate Gerwig '01; Shawn Robinson; Lauren Byrne Connelly; Grant Berry; Nick Bisceglia; Brad Calhoun; Courtney Zarra; Lauren Bachorski; Christopher Kempf; Molly Delaney; Josh and Amanda Hausman; Elizabeth Ross Radigonda; Carole Beck; and Debbie O'Dell-Seneca. Finally, thanks to Alina Laó Keebler, whose book, *The History and Architecture of the Henry Clay Frick School* (Pittsburgh: Frick ISA, 1996), inspired this one, and to Janine Jelks-Seale '00, whose accidental poetry became this book's working title, and ultimately the title of chapter 2.

Introduction

On a September morning in 1855, Pittsburgh's first public high school opened in a cramped, rat-infested storefront on Smithfield Street. Over the next 156 years, the unusually diverse school served as a social incubator in a largely segregated city, illuminating the raw effects of the Progressive Era, urban renewal, Martin Luther King riots, and court desegregation battles. Pittsburgh Central High School (known as "Central")—recast as Schenley High School in 1916—was at different times the subject of innovative investment and destructive neglect, providing a case study in both the best and worst urban public education practices. *The Schenley Experiment* tells the story of Pittsburgh and its public school district—of class, race, ethnicity, and collaboration—through the prism of its oldest and most dynamic high school.

The school often reflected the regional zeitgeist; its mere creation angered taxpayers, who viewed a high school in an industrial city as a public waste. However, the school also defied stereotypes of Pittsburgh as provincial and prejudiced. Central High was utterly cosmopolitan, offering rigorous, college-caliber instruction and serving as a pipeline to the Ivy League. Admission was exclusive but meritocratic, and black students enrolled at least nine years before the state banned school segregation.

When the Central school building became antiquated, the new Schenley building was designed as a forward-thinking comprehensive school where academic and vocational tracks—previously housed on separate campuses—would "learn to live and to work in happy, effective co-operation."[1] The triangular facility was considered luxurious, prompting a budget backlash when construction costs more than doubled. However, the school was prone to battling for big ideas, and anger ceded to civic pride when the building was completed. As at Central, Schenley's early faculty had collegiate credentials, drawing pupils throughout the county to the "educational palace."[2] In 1930, the majority of students came from distant city neighborhoods and suburbs—areas zoned for other high schools.

Most remarkably, Schenley often outpaced the nation's social progress. The school embraced diversity, bragging about its "cosmopolitan throng"[3] in 1905, and its twenty-five different nationalities a decade later. Indeed, Schenley's locale, in Pittsburgh's Oakland neighborhood, was proximate to numerous ethnic enclaves. Although the majority of students were white until the 1960s, students elected black, Jewish, and female class presidents by 1947. Ten years later, just months before the Little Rock Nine braved a mob, Schenley's senior class board featured black, white, and Chinese American students.

The school was no utopia, however, with instances of discrimination, latent class tensions, and no black teachers for nearly a century. Even into the 1970s, some counselors tried to talk college-track blacks into attending trade school. In the twenty years after *Brown v. Board of Education,* the loss of middle-income housing in Oakland, as well as civil rights unrest in the adjacent Hill District, dramatically reduced white enrollment, from 56 percent to 18 percent. Many middle-class blacks also abandoned Schenley. Soon the District diverted resources away from the shrinking school. Accordingly, the 1970s were marked by an antiacademic culture, with graffiti on walls and marijuana smoke in stairwells. Black leaders demanded that Schenley and other schools be integrated, observing that only schools with white students were adequately resourced. The District implemented forced busing and manipulated many schools' residency boundaries to overcome geographic segregation. Some whites obstructed with legal challenges, boycotts, and violence. Although busing brought balance to many schools, Schenley was not among them. In 1981, the state Human Relations Commission moved to disband the nearly all-black school, then the city's lowest achieving, for noncompliance with a thirteen-year-old desegregation order.

Instead, Schenley rose to become a national model of voluntary integration. The school's inventive reforms—a state-of-the-art teacher training center, a blue-chip faculty, and attractive magnet programs—drew students of all races, some of whom left private schools for Schenley. The experiment won praise from the *New York Times, Los Angeles Times,* and *Newsweek* as well as education trade journals, proving so popular that parents camped out in lines for six days in the winter to secure their children's enrollment. Still, some parents opposed all busing, particularly in working-class white areas, where resistance to magnets curtailed local curricular options. Thus, Schenley's renaissance bred resentment from neighborhood schools' stakeholders, who saw many top students and teachers recruited to Oakland.

Diversity at Schenley peaked in the 1990s, with a cross section of students from throughout the region and through specialized programs for preprofessional ballet students and English as a Second Language

(ESL) immigrants. Beyond mere equality, the school fostered meaningful synthesis across social strata. Laura (Sirbaugh) Ratica '97, a white student from Bloomfield, admitted she entered Schenley with prejudices but quickly built an eclectic social set and became fascinated with new friends' religious traditions. Similarly, G. Ryin Gaines '00, a black Catholic from Homewood, made so many Jewish friends that he "desperately wanted to be Jewish and have a bar mitzvah."

Moreover, the inner-city school was uncommonly successful. Graduates from the International Baccalaureate (IB) program matriculated at elite universities; the storied theater program claimed scores of awards, pulling pupils away from the performing arts high school; and the nationally ranked basketball team won its fifth state championship. Schenley flourished despite increasingly reduced funds, as the District balanced cuts in state aid by slashing site-based budgets and raiding reserves. Still, school board members refused to raise taxes, and despite dire finances and shrinking enrollment, the board actually opened fifteen new schools, mostly in white neighborhoods. These schools appeased a new push to end busing—led by a bevy of white politicians, including the mayor and state legislators—but further compounded the District's budget troubles.

In the early 2000s, the city's first black superintendent, John W. Thompson, began to stabilize finances, but some of his school closings riled board conservatives, who spent the next four years obstructing his agenda. When Thompson was ultimately terminated, black Pittsburghers cried racism, and the board's three black members boycotted the search for a successor. Notably, the new superintendent, Mark Roosevelt—a charismatic descendant of President Theodore Roosevelt—had impressive policy and law credentials but had never worked in education.

In 2005, Roosevelt proposed eighteen more school closings, including Schenley, which, despite thriving, required millions of dollars in asbestos remediation costs. The public fought hard to save Schenley, and the ensuing thirty-month battle dominated the news cycle in a region where school closings were common. Schenley supporters, particularly in the black community, felt "scammed," noting inconsistencies in the District's policy rationale, financial projections, and transparency claims. Roosevelt insisted that closure was unavoidable, but admitted communication failures and that his thin skin left him wounded by personal attacks.

The school shaped thousands of alumni—like Andy Warhol '45, Derrick Bell '48, Bruno Sammartino '55, Clifford Shull '33, Maurice Lucas '71, Vivian Reed '64, and Bob Prince '34—and was a staging ground for history through ties to notable institutions and events. Three different principals were honored at the White House, and math teacher Andy Kerr left

Schenley to become Stanford University's head football coach. Prominent visitors were also in evidence. Eleanor Roosevelt called for a nuclear test ban at a rally in the auditorium, and Jonas Salk promised the anxious PTA a "solution to the polio problem." Muhammad Ali and Jackie Robinson addressed students at Schenley; W. C. Handy and Marian Anderson performed; and Josh Gibson, "the black Babe Ruth," once "turned over the whole cafeteria" in confronting his son's bullies.

While Schenley's age, architecture, and historical footprint are impressive, the school was transformative because of its people. Accordingly, *The Schenley Experiment* represents a human experience, rooted in more than 150 interviews—with alumni of every race and class, aged 19 to 101 years, from dozens of Pittsburgh neighborhoods and five continents—and hundreds of other first-person sources. Their stories form this story, of Pittsburgh and its first public high school, where for more than a century and a half they built a community out of difference.

1 | Origin Story

The People's College and Why Schenley
High Almost Never Happened

Schenley is a lineal descendant of [Central High School]. In
fact, Schenley is Central re-named.
—PERCY B. CALEY, HISTORY TEACHER, 1926–57

Schenley High School opened in 1916, not as an entirely new institution, but as the recasting of Pittsburgh Central—the city's first public high school. Central, founded as an exclusive "People's College," offered college-caliber academic training and sent scores of graduates to elite universities. When the Central school building became obsolete, the new Schenley High School inherited its students, faculty, and traditions, yet this was almost not the case. Central's successor was initially sited for the edge of Squirrel Hill, and for years the school board proceeded with plans for a Magee High School. However, years of litigation, the involvement of two federal agencies, and a four-way trade (which required congressional approval) ensured that a high school would be established in Oakland.

Pittsburgh Central High School

At the dawn of the 1850s, Pittsburgh was not among the eighty US cities with a public high school, despite being the thirteenth most populous.[1] In the winter of 1855, the state legislature passed a law requiring the city's new Central Board of Education to establish high schools. The law stated, "[O]ne for the education of each sex, and one or more for the exclusive education of children of color."[2] Instead, the single, coed Pittsburgh High School—best known as "Central" and often simply called "the High School" in its first three decades—opened to 114 students on September

FIG. 1 The Quigg building on Smithfield Street was Pittsburgh Central High's first home. George Thornton Fleming, *My High School Days: Including a Brief History of the Pittsburgh Central High School from 1855 to 1871 and Addenda* (Pittsburgh: Press of Wm. G. Johnston, 1904).

25, 1855.[3] Black students were initially excluded by state law and relegated to poorly resourced "colored schools."[4]

Located Downtown, Central originally rented ten cramped, poorly ventilated rooms in a building on Smithfield Street near Fifth Avenue. The building—owned by the heirs of a John F. Quigg, who initially let the rooms to the District for $450 per year—sat opposite the post office and custom house. Rats and mice proved distracting, as did the noise from the cobblestone street outside, where horse-drawn wagons hauled iron products.[5] Admission to the school was free but exclusive to the highest-ranking elementary school students who could then pass an entrance exam.[6]

Central was initially unpopular, derided as "a very expensive public humbug" by the *Daily Post*.[7] The working-class public resented funding a "People's College"—where wealthy students studied Greek grammar, uranography, Roman mythology, and Virgil's *Aeneid*—while their own children went to work at age fourteen.[8] Despite this perception, the plurality of first-day students—39.5 percent—were children of laborers, while only 9.6 percent had professional parents. Pittsburgh's first high school students included fifty-seven girls and fifty-seven boys, and ranged from ten to twenty years of age, although more than three-fourths were between thirteen and sixteen years of age.[9]

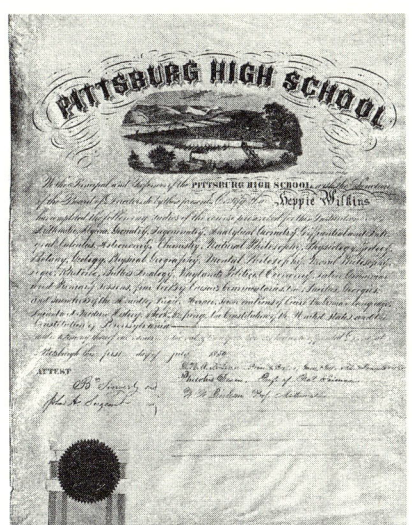

FIG. 2 The first diploma conferred by the District went to Hephzibah "Heppie" Wilkins Hamilton in 1859. George Thornton Fleming, *My High School Days: Including a Brief History of the Pittsburgh Central High School from 1855 to 1871 and Addenda* (Pittsburgh: Press of Wm. G. Johnston, 1904), 168.

Those students admitted did not stay long, in part due to the Panic of 1857 and the subsequent need for teenagers to generate income. Central graduated only three students at its first commencement in 1859, and, in a time when government provided few services, its perceived inefficiency was mocked in the press. The *Daily Pittsburgh Gazette* wrote, "[T]he mountain had labored for four long years at great expense to the city, and produced only three live mice."[10] Hephzibah "Heppie" Wilkins Hamilton '59, a female student, was the city's first graduate—out of deference from her classmates, William C. King '59 and Kuno Kuhn '59.[11] The Civil War seemed not to affect enrollment, although eighty-one Central boys fought for the Union Army. (Of these, nine died, ten were wounded, and one became a prisoner of war.)[12]

In 1868, Central relocated to the nearby Bank of Commerce Building at Wood Street and Sixth Avenue. The new facility was a substantial improvement, with "[l]arger, cleaner rooms" and "[b]etter light and ventilation."[13] The same year, Central broadened its appeal by adding vocational programs. The Commercial Department offered business courses, such as bookkeeping and commercial arithmetic, while the Normal Department trained pupils to teach in elementary schools.[14] Enrollment increased by 20.7 percent, and the building became so crowded that courses had to be staggered into the evening.[15] In 1869, Pittsburgh's recent annexation of six East End municipalities sent a crush of new students to Central, and

FIG. 3 The Bedford Avenue building was the first high school constructed by the District. Pittsburgh Public Schools Photographs, 1880–1982, MSP117.B004.F03.I09, Detre Library & Archives, Sen. John Heinz History Center.

overcrowding worsened.[16] It was not uncommon for two different classes to be conducted simultaneously in the chapel.[17]

Central now required its own building "planned and suited to its wants."[18] Principal Philotus Dean waged "an almost one-man campaign" to construct the facility, and in February 1869, the school board approved construction of the District's first high school.[19] The building was sited at Bedford Avenue and Fulton (later Fullerton) Street, in what is now the Crawford-Roberts section of the Hill District.[20] The school was then so popular that when the cornerstone was laid in September 1869, a parade of 10,000 people marched to the site to hear speeches and music.[21] In 1871, the state-of-the-art building opened to 436 students and boasted fourteen classrooms, a lecture hall with raised seating, a drawing room, a library, a 1,000-seat auditorium, and distinctive twin towers.[22]

Enrollment continued to surge, as shifting economic trends pushed teens out of the workforce and into classrooms.[23] Accordingly, the new building was soon overcrowded, with 572 students in 1877.[24] Normal and Commercial courses were diverted to nearby elementary buildings; the former took over Miller School (formerly for "colored" students) in 1878, and the latter moved in 1892 to rented rooms at Franklin School before finding a permanent home at the new Fifth Avenue High School in 1896.[25] This fractured school model, which segregated students by track—and, in doing so, by class and gender—was common throughout the country.[26] Incidentally, the Commercial Department's "second-class status" was partly fueled by its practice of admitting those who had failed the Academic Department's entrance exam.[27] However, Central seemed to become more accessible over time, as the exam's pass rate climbed from 74.4 percent in 1886 to 86.1 percent in 1906.[28]

Foreshadowing Schenley

Despite its divisions, Central resembled the future Schenley in celebrating its "cosmopolitan throng."[29] From 1876 through 1880, nearly one-third of graduates hailed from Pittsburgh's poorest neighborhoods (now Downtown, Uptown, and the Strip District).[30] "More is learned in a public than in a private school, from emulation," wrote Alice N. Bailey '85, reciting a Samuel Johnson quote that epitomized her high school experience. "There is the collision, of mind with mind, or the radiation of many minds pointing to one center."[31]

Diversity was more economic than racial, but Central's first black graduates—George G. Turfley '76 and James T. Whitson '76, who both became physicians—enrolled nine years before the state abolished school segregation.[32] Jewish students appeared as early as 1866.[33] "I can't remember any particular anti-Semitism," said Julian Hast '11, who attributed this to Central's Jews being from affluent, assimilated, German American families.[34] Female students were also atypically well received. Pauline Marks Frumerman '13, one of the city's first female physicians, recalled two teachers urging her to take the college entrance exams. "They even coached me," Frumerman said, "because high schools then did not prepare [women] for college."[35] Notably, female students could enroll in any of the three tracks—Academic, Commercial, and Normal—whereas males were excluded from the Normal Department.[36]

Central's three curricular tracks were unified by pronounced school spirit. Exuberant songs and yells filled the chapel, which hosted pep rallies and basketball games—including an inter-class contest that devolved into a thirty-minute brawl.[37] During the 1889 football season, the school adopted its colors, "bright red and deep black," which represented Schenley until its 2011 dissolution.[38] A matter-of-fact confidence was evident in the *High School Journal,* a student newspaper and antecedent to

High School Hymn

Joseph Haydn
Lyrics by Blanche A. Jones '88

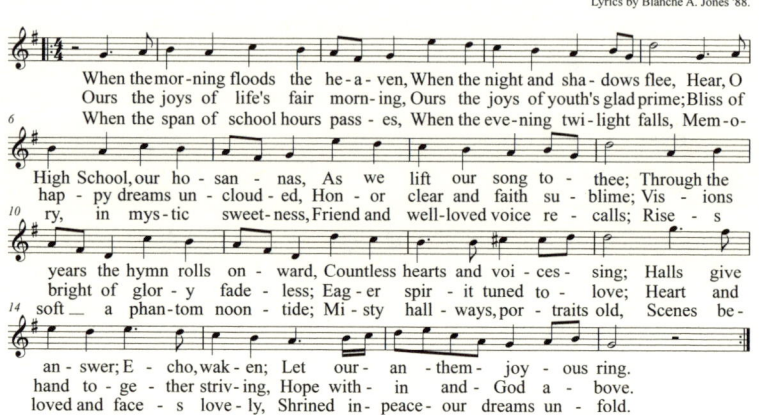

When the mor-ning floods the he-a-ven, When the night and sha-dows flee, Hear, O
Ours the joys of life's fair morn-ing, Ours the joys of youth's glad prime; Bliss of
When the span of school hours pass-es, When the eve-ning twi-light falls, Mem-o-

High School, our ho-san-nas, As we lift our song to thee; Through the
hap-py dreams un-cloud-ed, Hon-or clear and faith su-blime; Vis-ions
ry, in mys-tic sweet-ness, Friend and well-loved voice re-calls; Rise-s

years the hymn rolls on-ward, Countless hearts and voi-ces-sing; Halls give
bright of glor-y fade-less; Eag-er spir-it tuned to love; Heart and
soft_ a phan-tom noon-tide; Mi-sty hall-ways, por-traits old, Scenes be-

an-swer; E-cho, wak-en; Let our-an-them-joy-ous ring.
hand to-ge-ther striv-ing, Hope with-in and-God a-bove.
loved and face-s love-ly, Shrined in-peace-our dreams un-fold.

FIG. 4 Pittsburgh Central High's school song, "High School Hymn," was set to what was then the Austro-Hungarian anthem. Arranged by Leon Boykins.

Schenley's yearbook, which boasted of Central's "exceedingly high rank ... among high schools."[39]

This was not mere braggadocio, as Central—or, at least its Academic Department—remained the region's premier secondary school into the twentieth century. In its first fifty years, the school produced ninety-two attorneys, fifty-two physicians, thirteen clergymen, and six dentists.[40] Graduates matriculated at elite colleges, such as Harvard, MIT, and West Point, and the school booked notable assembly speakers, such as then Princeton University president and future president of the United States, Woodrow Wilson, politician William Jennings Bryan, evangelist Billy Sunday, controversial Harvard president A. Lawrence Lowell, Oregon governor Oswald West, and South Dakota governor Robert S. Vessey.[41] Central's reputation even attracted suburban students, who paid $100 per year in tuition, although some families schemed to evade the fee. "We had a fantastic faculty," said Harvey Thorpe '13, "they were better than the faculty that I had [at the University of Pittsburgh's] engineering school."[42] Not surprisingly, many Central instructors were also college professors, a few of whom were exceptionally accomplished.[43] Willa Cather, a composition teacher, later won the Pulitzer Prize; science teacher J. G. Ogden claimed the world's first brain x-ray in 1896; and Central's first principal— Jacob LaGrange McKown—had been president of a seminary.[44] Teachers'

FIG. 5 Architectural rendering of the proposed Magee High School. *The Builder* 28, no. 11 (March 1911).

salaries ranged from $200 to $1,050 in 1864, $800 to $1,700 in 1888, and $1,000 to $2,300 in 1912.[45]

Replacing Central

By 1895, the Bedford Avenue building was antiquated and overcrowded.[46] The infamous Pittsburgh Survey denounced Central's "unsanitary" and "injurious" facilities, and also noted, "[C]hildren from remoter districts left because they could not afford carfare."[47] The building lacked amenities that even newer elementary schools enjoyed, such as a gymnasium, pool, or cafeteria.[48] The school board was committed to a new Central High facility[49] but spent eighteen years waffling over locales.

A Negley Hill property was procured, but its steep incline was deemed too dangerous for book-toting students to climb in winter weather.[50] After flirting with an east Shadyside plot (now Sacred Heart Parish), the board purchased a site adjacent to Bloomfield's Friendship Park in 1900 (now West Penn Hospital),[51] but construction never commenced. Within three years, the board favored a location in Schenley Park's scholarly corridor, close to the Carnegie Library of Pittsburgh, the Carnegie Museum of Natural History, the Carnegie Art Galleries (now the Carnegie Museum of Art), the Carnegie Technical Schools (now Carnegie Mellon University), and soon, it was predicted, the Western University of Pennsylvania (now the University of Pittsburgh).[52]

Board members toured four Oakland properties, but most preferred a Squirrel Hill tract owned by Christopher Magee, a Common Pleas Court judge and cousin of Christopher Lyman Magee Jr., the city's late political boss.[53] The Magee site was well situated—on Forbes Street (now Avenue) between Craig Street and Morewood Avenue (now home to Carnegie Mellon's Hamburg Hall)—but the deal met fierce resistance and accusations of graft.[54] After nineteen months of contentious debate, the board voted 24–14 to acquire the plot in June 1905.[55] Plans for a Magee High School, alternatively known as the Schenley District or Schenley Park High School, began to take shape, with Frederick J. Osterling designing a stately, 190-by-254-foot Tudor-Gothic building.[56] However, ground was never broken, as a dysfunctional District bureaucracy and years of litigation delayed construction through 1911.[57]

The Bureau of Mines

In 1912, the US Bureau of Mines sought the Magee property for its proximity to Oakland's research resources. The federal agency had been operating out of the former Allegheny Arsenal property in Lawrenceville, which it offered to the District in exchange for Magee. When the school board rejected the trade, the Bureau threatened to leave Pittsburgh. The city council feared the Bureau's exit and offered the District additional property. To complicate matters, the Bureau did not own the Arsenal property and was a tenant of the US Department of War.[58]

After months of wrangling, the following proposal emerged:

- The Board of Education would convey the Magee property to the Bureau of Mines;
- The Department of War would convey the Arsenal property to the city of Pittsburgh; and
- The city of Pittsburgh would convey part of the Arsenal property, the entire Bedford Avenue Basin, and $218,774.50 to the Board of Education.[59]

The deal seemed inevitable, in light of pressure to keep the Bureau's federal dollars in Pittsburgh. Moreover, the new superintendent—Sylvanus L. Heeter—and several board members now favored the nearby Schenley Farms section of Oakland, approximately one-half mile northwest of Magee.[60] Primarily farmland in 1905, Schenley Farms had quickly become the city's most fashionable area, where a high-end "residential enclave" abutted "monumental civil institutions" (St. Paul Cathedral, Soldiers and Sailors Memorial Hall, Masonic Temple—now Pitt's Alumni Hall, the Pittsburgh Athletic Association, and the Concordia Club—now Pitt's O'Hara Student Center).[61]

In January 1913, a divided board consented to the convoluted swap, which was formally closed nine months later—with congressional approval and the president's signature. On October 14, 1913, the board acquired a tract at Centre Avenue and Grant (now Bigelow) Boulevard for a school building in Schenley Farms. Schenley High School was happening.[62]

2 | These Three Walls

The Comprehensive High School, Edward Stotz, and
the Fight to Make Schenley Extraordinary

The Schenley building's stateliness was largely a result of good timing, as
its conception coincided with a trend toward comprehensive high schools.
The movement aimed to integrate academic and vocational students
through common courses and activities, and thus required a single, comprehensive building to replace two or three specialized facilities. Architect
Edward Stotz was commissioned to make Schenley the District's first comprehensive facility, but his modern designs more than doubled the cost,
prompting anger and calls for austerity. The board persisted with plans for
an exceptional structure, and after three years of plans, budget debates,
and labor disputes, its critics marveled at the million-dollar high school.

The Comprehensive High School

Prior to the 1910s, most American school districts segregated students
by track, which entailed housing academic and vocational departments
in separate buildings.[1] As students often attended the most proximate
school, irrespective of its curricular focus, many were locked into programs ill-suited for their aptitudes and interests. Such pupils were more
likely to drop out than transfer, with those who did graduate stratified by
class.[2]

Reformers called for the comprehensive high school, with multiple
tracks in a single building. This integrated model allowed for sampling of
courses outside a student's department and convenient transfer between
programs. Moreover, this unified model engendered socialization, with
students mixing freely in corridors, elective courses, the lunchroom, and
assemblies.[3]

Meaningful bonds formed through common causes, such as school
clubs and athletics, were especially appealing to the National Education
Association's Commission on the Reorganization of Secondary Education.

The commission stated, "[P]upils in comprehensive schools have contacts valuable to them vocationally, since people in every vocation must be able to deal intelligently with those in other vocations, and employers and employees must be able to understand one another and recognize common interests. . . . Through friendships formed with pupils pursuing other curriculums and having vocational and educational goals widely different from their own, the pupils realize that the interests which they hold in common with others are, after all, far more important than the differences that would tend to make them antagonistic to others."[4]

Superintendent Sylvanus L. Heeter agreed and believed comprehensive schools would improve education and decrease truancy. In May 1912, Heeter called for the creation of such schools in seven neighborhoods, saying, "[A] big central high school in a city is just as inconsistent as a great central bathroom."[5] Although the District converted Fifth Avenue and Peabody High Schools into comprehensive schools—adding academic courses to the former and vocational courses to the latter—neither building had been designed for such a purpose.[6] Fifth Avenue High lacked an auditorium, library, gymnasium, and swimming pool—the very facilities that would foster interdepartmental socialization.[7] Thus, Heeter insisted that the new Schenley High should be the District's first comprehensive facility.[8]

Stotz Breaks the Mold, and the Bank

Edward Stotz, the city's most experienced school architect, was charged with Schenley's design. On February 16, 1914, Stotz unveiled his vision of a massive, triangular structure that utterly decimated the traditional school model. Stotz anticipated every conceivable need, curricular and otherwise, in what newspapers called "the last word" in American high school facilities.[9]

While Stotz's conception of Schenley was met with awe, many were concerned with its extraordinary cost. The *Pittsburgh Press* lambasted the District's "wasteful extravagance and insolent arrogance," as the original $600,000 price tag climbed to $1,430,014.72 ($31,241,492.23 in 2016).[10] Despite popular myth, Schenley was not the nation's first million-dollar high school. In 1902, Philadelphia Central High dedicated a $1,587,043.16 campus, and in 1915, Pittsburgh superintendent William M. Davidson referenced another million-dollar school—Jersey City's Dickinson High—when defending Schenley's cost.[11] It took twenty-six years to pay off the building's bonds, but the expense belied its efficiency. Schenley cost only 19.5 cents per cubic foot, whereas construction bids for Westinghouse, the

What's in a Namesake?
Mary Schenley

On January 5, 1914, Schenley High
School was formally named. The handle
was a geographic reference—shortened
from Bellefield-Schenley Farms, as the
neighborhood was then known—and
tied the school to Pittsburgh's burgeoning civic district. The name derives from
Mary (Croghan) Schenley (1827–1903),
whose family had long owned the land.
Mary was born wealthy, as heiress
to the extraordinary landholdings of
her grandfather, James O'Hara. At
age fourteen, she made international
headlines by eloping from her Staten
Island boarding school with Edward
Wyndham Harrington Schenley, a forty-
two-year-old British army captain. Both
Schenleys were abolitionists and braved
persecution in Dutch Suriname, where
the captain, then a diplomat, helped
emancipate thirty-four slaves. He was
"the 2nd 'great man' Washington,"
gushed Mary of her husband, who later
sought to fight in the Union's Civil War
effort, despite being sixty-one years old
and a British citizen.

Mary moved to her husband's native
England, but she owned considerable
land in Pittsburgh, where she was
"reviled" as a "heartless aristocrat."
She hoarded undeveloped land as
the region's population exploded,

FIG. 6   Portrait of a young Mary (Croghan)
Schenley by Thomas Lewis. Courtesy of the
Sen. John Heinz History Center, 86.1.167.
Photo: Liz Simpson.

leasing only tenement properties under
oppressive terms. Thus, critics accused
her estate of stunting development and
exploiting the poor. In 1889, Mary began
a historic giving spree that included
300 acres for Schenley Park, as well as
plots for the School for Blind Children
and West Penn Hospital. Despite her
largesse, Mary remained unpopular
with most Pittsburghers, who regarded
her estate as a "parasite." The modern
myth of Mary's popularity is likely a
symptom of forgetfulness, as newspapers have scarcely mentioned her estate
practices since the 1930s.[12]

FIG. 7 Schenley High under construction. *Journal*, June 1930, 8.

District's next new high school building, had to be advertised four times before the cost fell to 43.74 cents per cubic foot.[13]

Board member William Loeffler was a critic of Schenley spending. On September 22, 1914, Loeffler supplemented his dissent on an appropriations vote with a pointed diatribe: "It is an injustice to the taxpayers and an injustice to other sections of the city that are clamorous for additional educational facilities. The Schenley High School is located in a district where I have lived for 35 years and naturally I would welcome a magnificent educational palace in our midst. The people demand efficiency in the schools and desire good practical education, but they do not desire pomp and luxury at the expense of the taxpayers."[14]

Loeffler was routinely outvoted, but he personified a popular anger with the costly expansion of government services. While the public accepted the necessity of school supplies, there was backlash over nontraditional expenditures, such as $76,000 for Schenley's athletic field.[15] This frustration was compounded by expensive labor disputes, which caused construction to take three years.[16]

Looking Like a Million Bucks

Stotz's vision unfolded beautifully. The finished structure was utterly imposing, shooting seventy feet high over four uneven acres, with 250-foot sides and the northwest face forming its 468-foot isosceles base. The

FIG. 8 Facing south into Oakland from the Upper Hill District's Schenley Heights section. *Journal*, December 1916, 14.

facade's handsome plainness, punctuated only with a projecting, columned entrance, required 55,000 cubic feet of Indiana limestone.[17] Built with concrete and steel by the famous Thompson-Starrett Company, the fireproof school was constructed atop 1,700 concrete stilts to correct for unusually soft earth.[18] Schenley has been described as neoclassical "in demeanor and detail," with progressive features allowing for continuous corridors, natural light, and fresh air.[19] The interior boasted marble stairs, oak moldings, and fifteen-foot classroom ceilings, while the corridors, initially lined with famous art reproductions, were finished with terrazzo floors.[20]

Stotz's triumph was both aesthetic and utilitarian, merging curricular innovation with what were then impossibly modern luxuries. Engineers raved about the internal coal-fired power plant, which heated the school while fueling state-of-the-art machinery in the metal- and wood-working departments.[21] Schenley also had a bevy of electric appliances in the nation's "most complete" lunch department, as well as ovens for training "future housewives."[22]

Other novel amenities included a 1,600-seat auditorium with a balcony; two gender-specific gymnasia; the District's second-largest swimming pool, equipped with thirty-five showers; the region's most comprehensive school library, operated as a branch of the Carnegie Library of

FIG. 9   Schenley's then-state-of-the-art kitchen appliances, November 1916. Pittsburgh Public Schools Photographs, 1880–1982, MSP117.B006.F05.I02, Detre Library & Archives, Sen. John Heinz History Center.

FIG. 10   A physical education class in the boys' gymnasium, fall 1916. *Journal*, December 1916, 41.

Pittsburgh; a greenhouse; a 120-seat amphitheater with a grand piano and phonograph; and eleven science labs, equipped with hot and cold water, gas, steam, compressed air, and vacuums. Schenley also featured forty traditional classrooms, eleven shop rooms, seven home economics (then called "domestic science") rooms, and four crafts rooms. The million-dollar building was rife with utilities, including a large fountain aquarium, a master clock that controlled twenty-seven secondary clocks throughout the building, and 2,000 lockers—for increased security over cloakrooms.[23]

Accordingly, upon Schenley's completion in September 1916, cost concerns were eclipsed by civic pride. The building was ranked among "the finest high schools in the world" by the *American School Board Journal* and profiled in a number of national architectural trade journals. A full-page ad for back-to-school clothing called Schenley the "Pride of Pittsburgh."[24] The building was an "eloquent symbol" of the "city's progress," opined the *Pittsburgh Post*; the *Gazette Times* raved about its size and modernity; and the fickle *Press* compared its science equipment to that of the country's great universities.[25] Weeks before the school opened, citizens were so eager to inspect its facilities that the District promised public tours, and many in the city drew a circle around Schenley's first day.[26]

3

Enter to Learn

1916–1929

[T]hrough the happy and effective working together of us
all, for the common good, the life and comradeship of our
school will be helpful and wholesome and delightful. Our
school motto well expresses the directive aims of our school
life: "Enter to Learn, Go Forth to Serve."
—PRINCIPAL JAMES NOBLE RULE

Schenley opened in 1916, and its first years were marked by a robust academic culture. This reputation kept the school flush with students from throughout the region, whose diversity tested the principal's aim of "ensuring functional equality."[1] Students united over Schenley's frequent achievements, which quickly cultivated a shared exceptionalist identity.

People's College Redux

The demise of Central High initiated a move toward accessible secondary education. The District abolished its entrance exam and made Schenley the first of seven new high schools built in an eleven-year span.[2] These neighborhood schools were ostensibly equal, but Schenley was unusually popular. On Monday, October 2, 1916, when the building finally opened—a polio outbreak postponed the start of the school year for several weeks—a whopping 1,800 pupils appeared. Enrollment was nearly 10 percent higher than anticipated and so overwhelmed staff that lessons were delayed until the next day.[3] The modern building was part of the attraction for many, but Schenley's elite faculty, inherited from Central, was its primary draw.[4]

Many "professors," as they were then known, had advanced degrees from prestigious universities as well as collegiate teaching experience. According to Milton Susman '24, "The [Central] faculty, most of whom were offered college positions—which they turned down because they

MAP 1 Pittsburgh Public High Schools, 1929. Map by Lisa Christopher, using basemaps from the City of Pittsburgh.

didn't want to lose their tenure, and they could, in those days, make a better dollar in high school than they could in college—all came out to Schenley High School. And it had one of the finest faculties in the country."

Top instructors had been clustered at Central because of its status as the District's flagship high school.[5] However, when Central closed, its faculty was not dispersed among the new neighborhood high schools but was transplanted intact to Schenley.[6] Graduates thrived: in 1917, 7 percent of Harvard's high honor roll was from Schenley or Central. "I wish there were more schools like [Schenley]," wrote Frederick W. Burlingham, president of the Associated Harvard Clubs.[7]

Accordingly, enrollment swelled. Schenley was the District's largest high school for much of the 1920s, with 2,809 pupils in 1922.[8] The school drew students from throughout the region, making it an unintentional magnet school a half century before that concept existed. In 1927, its principal wrote that of all the District high schools, Schenley was "in the least sense" a neighborhood school.[9] More than 48 percent of 1929 graduates lived beyond adjacent neighborhoods, including 3 percent who traveled

TABLE 1 Pittsburgh Public High Schools, 1929

	School	Opened	Location	Format
A	Allegheny	1883	810 Arch St., Allegheny Center	Neighborhood comprehensive
B	Fifth Avenue	1896	1800 Fifth Ave., Uptown	Neighborhood comprehensive
C	South	1898	S. 10th & E. Carson Sts., South Side Flats	Neighborhood comprehensive
D	Peabody	1911	E. Liberty Blvd. & N. Beatty St., East Liberty	Neighborhood comprehensive
E	Ralston	1912	15th St. & Penn Ave., Strip District	Boys' vocational
F	Westinghouse	1912	N. Murtland & Monticello Sts., Homewood	Neighborhood comprehensive
G	Business	1916	1277–1433 Bedford Ave., Crawford-Roberts	Short course business
H	Schenley	1916	4101 Bigelow Blvd., Oakland	Neighborhood comprehensive
I	South Hills	1917	125 Ruth St., Mount Washington	Neighborhood comprehensive
J	Langley	1923	2940 Sheraden Blvd., Sheraden	Neighborhood comprehensive
K	Perry	1923	3875 Perrysville Ave., Perry North	Neighborhood comprehensive
L	Allegheny Vocational	1924	N. Lincoln & Galveston Aves., Allegheny West	Boys' vocational
M	Carrick	1924	125 Parkfield St., Carrick	Neighborhood comprehensive
N	Oliver	1925	2323 Brighton Rd., Marshall-Shadeland	Neighborhood comprehensive
O	Irwin Ave. Girls' Vocational	1926	Brighton Rd. & Wright Way, Perry South	Girls' vocational
P	Allderdice	1927	Shady & Forward Aves., Squirrel Hill	Neighborhood comprehensive
Q	Bellefield Girls' Vocational	1928	Fifth Ave. & Bouquet St., Oakland	Girls' vocational

Source: William D. McCoy, *History of Pittsburgh Public Schools to 1942* (Pittsburgh, 1959), 1:230–37, 239–40, and G. M. Hopkins maps at http://peoplemaps.esri.com/pittsburgh/.

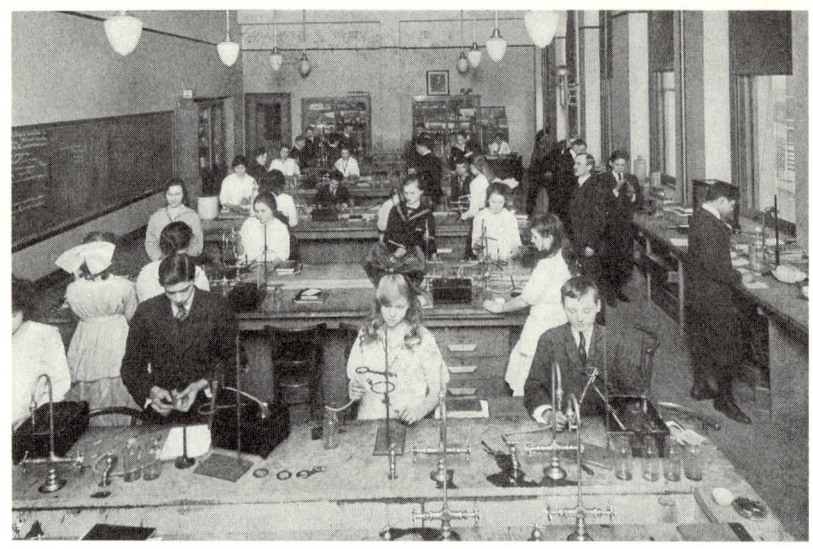

FIG. 11 Students working in one of the building's eleven science labs, fall 1916. *Journal,* December 1916, 28.

from suburbs such as Bridgeville, Mt. Lebanon, and Forest Hills.[10] Noncity residents paid $12 tuition per month in 1920, while those city residents equidistant from two District schools could seemingly attend either.[11] However, it is unclear how many students who were firmly in other schools' feeder patterns ended up at Schenley.

Susman was zoned for Peabody High but went through "a lot of red tape" to attend Schenley for its exceptional teachers, such as Elmer Kenyon. A Harvard-educated drama expert, Kenyon taught at St. Viator College before returning to Pittsburgh, where his father ran two prominent theaters. "Being of a very wealthy family, he needed to teach as you need another ear," quipped Susman, "but he loved teaching."[12] Nancy Newman Frank '27 remembered Kenyon as a "superlative" English teacher who taught her more about *Macbeth* than "any courses at [Carnegie Tech]."[13] Appropriately, Kenyon later headed Tech's drama department.[14]

Another teacher, Paul Dysart, was unique in having a doctorate, and according to Alexander Jackson '22, was "one of the outstanding teachers of the era."[15] Jackson went on to Cornell, where his physics courses lagged behind Dysart's high school curriculum. Schenley was an "absolutely superb school," with "marvelous teachers," Jackson raved.[16] Sara Soffel (Latin) became a trailblazing attorney, and, ultimately, Pennsylvania's first female judge.[17] Fred L. Homer (English) obtained a Harvard master's degree, edited Milton's *Shorter Poems*, and authored *Some Common Birds and Wild Flowers*.[18] Ruth Townley (math) and Emma Campbell (English) taught at what is now Chatham University, and Victor M. Rupert (commercial) published *The Drift of Wild Roses*, a collection of 235 original poems.[19]

Myrtle (Marcus) Fisher '24 lived much closer to Fifth Avenue High, but her mother felt Schenley was superior. In an interview in 1975, Fisher still marveled at her "outstanding" classmates.[20] Frank concurred, noting that although her era preceded enrichment programs, Schenley courses "naturally enriched themselves because of the high standard of teaching and the high caliber of students."[21]

The Meaning of the Motto

On Schenley's opening day, after registration, Principal James Noble Rule greeted students in the auditorium. After the singing of "America" and religious exercises, he shared the school's motto, "Enter to Learn, Go Forth to Serve," which was etched into the wall above the stage.[22] Rule's interpretation of the phrase—that one enters to learn to work and live for the common good, and goes forth to serve one's community and state— reflected his belief in the comprehensive school.[23] According to Rule, high schools should prepare pupils for college and industry but even more so for life in a democracy. He wanted Schenley to eschew social and curricular barriers, to be "pragmatic rather than dogmatic," and "democratic rather than aristocratic."[24]

Rule came from Central with most of Schenley's seventy teachers and was thrilled that his new school housed both academic and vocational courses. In 1919, a national trade journal explained the principal's pedagogy: "[Rule] says that a student is often guided in his choice of vocation by the fact that a commercial or a Latin high school is near his residence. He believes that the average student is not prepared for any sort of specialization until his senior year, and prior to this time should be getting a general broadening course of instruction."[25] The administration was adamant that curricular tracks be regarded equally and required every student to take one year of a vocational course.[26]

Twenty-Five Nationalities

The principal's egalitarian bend was appropriate, as the school's proximity to ethnic sections in Oakland and the Hill District engendered historic diversity. Schenley teemed with immigrants and first-generation Americans. Russian, Polish, Hungarian, and German students were the most

The Hill District: Crossroads of the World

The Hill District was Schenley's most prominent feeder neighborhood and often dictated the school's demography and character. Settled around 1800, the area had diverse ethnic enclaves by midcentury, with German, Irish, Scotch-Irish, and black residents. Arthursville, later known as Little Hayti—an upscale, racially mixed section near what is now Roberts Street—had 110 black families in 1830 and was a station on the Underground Railroad.

Between the 1860s and the 1880s, Eastern European Jews flooded the Lower Hill District—roughly bounded by Dinwiddie and Devilliers Streets, Fifth Avenue, what was then Tunnel Street, and the hill's northern cliff—where the foreign-born Jewish population jumped to 94 percent.

Italians, Greeks, and Syrians followed, carving their own Lower Hill colonies. When Schenley opened in 1916, the Hill was an eclectic hive of humanity—more densely populated than present-day New York City—with immigrants from at least a dozen nations.

During World War I, Southern black migrants crowded into Little Hayti. In less than two decades, Wylie Avenue at Fullerton Street was a black cultural axis. The era's jazz greats, including Duke Ellington and Louis Armstrong, played the Crawford Grill until sunrise, the Roosevelt Theater screened rare "Negro pictures," and Earl Hines and Billy Eckstine rocked Savoy Ballroom swing dances. The Hill was home to the storied Pittsburgh Crawfords baseball club—whose owner, Gus Greenlee,

FIG. 12 William "Woogie" Harris plays piano at the Crawford Grill No. 1. Teenie Harris Photograph Collection, 1920–1970, 2001.35.2499, Carnegie Museum of Art. Photo: Teenie Harris. Teenie Harris Archive / Carnegie Museum of Art / Getty Images.

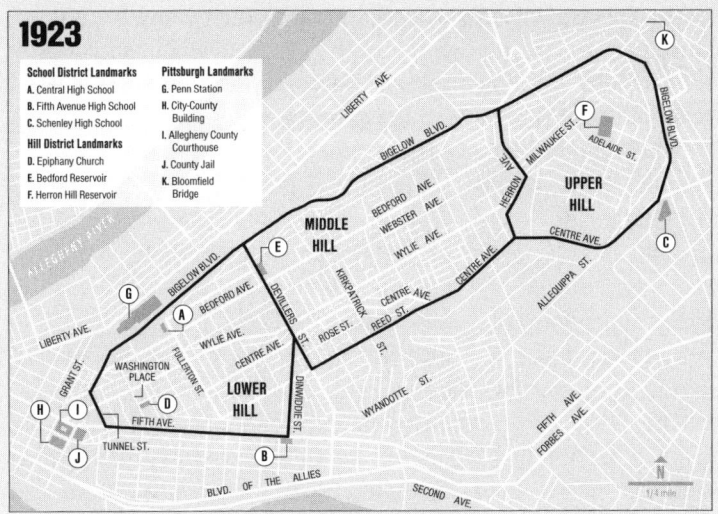

1923

School District Landmarks
A. Central High School
B. Fifth Avenue High School
C. Schenley High School

Hill District Landmarks
D. Epiphany Church
E. Bedford Reservoir
F. Herron Hill Reservoir

Pittsburgh Landmarks
G. Penn Station
H. City-County Building
I. Allegheny County Courthouse
J. County Jail
K. Bloomfield Bridge

MIDDLE HILL

UPPER HILL

LOWER HILL

MAP 2 The Hill District, 1923. Map by James Hilston, using basemaps from http://peoplemaps.esri.com.

had built the first black-owned Negro leagues ballpark—as well as burgeoning black artists, such as Lena Horne, August Wilson, and Teenie Harris. Pittsburgh's Little Harlem was the "Crossroads of the World," according to Harlem Renaissance poet Claude McKay, with its rare convergence of race and class.

This social mixing was remarkable, not only given Jim Crow policies in other neighborhoods, but also because financially stable residents—both black and white—had by then moved away from the Lower Hill but were willing to travel in order to patronize its nightlife. Despite the area's charms, poverty was endemic, prostitution was open and "without restraint," gambling was prominent, and even during Prohibition, 178 speakeasies operated freely with police protection. By 1930, the Hill District at large was 53 percent black, up from 25 percent in 1910.

Notably, many Jews and middle-class blacks moved only a few miles uphill, joining Irish and Scotch-Irish neighbors in the Upper Hill District, then known as Herron Hill. The Upper Hill, bounded by Bigelow Boulevard and Herron and Centre Avenues, offered scenic, high-altitude views, a high rate of home ownership, and little commerce. Like Harlem's Sugar Hill section, the Upper Hill became an "oasis of privilege for the black middle class," earning the nickname "Sugar Top."

Thus, the advent of Schenley split the Hill in half—with the Upper Hill zoned for Schenley and the Lower Hill for Fifth Avenue High—and added a tinge of class conflict to the schools' cross-neighborhood rivalry.[27]

populous, with Scotch, Greek, and Syrian rounding out twenty-five nationalities.[28] Jews initially had a pronounced presence, with an estimated 25
percent of Schenley's enrollment, despite representing only 6.7 percent of
the city's population.[29] Blacks were few, but those who did enter Schenley were bright and determined. "[E]very single one of them graduated,"
recalled Pauline (Savill) Wachs '21.[30] The school building itself was a shared
home base; ethnic clubs staged evening events, such as a Marian Anderson concert and Jewish holiday plays.[31] Already a multiethnic conflation,
Schenley soon welcomed blind students, who left the adjacent School for
the Blind to "mingle more constantly with sighted boys and girls."[32]

Students were also economically diverse, coming from a relative balance of middle- (50 percent) and working-class (42 percent) families.[33]
However, Schenley certainly attracted families of financial means. From
1916 to 1920, when obtaining higher education indicated wealth nearly as
much as aptitude, 52 percent of Schenley graduates went on to college—20
percent above the national average.[34] Moreover, the aforementioned
black and Jewish pupils were more likely to be upwardly mobile than
their counterparts elsewhere, as many lived in the middle-class Upper
Hill District.[35]

Democratic Experiment

Principal Rule's experiment may have mitigated prejudice, but most students still "thought, acted, and voted" in a sectarian manner.[36] Ethnic
slurs were likely common at Schenley, given a 1920 editorial in the *Triangle* discouraging epithets like "Dago," "Dutch," and "Wop."[37] All student
government presidents were white, Anglo-Saxon males, except for three
Jewish boys and Mildred West '23—the only female president until 1947.[38]
The principal denied that race engendered "any serious problems." Yet
despite relative civility among students, racism was systemic in the District, which had refused to hire black teachers since at least the 1880s.[39]

Biases notwithstanding, Schenley seemed to embrace those who
brought honor to its brand. In 1924, the overwhelmingly white school
organized a cheering section and "yelled itself hoarse" for William S. Randolph '25, a black student who trounced all-white fields at the city and
county oratorical competitions.[40] In 1917, the black community praised
Schenley's "broad American spirit" when Gerald Allen '17 was unani-
mously elected track team captain. The *Pittsburgh Press*'s "Afro-American
Notes" column declared Allen was the only logical choice but added that
he would have faced discrimination "in a majority of similar instances
elsewhere."[41] Moreover, Joseph "Ziggy" Kahn '17—the son of Finnish Jews

who grew up fighting anti-Semites in the Lower Hill District—was revered for his heroics in the WPIAL basketball championship series.[42]

Students' zeal for their new school often trumped factionalism—and this was by design. Rule emphasized a unified identity, as Schenley's first students were redirected from three schools—Fifth Avenue and Peabody, in addition to the majority from Central. The principal even organized a "Meet My Friend" campaign to dilute neighborhood cliques.[43]

Spirit of Exceptionalism

Schenley quickly established an uncommon esprit de corps, which was conspicuous to outsiders and inspirational to James Reed '25, who shared, "A little while after the average freshman enters Schenley, he is aware of a new feeling, which pervades the atmosphere of the place, something which makes him extremely proud to be one of the Schenleyites. He realizes that he belongs to Schenley's family, and begins to desire to perform some outstanding work."[44] Similarly, an early article in the *Journal* referenced a prevailing "premonition that our school is destined to become great."[45] This burgeoning tribalism was partly imported from Central, but also resulted from frequent shared successes.

In concert with traditional achievements—the first four graduating classes attended college at nearly twice the national rate, and seven different athletic teams won multiple Pittsburgh City League titles—a series of unorthodox accolades fostered a spirit of exceptionalism:[46]

- Visitors came from Japan, Wales, and North Carolina, as did the state superintendent from Harrisburg, who heaped praise on Schenley's facilities and innovative pedagogy.[47]
- Prominent speakers graced the auditorium, including muckraker Lincoln Steffens, suffragette Anna Howard Shaw, US senator Simeon D. Fess, comedian Sir Harry Lauder, and former US congressman and Indiana governor J. Frank Hanly.[48]
- School librarian Clara E. Howard was recognized as a national expert and lectured at universities and trade conferences.[49]
- Students performed concerts and gave speeches at the nearby KDKA station,[50] less than two years after the launch of commercial radio.
- Popular math teacher Andy Kerr helped the University of Pittsburgh win three national football titles as assistant coach and in 1922, left Schenley to become head football coach at Stanford University.[51]
- Harry Glancy won a gold medal in swimming at the 1924 Olympics, just one year after competing for Schenley.[52]

FIG. 13   The 1920–21 girls' basketball team. *Journal*, June 1921, 96.

FIG. 14   The 1922–23 football team. *Journal*, January 1923, 82.

Schenley also had White House connections. Two principals—Rule, who had by then been promoted, and his successor, Edward Sauvain— attended President Warren G. Harding's 1921 inauguration.[53] When former President Theodore Roosevelt passed away in 1919, the June graduates offered condolences to his widow, Edith, whose grateful reply was printed in the *Triangle*.[54]

World War I

After the United States declared war on Germany on April 6, 1917, at least fifty-seven current students and teachers went forth to serve with nearly 400 Central alumni.[55] Less than a year after coaching the basketball team to the WPIAL crown, Merle C. Knapp was on the front lines. "Remember me to the Schenley High family," he wrote to the *Journal*.[56]

Those students remaining were also active. Rule organized a 1,625-student Junior Red Cross chapter, the student government sold $10,000 in liberty bonds, and the library collected more than 34,000 magazines and books for soldiers. Even facilities contributed: shop rooms were made available six days a week to train seventy soldiers in sheet metal work, and the baseball field was sacrificed, along with the team's season, for a victory garden. Students saluted the flag when entering and leaving classrooms, and the *Journal* became a bastion of patriotism, filled with essays, poems, and letters from soldiers.[57]

FIG. 15 A tribute in the *Journal* to "Schenley Boys" serving in the war. *Journal*, January 1918, 73.

A Matter of Principals

Principal Rule was educated at Washington & Jefferson College and the University of Wisconsin, and he had been a high school principal since age twenty-three.[58] Rule orchestrated much of Schenley's exemplary war service, and in 1919, an appreciative Junior Red Cross tapped him as national director.[59] He later became Pennsylvania's state superintendent and was credited with keeping schools open at the height of the Great Depression.[60] Rule's successor as principal, Edward Sauvain—who had replaced Willa Cather as a teacher at Central in 1903—would lead Schenley through rapid growth and demographic change.[61]

4 Growing Pains
1930–1949

As the 1930s began, the exceptional faculty continued to draw pupils from distant city wards and suburbs. This phenomenon would wane, however, as the Great Depression, World War II, and shifting neighborhood demographics drastically recast the student body. By the 1940s, the school was largely constituted by working-class white ethnic families. However, the growing black population got along relatively well, as, outside of Schenley, discrimination was still common in employment, housing, and public accommodations. Achievement and morale remained high, but classrooms were increasingly overcrowded and underfunded, prompting several top teachers to retire.

The 1930s

The Great Depression affected everyone, even in the middle-class Upper Hill District, where Jewish unemployment hit 15.4 percent.[1] "Everybody was poor," recalled Bill McQuillan '33. "Everybody had to wear old clothes to school."[2] Budget cuts forced the District to scale back activities, although many students, like Walter Dassdorf '32, had no time for extracurricular entreprises.[3] "We were mostly concerned about the Depression," he said, "food lines, people sleeping under bridges." Dassdorf worked before and after school in a number of jobs, including construction, selling and delivering newspapers, parking cars at Pitt Stadium, and as an usher at Forbes Field. He even hustled his teachers, convincing the music director to pay him to arrange chairs for band practice.[4]

Schenley became crowded in the 1930s. Enrollment swelled from 2,182 in 1931 to 2,822 in 1936, with more than half of graduates living in distant city neighborhoods or suburbs.[5] Although Hill District Jews were rapidly migrating to Squirrel Hill, many initially eschewed nearby Allderdice High, which opened in 1927, and made the long commute to Schenley.[6] This was partly due to Schenley's strong reputation, but also because many students—especially those whose families moved in the midst of their high school years—were unwilling to leave their friends.[7] In June 1930, Squirrel Hill contributed 34 percent of Schenley graduates—including some who could see Allderdice from their bedrooms—compared with 18.3 percent from the Hill District and 17.6 percent from Oakland.[8]

Magnetic Faculty

The remarkable faculty was still magnetic, attracting Point Breeze's six Townsend children, who described selecting their high school in a letter to the *Triangle*. They wrote, "After consultation with neighbors, friends and teachers, Schenley was chosen over its two rivals, Peabody and Westinghouse. One of the most important reasons for the decision was the fine traditions which Edward Sauvain, as principal, had carried over from 'Old Central.'"[9] Similarly, Clifford Shull '33 endured a "troublesome" forty-five-minute streetcar ride from Glenwood (now Hays) but said choosing Schenley changed his life. Shull was so inspired by Paul Dysart's courses that he shifted his focus from aeronautical engineering to physics, in which he won the 1994 Nobel Prize.[10]

Faculty member Loretta Byrne was revered in her thirty-seven years at Schenley, teaching English, journalism, and "life—mainly by example."[11] She also supervised the *Journal* and the *Triangle* for ten years each.[12] The "superb" Miss Byrne "knew more about Medieval literature than any college professor I ever had," gushed Albert W. Bloom '36.[13] Byrne even helped Bloom become a journalist, when the devout Catholic called in a favor at the diocese. "I was the first Jewish boy from Pittsburgh who went to Columbia . . . with a recommendation from the Catholic bishop," Bloom said.[14] After retiring from Schenley in 1955, Byrne became a dean at Duquesne University.[15]

Other top teachers included J. Russell Clements—with degrees from Westminster, Columbia, and the University of Pittsburgh—who oversaw the makeup team for Schenley's class plays and moonlighted as a bee-keeper, and the charismatic Vaclav C. Veverka, whose biology course inspired Samuel E. Tisherman '47 to become a physician.[16]

This talented teaching corps paid dividends, as student achievement remained high. Ivan Getting '29 and Milton Dobrin '32 won national science scholarships to MIT, and the chess team won six regional titles in eight seasons, including four in a row, with captain David Foner '39 playing blindfolded to enhance his concentration.[17] Schenley also gained acclaim for vocational feats, as when Joseph Butler '40 constructed a functional miniature blast furnace to temper shop tools.[18]

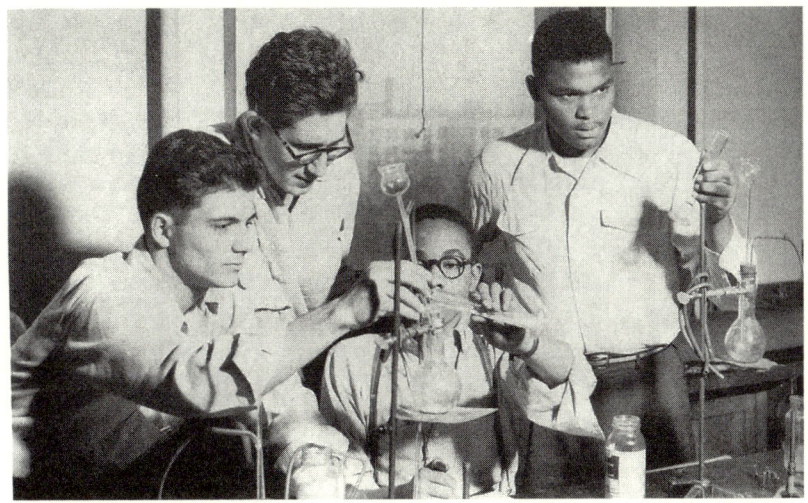

FIG. 16 Students experiment in a science lab. *Journal*, 1949, 46.

Principal Sauvain

Schenley's monopoly on elite teachers became diluted as faculty were transferred more freely between schools.[19] However, the school remained an attractive teaching destination because of Principal Edward Sauvain, who fostered a familial bond among staff. English teacher Elizabeth Malick recalled that new faculty were often welcomed with dinner at the Sauvain home, writing, "There, enjoying the hospitality at 400 South Lang Avenue, the new teacher had an opportunity to get really acquainted with her principal and his wife and she came away feeling that it was a rare privilege to belong to the Schenley family. . . . Yes, we knew that we were discussed at the Sauvain dinner table at the end of the day and we felt that Mrs. Sauvain's interest in her 'family' was one of the ties that made life at Schenley so pleasant."[20] Sauvain was good humored, and facetiously bragged that his mother could read in the dark, before revealing that she was blind and read Braille.[21] He headed Schenley for twenty-one years, by far the school's longest-tenured principal, and many teachers wept at the news of his retirement in 1940.[22]

Sauvin's successor, Harvey P. Roberts, had taught at Schenley decades earlier and had a personal touch with students.[23] When John H. Moore Jr. '43 was away fighting in World War II, Principal Roberts called Moore's parents and insisted that their son attend college upon his return. Moore obliged, ultimately becoming a pharmacist, and proudly told the story for the rest of his life.[24]

In 1935, popular history teacher and combat veteran Percy B. Caley used the school's Memorial Day program to denounce war—"the glamorous, romantic, thrilling wholesale slaughter of fellow human beings"—with the support of the principal and most students.[25] The same year, Hyman Milton '38 and Robert Sallows '38 wrote to Italian prime minister Benito Mussolini, expressing "their sympathy and admiration of [his] conduct in Africa." A thankful reply from Il Duce's secretary was printed in the *Triangle*.[26]

After the attack on Pearl Harbor, students gathered in the school auditorium on Monday, December 8, 1941, to hear President Franklin D. Roosevelt's Infamy speech.[27] Almost immediately, nine students quit school to join the military.[28] By June 1943, fifty-four pupils and one teacher, Mr. Caley, had enlisted, and the *Journal* was filled with letters from the front.[29] Many students were heroic, such as Milton Field '33, a code breaker who thwarted a Japanese attack, and Stanley A. Shepard '42, who was asleep when a torpedo hit his oil tanker, and floated for two days before being rescued.[30] The *Triangle* printed alumni casualties, although Stewart Brown '41 "came back from the 'grave,'" telephoning his mother after she was mistakenly told he was killed in action.[31]

Schenley aided the war efforts by initiating a student Victory Corps and adding defense-centered curriculum, with commando training and messenger courses.[32] New courses offered to "prepare [girls] for nursing or war-aid careers," and students in home economics courses sewed items for soldiers.[33] The halls teemed with patriotic fervor, and many students relished small acts—collecting tin foil, buying war stamps, singing "The Battle Hymn of the Republic" on the walk to school—that enhanced solidarity.[34]

A Woman's World

World War II caused a domestic labor shortage, which led to many teen boys leaving school to enter the workforce.[35] Accordingly, girls outnumbered boys at Schenley and across the District.[36] This female majority did not yield instant respect, as in 1945 many boys resisted a move to allow girls to be safety patrols. "Pupils are too boisterous for girls to manage," Joe Kowalski '47 told the *Triangle*. "Who can picture a sweet young thing saying, 'Hey, there, walk down those steps!'"[37] In 1947, Schenley girls parlayed a 14.8 percent enrollment advantage into a student government coup, claiming all four school-wide officer positions, and making Alice Dykema '48 the first female president in twenty-five years.[38]

Notably, Schenley girls were formidable well before the war. Alice McCloskey '30 was elected the *Triangle*'s editor-in-chief in 1930, the same year the chess club protested the admission of Marguerite Derdeyn '32.[39] Derdeyn was only granted membership by edict of her brother, Walter '30, the club president, but she subsequently whipped the boys, claiming one of four school championships and a varsity spot.[40] In 1938, Schenley girls rejected a lunch date with the boys, voting nearly two-to-one to maintain single-sex lunchrooms—the only District high school to do so. "You know perfectly well how boys talk," one girl told the Associated Press. "Who wants to listen?"[41]

Crowded, Poor, and Ethnic

Enrollment peaked at 3,025 in 1940, when a study hall of 100 students was forced to meet in the auditorium.[42] Teachers bemoaned their new conditions—crowded classrooms, suboptimal supplies, and uncompetitive salaries—and began to retire in frustration.[43] Enrollment thinned to 1,763 by the end of the decade, likely a consequence of World War II, the resulting labor shortage, and a 2.8 percent population drop in Schenley neighborhoods.[44] However, the Hill District grew rapidly, as tenants at new racially mixed public housing projects—Terrace Village and Bedford Dwellings—more than doubled during the decade.[45] Although the projects were zoned for Fifth Avenue High, many students used relatives' addresses to attend Schenley.[46]

Accordingly, student demographics changed considerably, with more low-income families in the feeder pattern. In 1945, 53 percent of Schenley students lived in the "poorest" or "below average" sections of Pittsburgh, although 47 percent lived in "above average" neighborhoods.[47] As the last remaining Jews left the Hill District for Squirrel Hill—where teens warmed to Allderdice and ceased commuting to Oakland—blacks arriving in the Second Great Migration rapidly replaced them.[48] Thus, Schenley's Jewish enrollment fell from 20.9 percent to 10 percent between 1931 and 1949, while black enrollment surged from 10.9 percent to 35 percent during the same period.[49]

Schenley grew increasingly integral to the black community, of which 39 percent lived in adjacent neighborhoods.[50] The auditorium hosted black fashion and hair shows, and in 1935, four black churches and 200 cast members collaborated on an Easter play.[51] The school was also the site of the city's inaugural George Washington Carver celebration—reportedly the first such observance endorsed by an American mayor.[52] Most white students were Italian (12 percent), Polish (11 percent), or Irish (9 percent), according to a 1949 survey.[53] In February 1938, Tong Wong '38, a Guangzhou, China, native, became the first Asian graduate.[54]

Fairness in Jim Crow Pittsburgh

While some inequity persisted, blacks fared much better at Schenley than in the region at large. Pittsburgh was "not much different from living in Mississippi," said Charles Greenlee, who arrived in 1932, and decried its redlining and segregation.[55] Black patrons were barred from many restaurants, hotels, and swimming pools, segregated at hospitals and movie theaters, and precluded from trying on clothes at department stores.[56] "While there were no Jim Crow signs, we knew where we could not go," said Byrd Brown '47.[57] Blacks were also excluded from unions, and thus, most high-wage industrial and hospitality jobs had even more racial restrictions than in the South.[58]

Teaching also had an unofficial barrier, and, in 1937, all of the District's 3,400 full-time teachers were white.[59] When qualified blacks sought employment with the District, Superintendent William Davidson would offer to find them jobs in other cities. "If you didn't want to leave Pittsburgh, you didn't teach," said Frank Bolden, who was told he was not hired because of his race.[60] After a protracted legislative hearing embarrassed the District, part-time music instructor Lawrence Peeler was promoted, becoming the first full-time black teacher since the 1880s.[61] Six years later, in 1943, the District employed only three black professionals, but Peeler noted that Catholics and Jews also faced discrimination. "Those jobs were for WASPs," he said.[62]

Given the city's racial climate, Schenley's frequent expressions of fairness were somewhat remarkable. David Jay Levy '31, a Jew, was elected president of a class that was over 80 percent Gentile, while Mary Strange '32, a black student, was elected president of a French club that was more than two-thirds white.[63] Morgan McDonald '33, a black student, began at Langley High, but upon joining the band, he "was shown clearly by the white students that he was not wanted." McDonald soon transferred to Schenley, where he not only got "along well," but where another black musician, James Young '32, was elected the band's first student director.[64]

In the 1946–47 school term, Schenley students—still approximately two-thirds white—elected their first black presidents in Henry Burwell '47, of the student body, and William Green '48, of his graduating class.

FIG. 17 Andy Warhol, the son of Carpatho-Rusyn immigrants, mostly socialized with Jewish girls, like Mina (Serbin) Kavaler. Andy Warhol's high school graduation photo, Schenley High School, Pittsburgh, PA, 1945. Collection of The Andy Warhol Museum, Pittsburgh.

Notably, the *Triangle*'s election coverage did not mention race, which was standard for student publications.[65] "There was very little problem between the black people and the white people," remembered Betty Kieffer '41, a white student. "If I'd see them on the street we'd hug each other," she said.[66] Similarly, Thelma Williams Lovette '34, a black Hill District resident, "had good relations with everyone," and she continued to socialize with both white and black classmates into the early 2000s.[67] Although some students reported "occasional" interracial fights, most found the school "unusually harmonious and dedicated."[68]

Jews also found atypical acceptance, despite dwindling numbers in the building and anti-Semitism outside. In the Strip District and Lawrenceville, where prejudice was flagrant, Jews were frequently in fistfights, but they had no problems at Schenley.[69] "We didn't have anti-Semitism," reported Mina (Serbin) Kavaler '47, a Jew, whose Jewish, Slavic, Greek, and black friends "were all intermixed."[70] "My Schenley experience made me think that helping race relations was a calling," said Kavaler, who spent seventeen years on the local NAACP's board of directors.[71] Bill Shaffer '46, another Jewish student, was undersized and insecure but found respite in an all-black jazz band.[72] Shaffer played "gigs on the Hill," "hung out with cats," and had a yearbook full of flirtatious notes from "cute black girls." "He would pull out his yearbook, and say, 'Look how diverse this is!'" said Matthew Shaffer of his late father.[73]

NOW HE IS A MAN!

O-o-o-h, do *you* go to Schenley now?

FIG. 18 Spirit was evident in this cartoon that appeared in the *Triangle*. *Triangle,* February 17, 1939.

Spirit of Loyalty

The era's alumni nurtured their school spirit, which in the case of Walter Dassdorf '32, endured over eight decades. Dassdorf followed Schenley's demise from his suburban Houston home and sought surviving class-mates on the *Post-Gazette*'s website.[74] In 2014, the day after his 101st birthday, Dassdorf recalled his "great school" with fondness and clarity.[75] Similarly, the Class of 1933 stayed remarkably close-knit, and Bill McQuillan '33 called the class directory "my bible." Nearly half of the class's living members attended their seventieth reunion, as, according to Ernest F. Thompson '33, "You have to have a certain amount of loyalty."[76] Mary McGregor Lee did not attend Schenley but said her mother, a 1940 grad-uate, always insisted they drive past the building on visits from Florida.[77]

This abiding spirit was rooted in a sense of cooperation. "There was a very good feeling among the students and the teachers," reported Betty Kieffer '41, who worked in the main office until 1977. "I'd stand there and cry if I ran into one of the people from the old days," she said in 2012.[78] Notably, this pride was also explained by the school's strong reputation. "It was one of the elite schools in Pittsburgh," remarked Milton Field '33 in 2003, and in an embrace of Schenley's later accolades, added, "I guess

Alma Mater

Lyrics by Anna R. Hunter

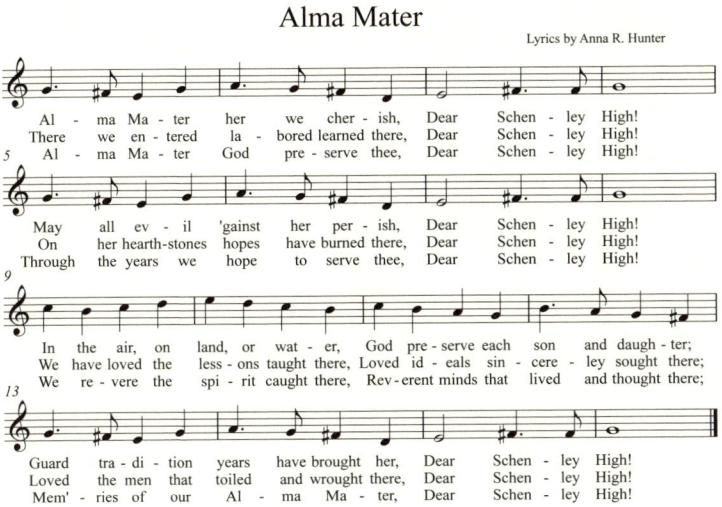

Al - ma Ma - ter her we cher - ish, Dear Schen - ley High!
There we en - tered la - bored learned there, Dear Schen - ley High!
Al - ma Ma - ter God pre - serve thee, Dear Schen - ley High!

May all ev - il 'gainst her per - ish, Dear Schen - ley High!
On her hearth-stones hopes have burned there, Dear Schen - ley High!
Through the years we hope to serve thee, Dear Schen - ley High!

In the air, on land, or wat - er, God pre - serve each son and daugh - ter;
We have loved the less - ons taught there, Loved id - eals sin - cere - ley sought there;
We re - vere the spi - rit caught there, Rev - erent minds that lived and thought there;

Guard tra - di - tion years have brought her, Dear Schen - ley High!
Loved the men that toiled and wrought there, Dear Schen - ley High!
Mem' - ries of our Al - ma Ma - ter, Dear Schen - ley High!

FIG. 19 The alma mater was penned by Schenley English teacher Anna R. Hunter in 1932. Arranged by Leon Boykins.

it still is."[79] In 1932, students were so convinced of future success that they autographed everything in sight, such as yearbooks, playbills, commencement programs, and even zoological specimens from science class.[80]

Almost Famous

Serendipitous associations with notable people continued during the era. In the late 1940s, the baseball team fielded sons of two active professionals, George D. Susce '48 and Josh Gibson Jr. '48.[81] Susce's father, George C. M. Susce '27, was a Major League catcher-turned-bullpen coach, while Josh Gibson Sr., "the Black Babe Ruth," was a Negro leagues legend and future Hall of Famer.[82] The elder Gibson was frequently on the road but made at least one appearance at Schenley, as told by his son: "[T]here was a bunch of guys, the neighborhood bullies, up at the school where I went, Schenley High, causin' me problems. So my grandmother told my father about it and he went there and turned over the whole cafeteria. He raised hell and told them, don't be messin' with my son no more. And, I mean, everybody stopped eatin' and just stared. And the guys that was hasslin' me, they ran out of the cafeteria. Yeah, that was the end of that."[83] Both sons were stars in their own right. Before each turned pro, they were praised by Pie Traynor, the Pirates Hall of Famer–turned-broadcaster, in a 1948 interview in the *Triangle*.[84]

Such celebrity interviews were common for the *Triangle*. Pop Warner, Knute Rockne, Otis Skinner, and Ida Tarbell spoke to student reporters, as did an unwitting Albert Einstein.[85] Prompted by faculty advisor Loretta Byrne, Herbert S. Parnes '35 ambushed Einstein—in Pittsburgh for a conference—who agreed to answer only one question. Parnes recalled, "What came out was, 'Dr. Einstein, what do you think of American youth?'" Einstein look at the flustered young reporter and "then threw back his head and roared with laughter."[86]

Still State of the Art

Even after three decades, the Schenley building was considered massive and modern, ideally suited for the District's flagship evening school. The program enrolled adults, was wholly distinct from the high school—with its own principal (L. L. Hartley), faculty, and yearbook (*The Schenleyan*)—and was the only one of the city's fourteen evening schools to offer an equivalent day school diploma.[87] Well into the 1960s, suburban districts sent adults to Schenley.[88] The building was also a political venue, and in 1938, it hosted tense debates between Charles Owen Rice, a prominent labor priest, and local Communist leaders.[89] In 1936, and again in 1939, Schenley was embroiled in a First Amendment squabble when the District blocked a Communist group's attempt to hold meetings in the building.[90]

The Renaissance Mayor

In November 1945, mayor-elect David L. Lawrence called for an ambitious civic revitalization campaign, but few anticipated its enduring impact on Pittsburgh's demographics, and, in turn, its public schools. The new mayor's agenda, later dubbed Renaissance I, included long-needed flood control and antismog measures that would end the "Smoky City" era.[91] A third initiative, a large-scale urban redevelopment, was the product of an unlikely partnership with Richard King Mellon, a scion of the famous banking family. Despite political differences, Lawrence and Mellon used their collective influence to combat industrial blight and launch three major renewal projects, which became Point State Park, Gateway Center, and Jones & Laughlin Steel's South Side plant.[92] On October 30, 1947, the city unveiled a fourth initiative: a seventy-acre civic center to remake the Lower Hill District.[93]

5 Running Uphill

1950–1964

In the mid-1950s, city planners demolished the Lower Hill District, and thousands of poor black residents were resettled in the Middle Hill neighborhood. Many such children went to Schenley, and amidst cool relations between poor and middle-class blacks, white flight intensified. These trends briefly brought historic racial balance, while quality of instruction, cooperation, and school spirit remained high.

Came in Like a Wrecking Ball

On March 22, 1956, the first of 8,000 Lower Hill residents was displaced with the signing of a sales agreement.[1] The neighborhood was once known as "the crossroads of the world," but it had long since devolved into a slum, with poverty, vice, and crowded, dilapidated housing.[2] To rejuvenate the area, Mayor David L. Lawrence razed over 1,300 buildings to make way for the Civic Arena—all that materialized from a proposed cultural "acropolis."[3] However, angry residents derided their eviction as "Negro removal." The project remains controversial in Pittsburgh, especially as the mayor's promise of "good homes and healthier neighborhoods" went unkept.[4]

Many of the 1,239 displaced black families moved up the Hill into the tenements or housing projects in the Middle Hill, Bedford Dwellings, or Terrace Village.[5] Schenley absorbed part of this diaspora, but there was "no great influx," as students from housing projects were assigned to Fifth Avenue High.[6] Even so, Schenley's black enrollment spiked, from 43.9 percent in 1955 to 65.8 percent in 1965.[7]

The 1960 school term would be Schenley's most racially balanced, with a 1.2 percent black majority.[8] However, white flight was at work, with 14,000 District students leaving during the era.[9] The University of Pittsburgh compounded this swift demographic shift with a 1950s land grab in the Oakland neighborhood that largely displaced white families.[10] Accordingly, Jewish enrollment continued to decline, from 9.7

FIG. 20 Buildings being razed in the Lower Hill District, 1957. Pittsburgh City Photographer Collection, 1901–2002, AIS.1971.05, Archives Service Center, University of Pittsburgh.

percent in 1950 to 3.8 percent in 1964.[11] Overall, Schenley had more departures than arrivals, and net enrollment fell 14 percent between 1950 and 1963, despite the baby boom's crush at many District high schools.[12]

In the early 1960s, Schenley gained dozens of students through a District-wide open enrollment policy, designed to alleviate de facto segregation. Under the policy, black students could transfer to any integrated school with excess capacity, regardless of its distance from their home, and Schenley was the most popular destination.[13] The school was trending toward racial imbalance, but its central location engendered other diversity. When disabled pupils from rural counties sought long-term treatment in Pittsburgh, they were welcomed at Schenley.[14] Moreover, new immigrants tended to land in Oakland, like Helga Barcs '62, who escaped the Soviet invasion of her native Budapest, Hungary.[15] Exchange students from Israel, Austria, British Guiana, and Italy, as well as a student teacher from Puerto Rico, provided additional diversity. Schenley also continued to serve students from the neighboring School for the Blind.[16]

TABLE 2 Hill District Population by Decade

	1940	1950	1960
Upper Hill			
Population	6,071	5,884	5,216
% white	63.4	27	14.7
% other	36.6	73	85.3
Middle Hill			
Population	17,029	14,929	11,849
% white	13.1	4.9	1.1
% other	86.9	95.1	98.9
Terrace Village			
Population	2,446	7,767	7,414
% white	49.4	44	37.2
% other	50.6	56	62.8
Bedford Dwellings			
Population	2,663	3,870	4,915
% white	35	16.8	7.4
% other	65	83.2	92.6
Crawford-Roberts			
Population	17,045	17,334	10,277
% white	43.8	19.4	7.1
% other	56.2	80.6	92.9

Source: Department of City Planning, *1990 Census of Population and Housing Reports, Report No. 1: Pittsburgh Population by Neighborhood, 1940–1990* (Pittsburgh, 1991).

Getting in the Door

While thousands of students fled the District, others went to great lengths to attend Schenley.[17] As an eighth grader, Ralph Falbo '55, a Bloomfield Italian, attended the Schenley-Westinghouse football game—a thrilling Schenley win before 10,000 fans at Pitt Stadium—and was instantly determined to join the team. Falbo's parents were set on Ralph's attending Central Catholic High, where he had earned a scholarship. Yet the next fall, Ralph simply showed up at Schenley. When Central Catholic administrators called the Falbos to check on their scholar, Ralph's parents were livid but ultimately allowed him to remain at Schenley.[18]

Arnold Sowell '53 grew up in the Bedford Dwellings projects, where he was zoned to attend Fifth Avenue. However, like generations of Hill District parents, his mother sent him to Schenley by using a relative's address. "My mother knew, or at least perceived, that Fifth Avenue wasn't academically rigorous," Sowell said.[19]

"One Human Race"

In 1957, the same year the 101st Airborne Division guided the Little Rock Nine through an angry mob, Schenley elected a diverse group of students to the same class board—one black female, one white male, one Chinese American female, and one black male.[20] Classes with a majority of white students chose black presidents in 1951 and 1952, and a Jew claimed the office in 1958.[21] Both blacks and whites have described positive race relations during the era, although whites were generally more effusive in celebrating their experience.

"Maybe I was naive, but it felt like we were all one human race there," said Meg Sandridge '64, a white Banksville resident. Sandridge attended Schenley for Continuum—an enrichment program with District-wide enrollment—but relished the diversity that came with it.[22] "There were a lot of racists in our neighborhood, but my dad was a born integrationist, and we were inculcated with the message of equality. Here I was, at age 13, taking a bus downtown and a streetcar (82 Lincoln), all by myself to go to a school that was predominantly black. My parents never batted an eye and hence neither did I. And neither did the other kids. We just

FIG. 21   Class of February 1958 officers, left to right: president Marva (Hord) Harris, vice president Ronald Kellner, secretary Helen Yee, and treasurer Eugene Harris. *Journal*, 1958, 16.

all blended."[23] Similarly, Falbo called the racial climate "phenomenal" and believed the "melting pot" enhanced camaraderie. "After [football] games, we all went to some player's house, whether it was in the Hill District, Bloomfield, or Oakland."[24]

Black students also spoke fondly of the era. The Upper Hill District's Leslie (Hill) Horne '64 said, "[A]ll neighborhoods and ethnicities interacted positively," while Bloomfield's Richard Nicklos '57 reported no racial tension.[25] Hubert Wilson '62, who came from all-black Herron Hill Junior High, credited Schenley with preparing him for the diverse world ahead.[26]

Simon Noel, a Squirrel Hill Jew and 1965 Allderdice High graduate, attended Schenley only for a summer typing class and came prepared for racial enmity. Instead, he formed a memorable connection with Eddie Salter '65, as the pair goofed off with their teacher's tacit approval. "[Mrs. Joan Peeler] knew that letting a kid from the Hill and Squirrel Hill get along—with the racial strife going on in the country—was so important."[27]

No Utopia

Schenley was not immune to prejudice, as some white students who were friendly at school then ignored their black classmates off campus. "It hurt like hell," said Ralph Proctor Jr. '56, a black Middle Hill resident, "because we thought these folks were our friends."[28] White and black students held separate after-prom parties, although the events were unofficial, and even Sandridge admitted there was no interracial dating "of course."[29] However, the dearth of black professional staff was arguably most harmful to black students. "Not seeing people like yourself in successful positions has a profound psychological impact growing up," said Proctor.[30]

In 1953, Schenley's 717 black students represented 42.2 percent of enrollment, yet the school had never employed a black teacher in its ninety-eight years since opening as Central.[31] White counselors exacerbated racial inequity, often telling blacks they "weren't college material" and should "learn to work with [their] hands."[32] The following year, Jody Harris '34 (instructional arts) became Schenley's first black teacher, yet in 1959, the school was 49.3 percent black, with just five black teachers.[33] Of these five, only Alice Bernice Wade (English) reported problems—standoffish colleagues, a heavier workload, and low-track teaching assignments—but found prejudice subtler than at her previous school, Fifth Avenue. Schenley "had a classier kind of bigot," she said.[34]

The Quirks of Being a Bellefielder, or Becoming Spartans

When Schenley opened in 1916, athletic mascots were ubiquitous in the professional and collegiate ranks but uncommon in high schools. Sportswriters employed informal, descriptive nicknames—usually in reference to a school's colors, geographic location, and coach—but this was purely to add color to their prose. Thus, newspapers generically called Schenley teams the "Red and Black," "Oaklanders," and "Grossmen" (after coach Walter S. "Pappy" Gross). A fourth unofficial name, "Bellefielders," was more precise to Schenley's home in the exclusive Bellefield region, which straddled eastern Oakland and western Shadyside. The name appeared as early as 1922 and had unusual staying power. When other District schools formally chose mascots in the 1930s, Schenley did not and remained the Bellefielders. This inertia persisted, and the handle became official, although seemingly by default.

Despite its longevity, the nickname was never popular, in part because the Bellefield area itself grew increasingly archaic. The neighborhood was slowly rebranded as Schenley Farms, and the Bellefield name became scarce. In May 1945, the *Triangle* called the bland Bellefielders moniker "a grave injustice" which "should be corrected immediately." No change came until October 1953, when the Student Board solicited submissions, from which a committee of teachers chose "Spartans"—a cinematic mainstay of the 1950s.

Regrettably, the new mascot was briefly an instrument of bias. Although a black student had designed the costume, only whites could audition to portray the Spartan. Administrators cited safety concerns, claiming that opposing white fans in rural communities might harm a black mascot. Most found this logic unsound, as black athletes competed in these communities, and the majority of games were in the city.[35]

A Hill Divided

While the black-white dichotomy was Schenley's most prevalent, there was also a rift within the black community, as long-simmering class tensions had been stoked by urban renewal.[36] Lower Hill blacks, largely poor and uneducated, had long felt ostracized by the Upper Hill's "little black aristocracy."[37] "Forget those niggers," said Charles "Teenie" Harris of professional blacks, who "wouldn't mingle with" their working-class counterparts.[38] Harris, a Hill District icon, did not attend Schenley but

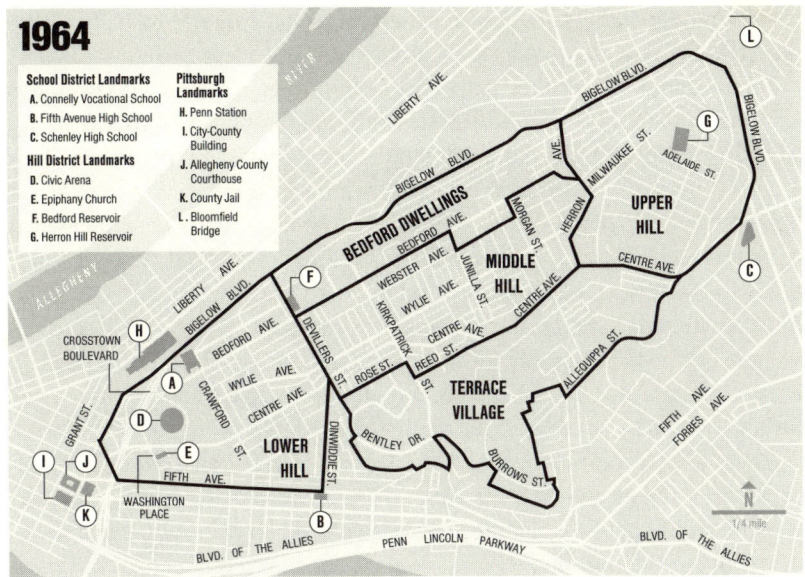

1964

School District Landmarks
A. Connelly Vocational School
B. Fifth Avenue High School
C. Schenley High School

Hill District Landmarks
D. Civic Arena
E. Epiphany Church
F. Bedford Reservoir
G. Herron Hill Reservoir

Pittsburgh Landmarks
H. Penn Station
I. City-County Building
J. Allegheny County Courthouse
K. County Jail
L. Bloomfield Bridge

MAP 3 The Hill District, 1964. Map by James Hilston, using basemaps from the City of Pittsburgh and the University of Pittsburgh.

navigated this chasm for nearly forty years as a photographer for the *Pittsburgh Courier*, the newspaper that covered the city's black community.[39] Many Upper Hill residents were OPs, or Old Pittsburghers: middle-class blacks preceding 1915, whose relative wealth inspired the neighborhood's "Sugar Top" moniker. OPs often withdrew into exclusive social clubs and felt Lower Hill blacks were "uncouth," "set bad examples," and "forced the black community upon itself."[40]

Before urban renewal, issues rarely arose at school, as the Lower Hill was zoned for Fifth Avenue, the Upper Hill for Schenley, and the "blue-collar" Middle Hill split between the two.[41] Tellingly, all housing projects—even those more proximate to Schenley—were assigned to Fifth Avenue, as were students expelled from Schenley, including pregnant girls.[42] This scheme was likely the result of white fear, admitted Ralph Proctor Jr. '56, and the fact that Upper Hill blacks fared better at Schenley as they were "almost white in culture and color."[43]

When the Civic Arena forced poor blacks into the Middle Hill, some felt unwelcome at Schenley. Sala (Samuel Howze) Udin initially attended Central Catholic, where he was regularly called "nigger[ ]," but said rejection at Schenley was "almost as traumatic." Udin shared, "I was just another 'kid from the projects.' Most of the students at the school were black, middle-class, and hailed from what was called 'Sugar Top.' We didn't know that the Sugar Top families had objected to the building of public housing so close to them. They fought against Bedford Dwellings and lost, which led to animosity toward the people who moved there. And that animosity was passed down from the Sugar Top parents to their children, who then passed it on to us. We never felt socially accepted at Schenley, even though it was all black."[44] The rift was less harrowing for Arnold Sowell '53, also from Bedford Dwellings, who said "kids like me" ate in one cafeteria, while whites and middle-class blacks ate in the other. This practice did not bother Sowell, who insisted, "We made that decision on our own."[45] Notably, class distinctions were irrelevant to some Hill District residents, who socialized, dated, and married across Kirkpatrick Street—which became symbolic as the Schenley–Fifth Avenue boundary.[46]

Despite its imperfections, alumni stressed that Schenley was more tolerant than the city outside its walls. "There were places [in Pittsburgh] where I would not be welcome," said Sowell, yet "there was never a racial problem" in the building. "I don't know how that happened," he continued, but "you were accepted."[47] Similarly, Sheldon "Skip" Monsein '52 was beaten up for being Jewish on his block in Oakland but had no problems while at school, despite his tormentors being classmates.[48] Although Bruno Sammartino '55 was bullied at Schenley—a target for his small frame and thick Italian accent—Maurice Simon '52, a competitive weightlifter, rescued him. Simon invited Sammartino to train at the YMHA (now the Jewish Community Center), and within ten years, the brawny Italian was the world's most famous pro wrestler.[49]

"The Lessons Taught There"

Schenley added rigorous academic offerings, even as it lost population.[50] The Continuum program, which allowed gifted pupils to progress through school at their own pace, led to several seniors enrolling in college courses. Funded by the Ford and Buhl Foundations, the program started at Frick and Falk Elementary Schools, continued at Schenley, and culminated at the University of Pittsburgh. For example, Frick's advanced eighth graders could take ninth-grade classes at Schenley, and Schenley's accelerated seniors could take Pitt courses at no cost.[51] The program was highly rated, and although open to students from across the District, most came from Schenley's feeder pattern.[52]

A new language lab boasted twenty soundproof booths with tape recorders, phonographs, and radios. A student could record and play back his or her own voice or listen to records or radio broadcasts in foreign

FIG. 22 A social studies class does research in the library, 1952. Pittsburgh Public Schools Photographs, 1880–1982, MSP117.B009.F03.I11, Detre Library & Archives, Sen. John Heinz History Center. Photo: Samuel A. Musgrave.

languages. Additionally, teachers could communicate with a single booth without disrupting others.[53]

Another curricular innovation, Schenley's social living course, proved popular for addressing real-world issues. Topics ranged from appropriate job interview attire to parenting skills, and the class took a field trip to Frick Elementary to observe the latter.[54] Social living was the brainchild of Bernard J. McCormick, the pioneering principal who established a special needs program, replaced class plays with operettas—allowing many more students to be involved—and organized the first official prom.

McCormick later became District superintendent, but in heading Schenley from 1946 to 1958, he nurtured a staff that was unusually accomplished.[55] Most decorated was ceramics teacher Virgil Cantini, who was an enamelist and sculptor. His works—such as *The Man* on Pitt's Graduate School of Public Health—were featured throughout Pittsburgh. Cantini was also a Pitt professor who won a Guggenheim Fellowship and the Pittsburgh Center for the Arts's Artist of the Year award.[56] Ralph Falbo '55 remembered Cantini's dynamism—hot-tempered Italian immigrant, former college football star, and distinguished artist—and thought it "amazing that a public school had guys with such credentials."[57]

TABLE 3 Pittsburgh Public High School Graduates in Higher Education, 1967

School	Format	4-Year College %	Junior College %	Trade School %	Total %
Allderdice	Neighborhood comprehensive	72.1	9.3	4	85.4
Peabody	Neighborhood comprehensive	47.7	6.2	9.5	63.4
Schenley	Neighborhood comprehensive	27.3	17.8	18.2	63.3
Fifth Avenue	Neighborhood comprehensive	21.1	17.1	18	56.2
South Hills	Neighborhood comprehensive	24.9	11.6	11.7	48.2
Carrick	Neighborhood comprehensive	26.9	8.1	12	47
Langley	Neighborhood comprehensive	25.1	9.4	11.4	45.9
Westinghouse	Neighborhood comprehensive	23.9	12.7	9.2	45.8
Oliver	Neighborhood comprehensive	15	11.5	17.5	44
Perry	Neighborhood comprehensive	20.6	9.7	7.9	38.2
Gladstone	Neighborhood comprehensive	9.9	8.2	13.2	31.3
Allegheny	Neighborhood comprehensive	14.2	5.3	9.6	29.1
Connelly Vocational	Boys' vocational	0	4.7	22.9	27.6
Washington Vocational	Boys' vocational	4.8	8.3	14.3	27.4
South	Neighborhood comprehensive	11.3	6.2	9.5	27
Arsenal Girls' Vocational	Girls' vocational	2.5	0	5	7.5

Source: "High School Grads Continue Education," *Pittsburgh Post-Gazette*, May 30, 1968, 26.

Other impressive teachers included Percy B. Caley (history), Ivan Hosack (science), Mary Jane Burwell (English), and Prudence Trimble (English). Caley had a doctorate, served in both World Wars—the first as a Marine, the second as an officer in what became the Air Force— had published a book on teaching, and later taught college.[58] Hosack also taught at Pitt and briefed elected officials and the public on health policy, education, and history. He left Schenley to become the county's audio-visual director and served twenty-four years on North Allegheny's school board before Hosack Elementary in McCandless was named in his honor.[59] Burwell had taught at Hood College and Ohio State University. Trimble, who spent more than twenty years at Schenley, was later editor of *Western Pennsylvania Historical Magazine*.[60] More enduring than credentials, teachers who served as mentors and demonstrated strong teaching aptitude were transformative for many alumni.[61] Choir director Howard Keister was levelheaded and unfailingly kind but most effective for his ability to reach both exceptional singers—such as future Broadway star Vivian Reed '63—and "regular folks."[62]

Eleanor, Jonas, Jackie, and W. C.

Schenley students continued to do exceptional things. Anita Heh '59 starred in *Swan Lake* and choreographed *Brigadoon* at Pittsburgh's International Theatre; William Harris '56 toured Mexico with the National Negro Opera Company Association; and Eva Tsang '61 made headlines as one of ten women among 1,500 men at the prestigious Case Institute.[63] Others were honored with unique experiences, as when the choir opened for a teenage Stevie Wonder in a concert at the School for the Blind.[64] Chuck Conroy '64 worked as a Pittsburgh Pirates batboy during high school, and even joined the team on West Coast road trips. Conroy was treated well by Pirates players and received Christmas cards from celebrity owner Bing Crosby.[65] In 1956, Schenley made its television debut, as students made at least three appearances on local station WQED.[66]

Even the Schenley building itself was fortuitously connected to notable people. Former first lady Eleanor Roosevelt drew more than 2,000 supporters to the auditorium for a 1956 rally, where she endorsed a nuclear test ban.[67] In June 1950, Dr. Jonas Salk told an anxious PTA that a "solution to the polio problem should be forthcoming in our lifetime"; seven years later, all Schenley students were vaccinated for free.[68] When Jackie Robinson spoke at a 1954 Christmas party, he was welcomed by Principal McCormick and baseball coach Coleman Kortner.[69] W. C. Handy performed at Schenley when he hosted "Big Break of 1953," a massive regional talent show. In 1956, Eddie Fisher—a teen idol and prolific hitmaker—sang with Diahann Carroll. Fisher was "greeted with swoons, screams, and cheers of delight from the feminine set" and also sang Schenley's senior class song.[70] Moreover, *Triangle* reporters consistently interviewed celebrities, including Jimmy Stewart, Bill Haley, Jimmy Dean, Richard Egan, Dinah Shore, Patty McCormack, Eddie Hodges, and Miiko Taka.[71]

FIG. 23   Left to right: unknown, US Senate candidate Joseph S. Clark, Alyce Lawrence, Pittsburgh mayor David L. Lawrence, activist Molly Yard, and former first lady Eleanor Roosevelt at Schenley for an Adlai Stevenson campaign rally, 1956. Teenie Harris Photograph Collection, 1920–1970, 2001.35.8675, Carnegie Museum of Art. Photo: Teenie Harris. Teenie Harris Archive / Carnegie Museum of Art / Getty Images.

"The Spirit Caught There"

John Young '53 was "involved in everything," which made him feel essential at Schenley. He kept a diary, and wrote, "I will probably never get over this high school," partially because of its uncommon sense of community. The school supported all student activities, not just athletics, which Young said "made you want to do well."[72]

Joni Perri also remembered that camaraderie, despite only attending Schenley for a few months in the mid-1950s. Perri's broken home left her ferried between orphanages, relatives, and myriad schools, where she often felt ostracized from classmates. The trauma of those years scattered her memory, yet Perri recalls her time at Schenley with unusual fondness and detail. Perri credits musical experiences—singing tenor in the chorus, and cutting class with other girls to play doo-wop on the piano—with helping her "connect a bit more" with her peers. Now in her seventies, Perri proudly belts out the alma mater.[73]

As the school entered its sixth decade, pride was amplified by the shared experience of generations. "My parents, aunts, uncles, and cousins graduated from Schenley," said Leslie (Hill) Horne '64, whose two children also taught there. "The school has a special place in the hearts of my whole family."[74]

6 | The Writing on the Walls
1965–1979

As racial unrest permeated the school district, most white families and many middle-class blacks began to abandon Schenley. By the early 1970s, the school faced deteriorating discipline and pervasive apathy. Hallways were frequently garnished with graffiti, stairwells and bathrooms were filled with marijuana smoke, and only a handful of students went on to college. Still, many teachers were unusually dedicated, and even at times when there was little to be proud of, students remained impossibly proud.

"Get the Hell Out of Here"

On Friday, April 5, 1968, less than twenty-four hours after Martin Luther King Jr.'s assassination, Schenley was simmering. "Folks came up from the [fourth] lunch period and were coming down the hall en masse," recalled Thomas Sumpter '68, a black Upper Hill District resident. "You could hear this chant, 'Long live Dr. King, Long live Dr. King!'"[1] Sumpter ducked into a stairwell, where he spotted his friend Gene Picciafoco '68 in a group of white classmates.[2] "You guys better get the hell out of here," Sumpter warned and quickly escorted them from the building.[3] Most students left in fear or protest, and some pupils—both black and white—punctuated their exit by stoning police cruisers and overturning a car.[4] "Schenley was in an uproar," reported Sylvia Jelks '69.[5]

Black Pittsburgh was in its own uproar, with the Hill District burning for four days.[6] By 9:30 P.M. Friday, throngs roved through the neighborhood: smashing windows, looting stores, and setting fires. The *Post-Gazette* described a riotous "gang of about 100 young Negroes" headed Downtown from Centre Avenue's 1900 block.[7] Denise (Fulton) Lamar '68 saw National Guardsmen marching down Bedford Avenue and watched Pennywise, the grocery store, burn to the ground.[8] Peace would not come until Tuesday, April 9, despite an official state of emergency, a strict 7:00 P.M. daily curfew, and 6,100 city, state, and federal law enforcement officers.[9]

FIG. 24 The National Guard used Pitt Stadium as a staging area during the Martin Luther King riots. David Blinky Photographs, 1968, AIS.2013.11, Archives Service Center, University of Pittsburgh.

The MLK riots ended with one dead, more than forty-five injured, 505 fires, and 926 arrests.[10] Wrenna Watson '72 remembered her father, J. Warren Watson, the county's second black judge, taking her to survey the damage. She said, "My dad rode me around the Hill District and showed me the burned up buildings. . . . He talked about what it meant to be a black person. He told me that it was going to be my responsibility to look out for my community. He also told me that the same people that you're responsible for wouldn't always accept you. But you're still responsible for your community."[11]

There was no residual racial violence at Schenley, but tensions remained high. Many white students stayed away for several days and "proceeded with caution" when they finally returned.[12] The school was then approximately two-thirds black. Picciafoco, fearing a "wrong place / wrong time" altercation, was anxious for the school year to end.[13] Before the term was over, Schenley students were linked to concurrent mobs that trashed Herron Hill Junior High and assaulted a Port Authority bus driver.[14]

White families now fled the school, although the trend had been gaining momentum since the mid-1950s.[15] To accommodate demand for Catholic education in Schenley's district and, admittedly, to "retain the white population," the diocese converted Lawrenceville's all-girls St. Augustine High into a larger, coed school.[16] "[A] lot of people send their kids to Lawrenceville Catholic High School just to avoid the blacks at Schenley," lamented Stan Lubarski, a progressive neighborhood pastor, in 1972.[17] Others finagled admission into Allderdice or Peabody: predominantly white, resource-rich schools with professional families nearby.[18] Schenley became increasingly segregated, with its black population climbing to 72.5 percent in 1970 and 89.8 percent by 1978.[19] Middle-class blacks also left the school, but to a lesser extent than whites.[20]

Fort Apache

Schenley's enrollment dropped 42.4 percent, from 1,709 students to 984, between 1965 and 1979.[21] Many of those remaining students were apathetic, while others were downright delinquent: bathrooms played host to occasional muggings and were often filled with marijuana smoke; two different freshmen, four years apart, were detained for alcohol-related incidents; and corridor walls were covered in graffiti. The *Triangle* was filled with admonishments for students to stay in school, go to class, and behave appropriately.[22]

In October 1972, Schenley became a punch line when the homecoming football game against Allderdice devolved into a battle royal. After several seemingly unfair penalties, Spartans fans stormed the field and attacked rival players with rocks, yard markers, and at least one golf putter.[23] Principal James Robinson '51 defended his players—who claimed the referees had insulted them with epithets and ejected those who protested—but Schenley's growing reputation for unruliness was substantiated.[24] "It was a Fort Apache–type place, wild school," said Al McGuire, Marquette University's Hall of Fame basketball coach, who visited Schenley to recruit Maurice Lucas '71. McGuire recalled that "the halls were like track meets"; math teacher Carol (Gift) Sperandeo concurred.[25] "After winning big games, kids wanted to celebrate immediately," remembered Sperandeo, who said students "would run around the halls" in lieu of waiting for a 2:00 P.M. pep rally.[26]

The school seemed to attract calamity and was strangely fire-prone during the era. A fire cleared the triangle in January 1967 and again that April—the latter igniting after school hours and causing $7,000 in damage to the auto shop.[27] In February 1972, a mysterious auditorium blaze burned for twenty minutes, completely consuming a piano and causing $15,000 in damage.[28]

Schenley's academic performance was also problematic. In 1972, only thirty-seven of 315 graduates went on to a four-year college.[29] Less than a decade later, 72 percent of students tested below the national norm in reading and language.[30] A pervasive "athletics first" culture hastened this decline, as teachers were pressured to pass athletes, regardless of proficiency or effort. When teacher Ann (Sharpe) Haley '59 flunked a baseball player—who waved from the street outside while he cut her English class—counselors and administrators urged her to change the grade. "But I stuck to my guns," Haley said.[31]

Other teachers were less principled, and even some athletes were annoyed by their indifference.[32] "[Some teachers] don't care," said Wayne Williams '75, a basketball star who hid his passion for poetry. "If you're a good athlete, they're going to pass you without any hesitation whatsoever," Williams added.[33] Nonathletes were also shortchanged; Michelle Terry '78 had teachers "who could[n't] care less whether you learn anything . . . because they get paid whether they teach or not."[34]

Poor counseling compounded students' academic difficulties. "The counselors would tell you that you weren't going to college," said Haley, "so they'd have you take nonacademic classes."[35] Wrenna Watson '72 earned an engineering scholarship, but counselors had never suggested she take calculus or physics, which caused her considerable difficulties in college.[36] Pupils were discouraged from taking courses that exceeded graduation requirements, the *Triangle* complained, and one white counselor notoriously deterred blacks from the college-prep track.[37]

The District also bore blame for low achievement as feeder elementary schools left students unprepared for Schenley. In 1978, Principal Robinson said the majority of incoming ninth graders could not "divide, use fractions, decimals or percents." Moreover, the District phased out three of Schenley's five foreign-language teachers, which forced some pupils to commute to Peabody for a single course.[38]

Admittedly, few students prioritized scholarship, and Watson reported that the school's culture was "absolutely" antiacademic:[39]

> There was a tremendous peer pressure, but it started long before you got to Schenley. It's not cool to be smart. If you're real smart, then you're nerdy, and you get picked on. At an early age, I succumbed to the whole peer pressure thing . . . I wanted to be cool. I didn't want to be smart. That really starts to kick in about fourth grade. . . . You go through all these years with this peer pressure, not wanting to do well. Then you go off to college, and it's cool to be the A student.[40]

Others would "deny themselves diplomas," lamented Mallorie Michael '78, in an editorial in the *Triangle*, "by not doing the required work to earn them."[41]

Despite Schenley's faults, Greg C. Young '73 insisted that "the teaching was there if you searched it out."[42] This was true for Gabriel Mejail '72, who went on to MIT and Harvard but nearly missed his high school's best courses. An Argentine immigrant, Mejail's limited English landed him in the mainstream track where "some of the classes were really too slow." Mejail languished for three years—often staring outside to "watch the blind kids play baseball"—before geometry teacher Catherine Jatkowski insisted he switch to accelerated courses. Mejail embraced the new curriculum, especially chemistry, which would be "the one class [he] didn't have trouble with [at MIT]."[43]

Stanley Page '70 attended mainstream courses, which left him academically unprepared for Bucknell. However, he felt Schenley trained him in other ways. "I knew how to navigate the university," said Page. "Schenley taught me to not be afraid to talk to a professor."[44] Schenley had quality teachers in both tracks, and Michelle Terry '78 praised those teachers who "really care[d]" and tried to help students solve their problems.[45] One such teacher, the "animated" Anthony Sgattoni (social studies), "made history fun by bringing it to life" and connecting with students of all abilities.[46] Mejail was inspired by Sgattoni, and later swapped a lucrative career in computer programming to become a middle school history teacher.[47]

Similarly, Virginia Musmanno Berardino (French) fostered student buy-in with enthusiasm and high standards. The Sorbonne-trained Berardino evoked French literature and details of her frequent foreign travels, which piqued a cultural curiosity in students.[48] English teachers were also engaging, including the "encouraging" Elizabeth Trumbull, the "refined" Robert Berkebile, and the "young, cool" Roberta Waldman—who later worked for the state Department of Education.[49]

Teachers of color were still scarce, which amplified the impact of Lois (Schrader) Golden '44, who later became Schenley's first female principal.[50] Golden held a law degree and served as a dean at Duff's Business Institute. As Schenley vice principal in 1977, she helped deliver the baby of a graduating senior's cousin, who went into labor moments before the commencement ceremony. Golden also fought to keep students in school, sometimes driving the "Skillsmobile"—a sound truck aimed at pulling dropouts back to Schenley's welding, bricklaying, auto mechanic, and plumbing courses.[51]

Similarly, Ernestine Gloster Parks '27—who headed physical education for girls and coached cheerleaders, majorettes, and pom-poms during the era—instilled self-esteem in generations of young black women. "We were never allowed to think of ourselves as victims because of our color," recalled Lois (Weaver) Watson '45, who preceded Parks at Schenley but was a member of her Upper Hill youth group, Entre Nous.[52] Other black teachers, such as Elizabeth Johnson Harper (biology) and Doris Douglas (English), stood out as mentors with their concern for pupils as people.[53]

A male black teacher, Fred Lucas (physical education), reached students through competition. From 1972 to 2000, Lucas published data from class activities—such as bench press, push-ups, and the infamous block run—in lists on the gymnasium wall, challenging the virility of recalcitrant students.[54] "We competed with history," said Anthony Williams '82, who was inspired to break the records of Larry Brown '65, a former NFL Most Valuable Player.[55] Lucas crooned "ze-ro" while failing nonparticipants in his classes. Yet, according to Darrick Suber '89, even "hard heads" "revered" his jovial toughness.[56] In addition to coaching the track team for decades, Lucas established a thirty-member weightlifting club and District-wide bodybuilding competition, which instilled discipline in many teens disinclined to traditional sports.[57]

"Schenley Came First"

Schenley was a decidedly black school in the 1970s, both statistically and culturally. Robert Burley taught the first black history course, while the *Triangle* featured Afrocentric poetry (e.g., "Pledge of Blackness," "To My Black Man") and editorials celebrating natural black hairstyles as well as the *Roots* television miniseries.[58] Diversity was quantitatively limited, but qualitatively eclectic, with immigrants—mostly Asian—and working-class whites constituting nonblack enrollment.[59] "All the foreigners would play soccer [in the hallway with a milk carton]," said Mejail, who used the games to connect with Greek and Taiwanese classmates, and relished "getting thrown into a piece of Americana."[60]

Schenley remained atypically cohesive, as racial violence at seven District high schools led to police patrolling the hallways.[61] Mejail had never seen a black person before emigrating from Buenos Aires in 1967, and despite being the school's only Latino, he was not only accepted but protected. When Mejail was jumped by Central Catholic students who targeted his letter jacket and called him a "nigger-lover," he told his homeroom. "Maurice Lucas ['71] and all these big black guys said, 'Let's all walk down to Forbes [Avenue] together.'" Lucas, a six-foot-nine-inch-tall tree of a teen whose future NBA teammates would dub him "The Enforcer," never got near Mejail's tormentors. "They went running," Mejail related with laughter. "Schenley came first, ahead of the race thing."[62]

FIG. 25 The 1972–73 pom-pom team. *Journal,* 1973, 115.

Black students also got protection, which they needed in certain parts of Pittsburgh. Before a volleyball game on the South Side, Stanley Page '70 and Ricky Del Vecchio '71 stopped into a soda shop on Carson Street. "They wouldn't serve me," said Page, who is black. "Ricky was getting ready to jump over the counter . . . I said, 'Rick, it's not worth it.'"[63] There were no racial problems inside Schenley, remembered Greg C. Young '73, a National Honor Society member who was frequently accosted by police during high school. "Color didn't matter," said Young, recalling how a predominantly black class elected a white president. "[H]e was the best student and a really nice guy."[64] Marvin Snowden '66, a basketball star, said the team's only white player, Phil Mazza '66, was always included in postgame parties. "We were really close at Schenley," said Snowden. "We were like family. The race thing never came in."[65]

Black alumni recall the era more rosily than their white counterparts. Some white students, especially those entering from all-white Catholic elementary schools, were prejudiced. However, Linda Leffakis '73, a Lawrenceville native, came without bias—having gotten along well at integrated Arsenal Elementary—but admitted Schenley could be racially tense. Leffakis was the target of animus at times and played hooky on Martin Luther King Jr.'s birthday and death anniversary ("there was always trouble"). Yet she felt protected by her many black friends. Even at Westinghouse and Fifth Avenue High Schools, where students threatened white Spartans fans during basketball games, Leffakis insisted, "Our school took care of us."[66] Varsity Club president Jim Burwell '65, a Hill

District native, conceded that white nonathletes were somewhat isolated, but Roberta (Thompson) Woods '66, a white student from the integrated Terrace Village projects, "felt part of the community" and "didn't think of race differences."[67] Despite the absence of varsity athletics for girls, several black women, such as Nancy Primus Greene '65, Linda Tardy Wilson '67, and Marlene Gary Hogan '67, cited interracial friendships with fondness.[68]

While interracial camaraderie was strong, subtle divisions persisted within the black community. In the mid-1960s, middle-class black students were then still at critical mass, and many did not socialize outside the scholars track.[69] This was no longer the case by the early 1970s, said the Upper Hill's Page, who frequently visited friends at the Whiteside Road projects. Page insists that "there was never an economic divide," but this spirit of equality may not have pervaded the faculty.[70] Auxiliary teams were allegedly segregated by class: only Upper Hill girls could be cheerleaders, while those from the projects were relegated to the pom-pom squad.[71] "It was almost like a little caste system that was imposed upon us," said Wrenna Watson '72, "because that wasn't our doing or our choice."[72]

Impossibly Proud

Despite students' struggles and the school's poor reputation, spirit was pronounced. "Schenley was not just a high school," wrote Joseph M. Winbush Jr. '74, "it was more of a life experience."[73] The school naturally coalesced around basketball. The Spartans won four state championships and eight City titles during the era, and compiled a four-year, sixty-one game, regular season league winning streak.[74] The team sold out gyms across the region, and most home games were moved to Pitt's Field House, where even regular season contests drew up to 4,000 spectators.[75] In the era alone, eighteen Spartans played at Division I colleges, and two played in the NBA.[76]

The first state crown in 1966 precipitated an impromptu Hill District block party when a jubilant throng intercepted the returning team bus. "We got off the bus at Centre and Kirkpatrick," said Marvin Snowden '66, who estimated "hundreds of people were there, partying and having a good time."[77] Back at school on Monday, Denise (Fulton) Lamar '68 heard a commotion outside her classroom. She said, "[W]hat started as a low rumble was actually students running through the halls shouting, 'Schenley's in an uproar! Hoop-Hoop!' Classroom doors opened as we all ran out of class and joined this peaceful crowd, running through the halls on

FIG. 26 Students celebrate Schenley's fourth state basketball title on the building's front steps, 1978. *Pittsburgh Press*, March 20, 1978, A-1. Photo: Lynn Johnson. Copyright © *Pittsburgh Post-Gazette*, 2016, all rights reserved. Reprinted with permission.

Nice and Sharp

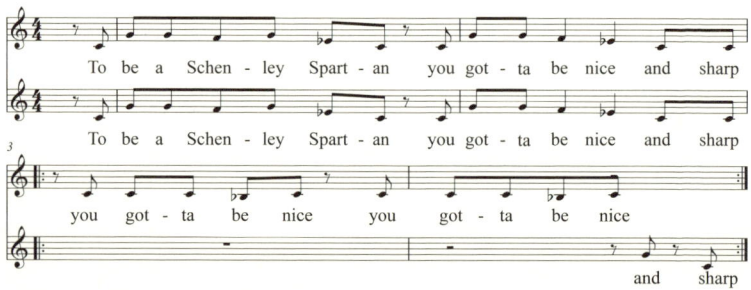

FIG. 27 "Nice and Sharp" was sung soulfully at basketball games, and intimidated, or at least distracted, opposing teams. Arranged by Leon Boykins.

all floors. The teachers just stood by laughing. It was great fun!"[78] Donna (Fox) Vlassich '67 said classes were canceled for the day, and Schenley rejoiced, with game films in the library, music in the gym, and open classrooms so students could chat with players.[79]

Even Schenley's rivals contracted Spartan spirit. "[Schenley basketball players] were very, very friendly to us," said Simon Noel, whose Allderdice team was taunted by Fifth Avenue High. After graduation, Noel and his friends, self-professed "old Jewish guys from Squirrel Hill," cheered Schenley in games at Johnstown, Uniontown, and Braddock. "We were like groupies," he joked.[80] Beyond basketball, accolades were far fewer than in past decades. Yvonne Walden '77 sang Heinz Hall solos and made trips to Manhattan to audition for musicals.[81] Additionally, Jerry Mages '77 was part of the Lawrenceville-based marbles team that won the 1975 world championship, competing in Crawley, England, over spring break.[82]

However, greatness did come to Schenley during the era—or, more specifically, "The Greatest" came. In May 1970, Muhammad Ali appeared unannounced on the lawn. Ali pretended to box with students, until the flustered principal, Arthur Outen, called an impromptu assembly. "[Y]ou very seldom see real champions in this neighborhood," Ali needled, but the 1,500 students—apparently more proud than starstruck—were "unresponsive." The former champ recovered, saying, "They thought it was fittin' for me to visit the school with the *baddest* basketball team," after which, according to the *Pittsburgh Press*, "The auditorium rocked."[83]

Students also took pride in their appearances. Early in the era, "everyone dressed up every day." Expensive gauchos and pressed collars were standard for boys, and girls favored shirtwaist dresses or plaid, pleated skirts with knee socks. While formality comported with a District-wide dress code—no football jerseys, facial hair, spaghetti straps, or short skirts—Schenley students were admittedly keen on looking sharp, and most never thought of dressing down.[84] Rules were relaxed by the 1970s, and students' sensibilities were more expressive and rebellious. Cut-off shorts and leotard tops were common. Andra Powell '73 recalled one flamboyant pair of bell-bottoms with "sex" bleached across the rear and "machine" bleached down the side.[85]

Morale waned slightly in the mid-1970s, undermined by the steep decline in academics and discipline. Jackie Collier '80, who attended Peabody for two courses, lamented the contrast with the East End school—then integrated, intellectual, and supportive of diverse activities.[86] Peabody's relative racial balance, unique among successful District schools, resulted from thousands of displaced Lower Hill residents settling in East Liberty and Larimer. Yet Peabody retained its white majority, flush with middle-class families from Highland Park, Stanton Heights, and eastern Shadyside.[87] As Schenley's decline continued, parents in the Hill District and in every black neighborhood coveted white schools' resources, and demanded integration.

7 | If You're Going to Drop a Bomb

The PHRC, Richard Wallace, and the Teacher Center

By the 1980s, Schenley's racial imbalance was a legal albatross, as the District had spent twelve years in defiance of a desegregation mandate. Despite the low-ranking school's toxic reputation, Superintendent Richard C. Wallace Jr. favored drawing diverse students voluntarily through exceptional academics. The District spent three years planning Schenley's renaissance, which would include a first-in-the-nation training center for teachers; a revamped, blue-chip faculty; and three rigorous magnet programs.

Pittsburgh's Desegregation Battle: A Brief History

In 1961, a federal court ruled that de facto segregation in New Rochelle, New York, violated the Fourteenth Amendment, and issued the first-ever desegregation order to a northern school district.[1] Pittsburgh was proactive, implementing an open enrollment policy in 1962. This led to 900 pupils, mostly black, transferring to predominantly white schools.[2] In 1966, the District embraced the Great High Schools plan, which called for five new "super high schools" in strategic locations, with each school housing 5,000 to 6,000 students at a fixed ratio of one-third black. Schenley would be converted into a middle school, along with nine of the other thirteen existing high schools.[3] White opponents called the proposal "an affront to freedom," as many students would have to travel outside their neighborhoods, while the NAACP decried its failure to address inferior elementary schools.[4] After four contentious years, the plan was scrapped because of its $236 million price tag and impracticality.[5]

Consequently, the District was without a desegregation plan in 1970, which by then ran afoul of a 1968 order from the Pennsylvania Human Relations Commission (PHRC).[6] The state defined racial balance with a formula measuring a school's black enrollment against the district average in pertinent grade levels.[7] Several District schools, including Schenley, were noncompliant.[8] The school board adopted piecemeal reforms, such as manipulating feeder patterns, which opponents called "forced busing,"

FIG. 28 Antibusing signs reflect the mood at a public meeting at Frick School, 1972. *Pittsburgh Press*, November 16, 1972, 2. Photo: Michael Chikiris. Copyright © *Pittsburgh Post-Gazette*, 2016, all rights reserved. Reprinted with permission.

but did not pass a comprehensive plan until 1973.[9] The PHRC rejected its attempt, and the board used six years of legal appeals to delay submitting a new plan.[10]

The board's ineffectiveness was due in part to politics: black groups criticized most proposals as insufficient and one-sided, while some whites opposed integration per se.[11] Antibusing fervor was rooted outside the rivers—working-class neighborhoods in the South Hills, West End, and North Side—where whites protested with sit-ins and boycotts. More than 10,000 pupils participated in a 1980 District-wide boycott, with paltry attendance at Carrick (16 percent), South (19.3 percent), and South Hills (29.2 percent) High Schools, and no students showing up at Carrick's Bon Air Elementary.[12] Notably, Pittsburgh mayor Pete Flaherty was a vocal busing opponent, cruising to reelection in 1973 and claiming every demographic except black voters, after urging the board to defy the PHRC's mandate.[13]

In 1976, the District opened Brashear High School in Beechview, combining whites from nearby South Hills neighborhoods with black students bused from the Lower Hill District and Hazelwood. The move was unusually bold for the board, as it instantly created a racially balanced school (59 percent white) and entailed closing Fifth Avenue and Gladstone High Schools. Notably, Brashear would replace Fifth Avenue as Schenley's intra-Hill District rival, despite its remote location and white

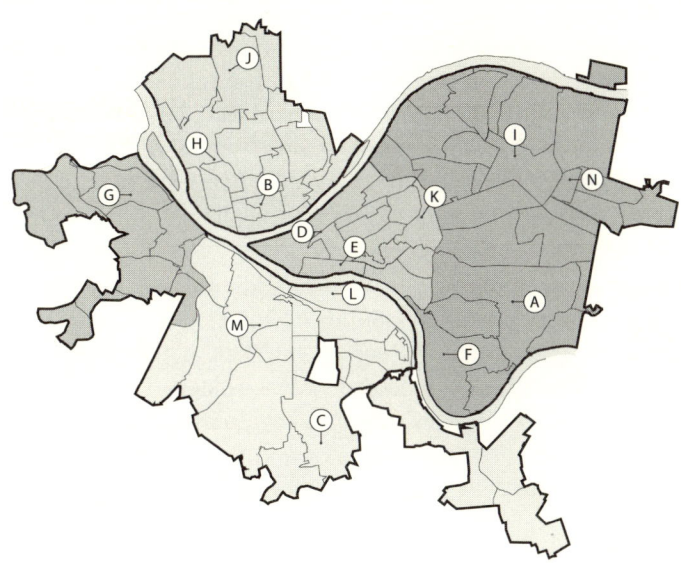

TABLE 4 Pittsburgh Public High Schools Enrollment by Race, 1974–1975

	School	Opened	Location	Grades	Enrollment	% Black	% Other
A	Allderdice	1927	Shady & Forward Aves., Squirrel Hill	9–12	3,099	9.1	90.9
B	Allegheny	1883	810 Arch St., Allegheny Center	9–12	1,562	35.7	64.3
C	Carrick	1924	125 Parkfield St., Carrick	9–12	2,521	8.6	91.4
D	Educational-Medical	1965	1530 Cliff St., Crawford-Roberts	7–12	94	97.9	2.1
E	Fifth Avenue	1896	1800 Fifth Ave., Uptown	7–12	1,104	98.5	1.5
F	Gladstone	1958	327 Hazelwood Ave., Hazelwood	7–12	572	54.7	45.3
G	Langley	1923	2940 Sheraden Blvd., Sheraden	9–12	1,908	13.4	86.6
H	Oliver	1925	2323 Brighton Rd., Marshall–Shadeland	9–12	1,393	33	67
I	Peabody	1911	E. Liberty Blvd. & N. Beatty St., East Liberty	9–12	2,654	39.1	60.9
J	Perry	1923	3875 Perrysville Ave., Perry North	9–12	1,050	42	58
K	Schenley	1916	4101 Bigelow Blvd., Oakland	9–12	1,471	81.7	18.3
L	South	1898	S. 10th & E. Carson Sts., South Side Flats	7–12	1,618	17.4	82.6
M	South Hills	1917	125 Ruth St., Mount Washington	9–12	2,358	16.8	83.2
N	Westinghouse	1912	N. Murtland & Monticello Sts., Homewood	9–12	2,251	100	0

Source: Pittsburgh Public Schools, *Membership Report of September 29, 1975* (Pittsburgh, 1975), 9.

majority. Some Lower Hill residents mourned their neighborhood school, while many South Hills parents feared "trouble" from the influx of black students. In fact, Brookline's Bob Corbin admitted that, before attending Brashear, he "pictured Fifth Avenue as a big, black school where the kids were nothing but bad." In 1978, the school experienced a twenty-five-person race-based brawl, after which knives, baseball bats, an ax handle, and unloaded revolvers were confiscated.[14]

Throughout the city, some whites were candidly racist, demonstrating anger reminiscent of the bloody South Boston riots.[15] "If you think they had it bad in Boston you ain't seen nothin'," a Carrick parent told District and PHRC officials in 1979. Racial violence plagued at least nine Pittsburgh high schools during this time.[16] In 1971, more than 200 white students blocked the Carrick High entrance and threw bricks at buses bringing blacks from the St. Clair Village projects.[17] Forty-nine whites were arrested, and though the school was only 6 percent black, Superintendent Louis J. Kishkunas said phone calls from the neighborhood were "dripping with hate."[18] However, Jean Fink, who led the antibusing Carrick Community Council, insisted that it "was not a racial issue" but one of community and autonomy.[19] In 1976, Fink won a seat on the District's first elected school board, where a conservative majority made PHRC compliance even more unlikely.[20]

Schenley's First Magnet: Health Careers

In 1977, Superintendent Jerry C. Olson proposed establishing magnet schools across the District, including a health careers program at Schenley. The magnet model—designed to draw students to nonfeeder schools with specialized curricula—offered a path to legal compliance while maintaining school choice.[21] Blacks were skeptical about whites' willingness to attend schools in predominantly black areas, while whites again opposed the busing component.[22] "If you're going to drop a bomb it might as well be hydrogen," laughed Fink, whose conservative faction initially rejected magnets.[23] The board's most vocal detractor, the provocative Frank Widina, alleged magnet students would be "snobs, snippy and stupid."[24] Notably, Widina opposed any integration plan ("wait until housing patterns change and schools become integrated naturally"), advocated ignoring court orders, and once called a black colleague, Jake Milliones, "boy" during a board meeting.[25] However, the board reversed course after losing a state Supreme Court appeal, preferring its own plan to one imposed by a "master of desegregation from Harrisburg." On March 21, 1979, the board created sixteen magnet programs, including Health

Careers at Schenley. The 5–4 vote was split ideologically, with opposition from both liberals and conservatives.[26]

Enter Richard Wallace

One year later, the board fired Olson, whose seven-year tenure as superintendent was marked by racial unrest and plummeting enrollment.[27] More than forty candidates sought to replace him, and Bill Cooley, an education expert at the University of Pittsburgh, urged his friend Richard C. Wallace Jr. to apply.[28] Wallace, then superintendent in Fitchburg, Massachusetts—with an enrollment and budget less than nine percent of those in Pittsburgh—was building a national reputation as an innovator.[29] Wallace huddled with Cooley and his Pitt colleagues, Bill Bickel and David Engel, the latter of whom was also a board member. Wallace recalled, "I kept asking, 'Can you do anything in Pittsburgh? Is the political and educational climate such that I could get something done?' The answer I kept getting was, 'Yes, yes, yes, yes.'"[30]

Wallace was hired in August 1980 and formally asked the board to define their priorities. "It worked," he said, "because I was working on their agenda, not mine." Top action items included desegregation, closing the achievement gap, managing enrollment decline, and attracting students back from private schools. The new superintendent also commissioned a comprehensive needs assessment survey of the District's stakeholders. The survey revealed that parents who had abandoned the District were concerned about discipline—tellingly, those with children in city schools had no such worry—and all parents feared another teachers strike, as three had occurred since 1968.[31]

Wallace assuaged discipline concerns through his "phenomenal PR director," Pat Crawford, who drew local and national press to the District's successes. To curtail labor worries, Wallace invested in a relationship with Al Fondy—president of the teachers' union—and negotiated a new contract "way ahead of time."[32] The superintendent's efforts bore fruit, and by early 1981, parents waited in the cold rain, some as long as twenty-four hours, to enroll their children in choice magnet programs.

Schenley's Health Careers program was not especially popular. Despite drawing slightly more students than magnets at South and Westinghouse, it was far under capacity.[33] The program gave students field and clinical experience at Presbyterian, Magee, Mercy, and other area hospitals, and inspired some to seek careers in the medical field.[34] While the Health Careers program challenged and engaged those enrolled, it attracted few whites. Thus, despite the program's growth to 137 students by its fourth year, Schenley overall remained 84.9 percent black.[35]

The John Young Era

In the fall of 1979, John Young '53 became Schenley's new principal. Young quickly made inroads at improving the culture by restoring basic discipline, fostering faculty buy-in, and resurrecting the PTA. Weeks into his tenure, the *Triangle* noted the newsworthiness of empty hallways and busy classrooms.[36] The new principal ended the "athletics first" mentality, which briefly made him unpopular, but his most effective move was banning snack trucks. The trucks sold junk food—and allegedly marijuana—but when the trucks stopped camping outside during school hours, so did students.

Admittedly, Young's early successes were nonacademic.[37] In 1980, only thirteen of 176 students graduated with honors.[38] Schenley was hamstrung by teachers who "were no longer really teaching," said Young. The school offered no Advanced Placement (AP) or calculus courses and lacked a culture of achievement. Middle-class pupils were nearly nonexistent, and Young's friends confessed they "could not sacrifice their kids to stay at Schenley."[39]

One obvious outlier was Diane Thompson '85: a white, type A, Shadyside resident whose progressive mother was committed to public schools. Zoned to attend Peabody High, Thompson's path to Schenley began in fifth grade, when a visit to Reizenstein, her neighborhood middle school, was "chaotic and scary."[40] Although Reizenstein offered

FIG. 29   Principal John Young assists a student using a computer. *Journal*, 1983, 69.

strong academics and a white, middle-class peer group—the school was strategically proximate to neighborhoods spanning racial and economic strata—Thompson preferred the Upper Hill's Milliones Middle School (formerly Herron Hill).[41] "People were friendly . . . discipline was not the uppermost preoccupation," said Thompson, likely the only nonfeeder white student to seek placement at Milliones, then 98.3 percent black.[42]

Unfazed by its racial composition, Thompson enjoyed the Upper Hill middle school and followed her classmates to Schenley, which seemed "so white" in comparison. While Thompson had few academic peers at Schenley, the National Merit Scholar "felt very protected" by her classmates, who elected her student body president. At a regional student government convention, Thompson's cohort laughed when she reflexively said, "We're the only black people here."[43]

Red and Black . . . and Orange?

Despite Wallace's relative success, the PHRC was losing patience. Schenley, South, and Westinghouse High Schools were still legally segregated, as were nineteen elementary schools.[44] In February 1982, the PHRC asked the Commonwealth Court to hold the District in contempt for noncompliance with past court orders. Further, the Commission sought forced mergers of four unbalanced schools: Schenley with South, and Allderdice with Westinghouse.[45] There was precedent for such action, as months earlier a federal judge had consolidated five nearby school districts to form Woodland Hills, causing considerable white anger.[46]

The PHRC argued that a Schenley-South merger would result in "a 50 [percent] balance." However, the Court refused the proposal based on the Commission's mathematical error, noting that a Schenley-South hybrid would in fact be 58 percent black. As the state's definition of a desegregated high school was between 28 percent and 53 percent black, the move would still produce a segregated school.[47] Notwithstanding the reprieve, it was clear that Schenley, with a 34 percent dropout rate, could only be saved through a drastic solution.[48]

The Teacher Center

Wallace needed to integrate Schenley, but he also faced personnel problems. According to the stakeholder survey, District staff believed there were "too many incompetent teachers and principals." In response to both issues, the superintendent proposed a teacher training laboratory at Schenley. Wallace could have placed the Teacher Center at South or Westinghouse but chose Schenley for practical reasons. He shared, "There's a saying among superintendents, 'A school district is only as good as your weakest high school.' Schenley clearly was failing. It was the lowest achieving high school in the District in 1980. It was a nonfunctioning school. It was also close to [the Board of Education building], where I could keep an eye on things, and in an area with a sufficient number of white students to desegregate the school."[49]

The Schenley High School Teacher Center, through which all 750 District high school teachers would cycle for nine-week mini-sabbaticals, would refresh and enhance teaching knowledge and techniques. "Let's make marginal people competent and competent people extraordinary," said Wallace of his mind-set. The Teacher Center was modeled after the Harvard-Lexington program in which Wallace had participated; he had implemented a similar model as an administrator in Holliston, Massachusetts. However, those centers served elementary and middle school teachers, and had taken place in the summer. Schenley's in-service training program would be the nation's first to operate in a high school during the school year.[50]

Wallace ensured buy-in by involving District staff in the planning, and more than two hundred staff volunteered to participate. It was important that the venture be collaborative, said Wallace, as the teachers' union was "powerful enough to pull the plug at any time." The superintendent frequently met with union head Al Fondy "at out-of-the-way restaurants," and he persuaded Fondy to approve fifty positions at the Teacher Center. The rest of the project was financed by grants, such as one from the Ford Foundation. As Wallace exceeded his fundraising goal by $10 million, the board was initially off the hook financially. "The board does not like to fund experimentation," Wallace said. However, the Teacher Center earned the board "so much national notoriety that they were eventually willing to fund it."[51]

Effective leadership would be critical. Judy Johnston, a Brashear vice principal, had impressed the superintendent with her work on the staff development team. "[Johnston] knew exactly what we were trying to achieve," remembered Wallace. Moreover, Johnston knew, liked, and worked well with Principal Young, who would remain head of the high school. Wallace felt it obvious to put the two together, and in July 1982, Johnston was named director of the training center.[52]

Staff Selection

Revitalizing Schenley required a veritable teaching all-star team. Wallace effectively reset the faculty and asked instructors across the District—including those already at Schenley—to apply for positions at the new

Teacher Center. The application process was exhaustive and competitive, with one hundred candidates for fifty positions.[53] Despite a deep talent pool, Principal Young personally recruited Carol Dyas, the 1980 state Teacher of the Year, whose skills were "ideal" to "change a culture in a school."[54] However, Dyas was happy at Langley High and only acquiesced when Wallace intervened, promising her a reduced teaching load and the activities director post.[55]

Not surprisingly, Langley's principal was angry, as were other administrators whose best teachers were poached.[56] Vincent Carr, principal at four District high schools during the 1980s, found the resource diversion "galling."[57] "If looks could kill, I would've been dead on the spot," said Wallace, describing meetings with District department chairs.[58] Some instructors also resented the Teacher Center, particularly veterans who were insulted by the suggestion that they needed to be retrained.[59] Neretta (Troxell) Brobst, then a Brashear English teacher, became a "virtual pariah" at the Beechview school when her Teacher Center appointment was made public.[60]

Schenley teachers were especially bitter at having to reapply for their jobs.[61] The process "caused anxiety," admitted Ann (Sharpe) Haley '59, one of sixteen teachers retained in Schenley's new incarnation. Unsuccessful candidates were dispatched to other schools.[62] "It was like saying, 'you're not good enough to be here,'" said math teacher Carol (Gift) Sperandeo, who was also selected to stay.[63]

Principal Young, Judy Johnston, and assistant superintendent Helen Faison chose the staff. "There was not a lot of dialogue about whether we'd keep Roger Babusci or Fred Lucas," said Young of effective, popular teachers who "had a following."[64] Decisions were mailed just before spring break in 1983, making the term's final months decidedly uncomfortable.[65] A long-time English teacher protested not being selected by wearing a black armband for the remainder of the year.[66] Haley suspected the process dismissed "older people who weren't amenable to change," but recognized that some Schenley teachers were unhappy and seized the opportunity to leave.[67]

More Magnets

While the Teacher Center could improve Schenley's toxic brand, it would not be sufficient to attract white students. Thus, the District announced three new Schenley magnets—International Studies (IS), High Technology (High Tech), and Classical Studies—to debut with the Teacher Center in the fall of 1983. Additionally, qualified IS juniors and seniors

Magnets Explained

- International Baccalaureate (IB): Developed and facilitated by the Geneva, Switzerland–based IB Organization, the program emphasized critical thinking over memorization, and its diploma was seen as equivalent to a full Advanced Placement (AP) course load, the United Kingdom's General Certificate, France's Baccalaureate, and Germany's Abitur. The IB diploma could help a student earn sophomore standing in college, but required a two-year course and exams in seven subjects—English, a modern foreign language, math, science, social science, art, and theory of knowledge—plus a 4,000-word independent research essay, and community service.

- International Studies (IS): This program was built around a language concentration in French, German, Japanese, or Spanish, which most students began in kindergarten. Other academic courses were also globally oriented. English

emphasized world literature; social studies emphasized international relations; and science emphasized global ecology.

- High Technology (High Tech): This program required a bevy of technical courses—electronics, technical drawing, computer-aided design, technical writing, computer applications, and robotics—but was not traditionally vocational. Students also took honors-level academics, and most went on to four-year colleges or technical schools.

- Classical Studies: This curriculum focused on philosophy, science, arts, and Greek and Roman culture. While the magnet proved popular at Sterrett Middle School, it failed to attract students to Schenley and was quickly abandoned.[68]

could merge into the International Baccalaureate (IB) program, a rigorous, globally focused, college-level curriculum.[69]

"My God!" thought Brobst, "Richard Wallace really thinks he can pull this off?" Brobst's reaction to the Schenley proposal was more optimistic than most.[70] The board's four liberals, including its three black members, rejected the magnets.[71] The Hill District's Jake Milliones called the plan "repulsive and an insult to the black community," while some Upper Hill parents resented the idea that a functional school required white students.[72] The plan passed, 5–4, in October 1982.[73]

"What's our drawing card here?" asked Frances Vitti, a nay vote, who noted that the IS program's foreign-language courses were already offered at every high school. The District countered that the IB program would attract students, but many did not believe whites would voluntarily attend an all-black school.[74] The PHRC conditionally approved the Schenley reboot, but cautioned that failure to draw 115 white students annually would trigger a mandatory integration plan.[75] Soon Schenley staff and parents were recruiting as if their school depended on it.[76]

8 | Renaissance
1983–1993

> Schenley was the worst school in the system. They took the
> worst and made it a model.
>
> —SUZANNE DAVENPORT, DESIGNS FOR CHANGE

Schenley worked hard to sell apprehensive students on its magnet programs and enthusiastic teaching corps. The first magnet students took a
chance that the failing school would improve, and within four years, the
vision of Superintendent Richard C. Wallace Jr. was thriving. By the late
1980s, Schenley was a national model of voluntary integration and scholarship, and parents from across the city braved days-long lines to enroll
their children.

Leap of Faith

Schenley needed to draw whites to avoid state intervention, but many
were hesitant to gamble on the city's lowest-rated high school. "It was
a scary idea," admitted Jason Brown '89, who had wanted to follow his
friends to Allderdice High and was initially "not super happy" that his parents picked Schenley.[1] Dawn (Gust) Vero '89 was allowed to choose her
high school but struggled with the decision all summer, and said leaving
her Carrick-bound twin "was a huge leap of faith."[2]

Despite its reputation, some early magnet students found it easy to
choose Schenley, such as Leah Wahrhaftig '87, a white Regent Square
resident in the first International Studies (IS) class. Wahrhaftig's mother
and father had grown up amidst systemic racism—in Rhodesia and South
Carolina, respectively—which inspired them to work for civil rights.
Moreover, her parents "had huge faith" in the District, and Leah herself
"was quite happy" to join the experiment.[3] Similarly, Andrea Boykowycz
'89 "almost kissed the ground" when she got to Schenley in 1985, pleased

FIG. 30 A billboard advertising enrollment at Schenley. *Journal*, 1984.

to leave an unpleasant private school experience. Still, the Oakland resident admitted some risk and that, upon enrolling in the third year of the reboot, "it was not yet clear that it was going to be okay."[4]

Notwithstanding a few eager families, most still saw a school in tumult. "Where you see tumult," laughed Mary Ellen Kirby in 2014, "many of us saw the brink of greatness and dared to make that leap."[5] Kirby, a white Stanton Heights parent, allayed fears through grassroots recruiting, and was so effective at selling Wallace's vision that the District hired her to attract white students. She "gave the pitch" at East End coffees, District middle schools, and even Polish Hill's Immaculate Heart of Mary School, where working-class whites had long escaped integration. Kirby targeted exceptional students by cold-calling seventh grade Hopkins Scholars and pushing the International Baccalaureate (IB) diploma.[6] "[Kirby] was very, very sharp, very, very savvy," remarked English teacher Neretta (Troxell) Brobst.[7]

Jackie Perhach, a Knoxville parent, was Kirby's High Technology (High Tech) counterpart and later became the program's full-time manager.[8] Principal John Young credited Kirby and Perhach with "recruiting the white students that we needed to make that school go as it should." Young, who is black, clarified, "I didn't mind going with a school that was all black, but I knew that an all-black school wouldn't get the resources it needed."[9]

FIG. 31 One hundred twenty-five parents camped outside Reizenstein Middle School to secure their children space in magnet programs, 1986. *Pittsburgh Press*, November 7, 1986, A1. Photo: John Sale. Copyright © *Pittsburgh Post-Gazette*, 2016, all rights reserved. Reprinted with permission.

Call It a Comeback

In September 1983, Schenley launched its long-awaited upgrades, which included an in-house teacher training center, a blue-chip faculty, and three new magnets. Rebranded as the Schenley High School Teacher Center, the school yielded results—and praise from the *New York Times*, *Los Angeles Times*, *Christian Science Monitor*, and *Education Week*.[10] "[The Teacher Center is] the most exciting development in in-service teacher education in America," gushed Lee Schulman, president of the American Educational Research Association.[11] In its second semester, the program attracted tuition-paying suburban teachers, who raved about the value of constructive, clinical feedback in a largely isolated profession.[12]

The most persuasive endorsement was student achievement. In 1981, only 27 percent of students scored at or above the national norm in language, but the figure spiked to 77 percent by 1987. Accordingly, Schenley's ranking surged, from last place to third of eleven District high schools.[13] By the era's end, there was a 53 percent uptick in honors graduates, and many landed at elite universities, such as Harvard, Columbia, Cornell, and Georgetown.[14] Rachel Pottinger '93 was prepared for Duke, where the advanced French class read the same books used in her high school courses.[15] Additionally, Miriam Allersma '87 entered Bryn Mawr College as a sophomore, with credits earned from Schenley's first IB diploma.[16]

The renaissance even impressed the White House, with US secretary of education William Bennett observing classes in 1986.[17] The following year, President Ronald Reagan honored Schenley with the Flag of Excellence in a Rose Garden ceremony.[18] Geometry teacher Catherine Jatkowski also earned executive honors, receiving the 1986 Presidential Award for Excellence in Science and Mathematics.[19]

These results made magnets wildly popular at Schenley and other District schools, and parents camped out to reserve space in the registration line. Even school board member Jake Milliones—who had decried magnets as "a joke" that were "not going to work at Schenley"—waited out the queue to enroll his daughter in the IS program.[20] In 1987, the line morphed into a "six-day vigil," where record-breaking winter weather and angry parents prompted a pivot to a lottery system.[21] Recruiting had mostly targeted East End whites, but many nonfeeder blacks and at least one suburban student were also pulled to Schenley's magnets.[22]

Integration: It's Elementary

By 1993, Schenley's enrollment had increased by 56.6 percent.[23] "If you build it, they will come," laughed English teacher Carol Dyas.[24] This influx eased racial imbalance, as nonblack students—which the District collectively classified as "other" through at least 2001—more than tripled, from 122 (15 percent) to 445 (43 percent), between the 1982–83 and 1990–91 school years.[25] The ratio was primarily driven by white arrivals, but District interventions also had an impact. New feeder boundaries diverted some black students to Brashear and Allderdice, and in 1985, Schenley's predominantly black Health Careers magnet was moved to South High.[26]

Notably, white families' interest in Schenley took years to cultivate. Superintendent Richard C. Wallace Jr. favored early integration and saw its success in foreign language-based IS magnets at East Hills, Liberty, and Linden Elementary Schools.[27] To maintain this momentum, Wallace established a middle school IS program—which quickly outgrew Dilworth and moved to Frick in 1986—"as a steppingstone" into Schenley's high school iteration.[28] Thus, students followed the magnet, studying the same language with many of the same classmates from kindergarten through high school. "None of the cultural mixing [at Schenley] was remarkable, having gone through East Hills," said Esther Wahrhaftig '90.[29] This continuity fostered "true integration . . . not

TABLE 5 Schenley High School Enrollment by Race, 1982–1993

Year	Enrollment	Black	Other	% Black	% Other
1982–83	808	686	122	84.9	15.1
1983–84	814	650	164	79.9	20.1
1984–85	1,058	759	299	71.7	28.3
1985–86	1,038	731	307	70.4	29.6
1986–87	1,062	703	359	66.2	33.8
1987–88	1,089	706	383	64.8	35.2
1988–89	1,025	656	369	64.0	36.0
1989–90	948	580	368	61.2	38.8
1990–91	1,043	598	445	57.3	42.7
1991–92	1,035	591	444	57.1	42.9
1992–93	1,182	676	506	57.2	42.8

Source: Pittsburgh Public Schools, *Membership Reports*, 1982–1992 (Pittsburgh, 1992).

just desegregation," according to Mary Ellen Kirby, a Schenley parent-turned-District recruiter,[30] and the distinction is evident in career IS pupils, such as G. Ryin Gaines '00—a black Catholic from Homewood—who made so many Jewish friends that he "desperately wanted to be Jewish and have a bar mitzvah."[31]

All-Star Teachers

Schenley's revamped faculty was essential to the school's quick turn-around. "In general, the teachers were kind of amazing," said Esther Wahrhaftig '90.[32] Some new additions yielded instant credibility, such as Bob Dilts (math), who held a doctorate and had taught at Pitt.[33] Dolores Kubiak (chemistry) added rigor, as the quirky former pharmacist "beat the bejesus out of [students] academically."[34] Geraldine McFarland (computer applications), a 1992 state Teacher of the Year finalist, guided multiple High Tech students to victories in statewide competitions and was chosen by the Smithsonian to field test aerospace lesson plans.[35] Similarly, Neretta (Troxell) Brobst (English) brought demanding standards, exacting elocution, and incisive real-life lessons.[36] Her courses taught "everything of value," recalled Andrea Boykowycz '89, and Bill Mitchell '85 followed Brobst's advice ("dream a little bit bigger") from the Terrace Village projects to Harvard to a US Navy commission.[37]

The faculty was also well rounded, as Norman Brown and Karen Price joined Pam Haywood for a formidable art department.[38] Haywood's free spirit—speaking bluntly, bringing her dogs to class, and modeling for figure studies—put students at ease with their own creativity.[39] These enthusiastic instructors implemented Arts Propel—a Harvard collaboration that nurtured artistic talents as forms of intelligence—earning Schenley a mention in a *Newsweek* piece, "The Best Schools in the World."[40] The department also solicited Raymond Saunders '53, an internationally known painter, to help students create a mural.[41]

The teaching team excelled, not only for their individual talents, but also because universal buy-in fostered exceptional morale. "The difference was everyone in that building was there because they wanted to be," said Ann (Sharpe) Haley '59 (English).[42] Brobst agreed and likened the faculty's commitment—enduring weekend and summer trainings, and occasional travel for conferences—to that of "missionaries or disciples." She said, "This led to camaraderie being through the roof. . . . The staff became amazingly close, and that was one of the elements of being chosen for this grand experiment in Oakland. We lived and breathed Schenley High School for a decade. It was just real craziness until it got off the ground. It made us really reassess our purpose and our dedication. This makes it all sound very mystical or religious, but maybe in a sense it is." Schenley staff had no choice except to be friends, joked Brobst, because "the rest of [the District's] teachers hated us."[43]

This exceptional faculty—and Schenley at large—was anchored by Carol Dyas (English).[44] Her enthusiasm and expectations, both high and uncompromising, were essential for a school relearning to believe in itself. "[Dyas] was exactly what I needed," said Missy (Kaefer) Stokes '97, who hated to read and initially thought she was "never gonna make it." Stokes, a mainstream student, was overwhelmed by Dyas's knowledge of Shakespeare and ability to quote books from memory. "She was hard and made me read, and told me the importance of reading and of my future," said Stokes, who now works for a literary journal.

Dyas's attitude also inspired students, and Stokes, like most of Schenley, "wanted that spunk."[45] As activities director, Dyas's zeal permeated the building, and alumni described her pep rallies as "unbelievable," "incredible," and "epic." The diminutive Dyas would bark cheers as she strutted the stage frenetically, whipping the toughest, most disaffected teens into hysterics.[46] "Spartan Spirit," Schenley's signature cheer in its final twenty-eight years, followed Dyas well into retirement, as one day on a trip to the mall, she was startled to hear the distinctive call from hundreds of feet away.[47]

Crucially, Schenley's overhaul engendered a culture of ambition and helped narrow the racial achievement gap. By the Teacher Center's fourth year, black students' standardized test scores had more than doubled, and honors assemblies were filled with applause instead of jeers.[48] The principal's office even got a call from a Schenley Farms neighbor who was shocked to see students carry books.[49]

However, change came with difficulty. Hill District residents initially resented the magnets, which the majority felt were only motivated by the integration mandate. "There was a racial issue," said Bill Mitchell '85, who, despite being black, was bullied by black neighbors for his studiousness. Mitchell grew up in Terrace Village, where low expectations and taunts of "acting white" led capable black students to resist magnet courses.[50] Notably, some black parents eschewed magnets in protest, complaining, "[Schenley] didn't have these programs when it was all black."[51]

After much prodding, mainstream students began to migrate into magnets, which demonstrated the utility of housing diverse students and programs together. "Kids from difficult backgrounds have to be able to see that these opportunities exist and have to be exposed to people who are succeeding," Brobst said. "They need to be part of that in order to become those other things."[52] Black achievement had jumped by the mid-1980s, and a decade later, the IS program was racially balanced.[53] "It wasn't cool to be smart when I started [seventeen years ago]," English teacher Roger Babusci told the *Post-Gazette* in 1988, "[b]ut now the priorities for the kids have shifted."[54]

Spartan Classics Academy

The shrinking achievement gap was also the result of the Spartan Classics Academy (SCA), which addressed the unique needs of mainstream pupils. These students were "getting lost," worried Principal Young, who allowed Schenley teachers to design the new curriculum.[55] Partly inspired by Theodore Sizer, a Brown University education reformer, the SCA program launched in 1988.[56] SCA was not a magnet—serving only mainstream students from feeder neighborhoods—but it was arguably the school's most specialized program.

As most SCA students had remedial needs, with many considered at-risk, the program was structured to enhance personalization and extend teaching time. The SCA program pioneered looping: the now-popular practice of advancing students to the next grade level with the same teacher.[57] Looping fostered trust, reduced introduction time, and illuminated individual students' issues.[58] The staff was exclusive to the program and conferenced daily about students' barriers and breakthroughs. Additionally, an on-site social worker helped navigate behavioral and personal problems. "We were teaching to the child," said program director Ann (Sharpe) Haley '59.[59]

The SCA program also used alternate day block scheduling, with fewer classes per day, but in longer installments. The 130-minute morning block, with two consecutive classes in the same room with the same teacher, allowed sixty-five minutes per subject without disruptive classroom changes. "Nobody does anything in forty-five minutes," said Haley, who was sold on the model at the Brookings Institution. While the weekly schedule stayed fixed, class sequence varied by day. "You know there's always a kid coming to school late," Haley reasoned, "and some kids are better up in the morning than the afternoon."[60]

Some IS students pitied or feared their SCA counterparts, and many middle-class blacks were uncomfortable with the idea of poor, minority students being "hidden" in the basement.[61] However, Haley remains resentful of such notions and clarified that SCA classes—actually on the first and ground floors—were located to avoid disruptions from the magnet programs' divergent bell schedule. "Nobody was in the basement," insisted Haley, who said, "those kids got more than [IB students] upstairs."[62] To be sure, the SCA program's personal touch was unprecedented. In addition to after-school tutoring and make-up classes, teachers occasionally telephoned students' homes to wake them up, or made house calls to conference with parents.[63] "[The SCA program] treated us like we were more than just students," wrote Tom Podgorski '96, who felt the staff was "like another family."[64] While teachers encouraged thriving students to transfer into accelerated courses, many were reluctant to sacrifice the SCA program's personalization. "Kids really felt like teachers cared about them, which we did," said Haley.[65]

SCA was costly: $100,000 per year for a program with fewer than 100 students per grade. However, expensive amenities such as a social worker and full-time program director were invaluable in many students' lives. When the Heinz Foundation's initial funding expired in 1994, students personally lobbied the school board, which ultimately financed the program.[66]

Schools Within a School

Schenley's new composition, which included several diverse curricular programs—or schools within a school—enhanced esprit de corps. "The concept of the school should not have worked," said Matt Rahuba '98, "but it did."[67] Magnet programs were especially cohesive in part because students were there by choice. Graduation "was like leaving your family," said Dawn (Gust) Vero '89, an IS student who shed tears with classmates and teachers.[68] This familial trope was a cultural anomaly, observed Jason Brown '89, who noted "[most] people don't talk about high school with any sort of reverence."[69]

Pride was just as high in the Hill District, where Schenley was entrenched in the culture.[70] "Growing up on the Hill, you were keenly aware of [Schenley's] history," said Darrick Suber '89, who felt the school and its successes were critical to "a neighborhood in the process of decaying." In contrast, Brashear, the Hill's other high school, was "tougher." Jack Higgins '01, a Whiteside Road projects native, said, "I had friends who went [to Brashear] who ain't even alive no more."[71] Although most Hill residents were zoned for Schenley, many others "engineered a way" in, such as using a relative's address. "There was no way I wasn't going to Schenley," insisted Suber, who lived on the Brashear side of the boundary.[72]

While Schenley students were happy within their programs, there was initially little symbiosis between magnet and mainstream tracks.[73] Race and class compounded this divide: magnet students were overwhelmingly white and middle-class, while the SCA program served mostly black, working-class pupils.[74] SCA students resented a double standard for magnets, while some students in the IB program, such as Michelle Allersma '89, felt "like a fish out of water" during integrated electives.[75] "We [IB students] were a bit of a clique," admitted Tracy Kroner '89, but qualified that they were a "nerd clique" and had to work for acceptance from black groups.[76] Acutely aware of this chasm, Principal Young emphasized extra-curricular activities, the primary fora for inter-track socialization, and defended them to teachers who found them disruptive.[77]

Despite this "feeling of separation," Schenley was unusually harmonious.[78] When a journalist asked if racial tensions were resolved, Dana Boswell '90 replied, "*And then some. We're like a big family here.*"[79] The majority black school elected three nonblack student body presidents— two white, one Arab, all female—and an interracial homecoming king and queen.[80] Immigrants also felt welcome, such as China's Xiaowei (Gao) Nguyen '89, who recalled classmates in her gym locker room cheering her name "for no reason."[81] Moreover, inter-track relations warmed with time, especially as students from the District's integrated elementary magnets reached Schenley.[82]

Schenley Theater: The Sound of Magic

Schenley initially produced semiannual class plays, which flourished in the 1920s under Theodore A. Viehman, a Carnegie Tech drama instructor. Viehman would later direct at least one Broadway play and dozens of professional shows. His successor, Chester B. Story, had acted and directed professionally, taught at Harvard, Tufts, and Carnegie Tech, and brought an "almost professional" standard to Schenley. After 1951, plays were largely abandoned at the school for two decades.

In 1971, Roger Babusci, a "young, cool" twenty-nine-year-old English teacher, arrived at Schenley. The next spring, students asked him to revive the tradition. His no-frills production of *Five on the Black Hand Side* was plagued with difficulties but challenged the perception that theater was uncool. Three years later, he tried his first musical, *Purlie*. Schenley was still predominantly black, but Babusci refused to be confined creatively, and in 1976, he "may have staged the first all-black version of *Guys and Dolls*." The spring musical became an annual event in the neighborhood, and by 1980, shows sold out, with long lines down Centre Avenue.

In the classroom, Babusci won respect through humor—drawing apathetic pupils to class on time for the "teaching comedian." Moreover, Babusci believed in students before they did. When he was named the 1983 Pennsylvania Teacher of the Year, he was introduced at the award ceremony by Kim Cobbs '83, who had auditioned to be a dancer in *West Side Story* but ended up dazzling as Maria. The director was beloved, even though he could be demanding, cantankerous, and "slightly terrifying." He often yelled and threw things, but his tantrums reflected his commitment, and students saw the "intimidating teddy bear" cry after every show.

FIG. 32 Schenley's *West Side Story*, 1982. *Journal*, 1983, 31.

FIG. 33 Roger Babusci, with student Kim Cobbs, is named the Pennsylvania Teacher of the Year by Governor Dick Thornburgh. *Journal*, 1983, 65.

As magnet programs integrated Schenley in the 1980s, the musical bridged demographic gaps, and Babusci maintained colorblind casting. The school was less stratified by the 1990s, but the musicals continued to defy convention by drawing "cool kids," "not-so-cool kids," scholars, "band geeks," and even "jocks." The shows established a broader following as they racked up Gene Kelly Awards, a Tony-like showcase for regional high schools. Schenley won forty awards in twenty-one years, but students insisted the experience was greater than the accolades. "You were doing it for the ghost in the auditorium," said Babusci's daughter, Alison '88, in reference to "the reputation of every musical that had been done there." This legacy helped recruiting, as some middle school students chose Schenley over the District's Creative and Performing Arts (CAPA) high school after seeing a Babusci musical.

In 2006, after thirty-five productions and four heart attacks, Babusci retired from directing, and the auditorium was named in his honor. English teacher Kelly McKrell '95 replaced Babusci. A musical alumna who had been Babusci's assistant director, McKrell also demanded perfection. "When she directs, it's like watching myself direct [twenty] years ago," Babusci said. When Babusci passed away in 2008, dozens of alumni crashed that evening's rehearsal, sitting in the auditorium's dark last row in silent tribute to their director. Eight days later, the Schenley building's final production, *All Shook Up*, was a "truly magical" send-off, declared the *Post-Gazette*. "[T]he weight of the situation could have easily overshadowed the performance itself. Schenley, however, had other plans."[83]

Furthering its diversity, Schenley soon added English as a Second Language (ESL) and Pittsburgh Ballet Theatre (PBT) programs. The ESL program began at Allderdice in 1983 but was moved to Schenley the following year to improve racial balance, complement IS, and convenience immigrants who mostly lived in Oakland. Students had intensive English-language courses with Carolyn Burgh until they were proficient enough for traditional coursework. By 1990, Schenley had thirty-seven ESL students representing sixteen nations and four continents.[84]

In an essay in the *Triangle* detailing her family's escape from Cambodian genocide, Ly Hong '93 shared a jarring sense of perspective. "Sometimes in our lives, even here at Schenley, we feel trapped and restricted," wrote Hong. "We don't feel free, but we are."[85] Some American students relished the international flavor, such as Sharice Smalls '88, who actually transferred to Schenley for the chance to interact with different ethnicities. Smalls soon became close with a Japanese classmate and wrote in a 1987 op-ed in the *Triangle* that Schenley fostered "open-mindedness" by "bring[ing] the world under one roof."[86]

Schenley's PBT program, launched in 1986, was a partnership between the District and the dance company. Gifted student dancers, affectionately known as "PBTs," received intensive training in the morning (8:00 A.M. to 9:30 A.M.) and afternoon (3:00 P.M. to 6:00 P.M.), with an abbreviated academic schedule in between. On Saturdays, they trained from 10:30 A.M. to 4:00 P.M. The program, patterned after those attached to the Paris Opera and Royal Ballets, gave students a leg up on post–high school professional opportunities.[87] "I think it's really impossible to get a job without it," said Eva Trapp '01, of full-time ballet schools, which were then scarce outside of Manhattan.[88]

Schenley's first class of fifteen dancers included six from outside the region, who moved to Pittsburgh without their families and boarded with company-approved host parents.[89] Danielle Sunseri '87 left friends and familiarity in nearby Wintersville, Ohio, to begin Schenley as a senior. "I can't live without [ballet]," Sunseri told the *Triangle,* "and sometimes I can't live with it."[90] The PBTs fed Schenley's culture of ambition; early alumni—Sunseri (Colorado Ballet), Crystal Conway (Boston Ballet), Valentine Liberatore '91 (Cincinnati Ballet), and Todd Jost '89 (Miami City Ballet)—were decidedly successful.[91] The program's steep tuition—$4,095 for local students and $6,945 for boarders in 1988—added socioeconomic diversity to Schenley.[92]

A Historic Facility

In the midst of Schenley's renewal, the seventy-year-old building was added to the National Register of Historic Places in 1986.[93] Days later, the school christened a long-awaited athletic addition—including a six-lane, twenty-five-yard pool with seating for 200, and a standard high school basketball court with seating for 600—adjoining the building's southwest corner.[94]

Students delighted in the $9.2 million upgrade, as the old facilities had become decidedly dangerous.[95] The original gymnasia—located on the basement floor—were also tiny by contemporary standards, with varsity basketball games moved off campus in the 1960s. Team practices and gym classes were plagued by "poor lighting," "obstructive poles," and exposed brick walls less than a foot from boundary lines.[96] The original pool, located on the ground floor, was also archaic, with a ceiling so low that the diving board was removed to protect students from hitting their heads.[97] After the addition in 1986, the original gymnasia were converted into a weight training/wrestling room and vocational classrooms, while the original pool was converted to counselors' offices.[98]

Might as Well Jump

As in past decades, students again had exceptional experiences, even beyond academic achievements. In 1991, Thomas Buschek's world cultures class was chosen to correspond with Soviet students in what were likely Schenley's first e-mails.[99] Melvin Plowden '85 made the silver screen, as the senior appeared in *Rappin'* with Ice-T, Mario Van Peebles, and Eriq LaSalle.[100] Prominent visitors were also in evidence, such as NYSE chairman William Donaldson, future college basketball coaching legend John Calipari, and Pittsburgh Steeler Merril Hoge.[101]

However, the era's most surreal moment involved an open third-floor window. On April 30, 1985, Bob Pack attended school—despite being suspended—and got into a fight before 9:00 A.M. Warned that he was trespassing, Pack shouted, "I can't go to jail!" and dove head first out of a window. According to the *Pittsburgh Press*, Pack fell fifty feet, flipped over twice in the air, and landed in the bushes outside the main office. "He then got up and walked away" and was unharmed except for "minor bruises."[102]

Wallace's Legacy

Superintendent Wallace, the architect of Schenley's renaissance, retired in 1992.[103] Some question whether the Teacher Center produced demonstrable, sustainable results. However, Wallace's critics were few—mostly stakeholders in neighborhood schools that suffered from Schenley's resurgence.[104] Most former District staff still heap praise on the "visionary," and Howard Bullard—Schenley's thirteenth principal and a teacher at Allderdice in the 1980s—called him the city's best superintendent "bar none."[105]

Notably, Wallace's successes were District-wide, as he raised overall proficiency, halved the achievement gap, and made Pittsburgh a national model of urban education.[106] While the city hemorrhaged population, he mitigated enrollment decline, growing the District by 2.9 percent in his final three years.[107] "We had so many students coming back from private schools," remembered Wallace, "we had to buy parochial school buildings and reopen some closed schools."[108] Despite myriad achievements in his twelve-year tenure, Wallace today remains "most proud of" the turnaround at Schenley.[109]

9 The School of Choice
1994–2007

Schenley was red-hot, with prospective students facing long odds in a magnet admissions lottery. The school's record of achievement drew diverse pupils—including some from prestigious private schools—while its community proved unusually inclusive for pregnant teens, sexual minorities, and political refugees. The District at large was less successful, as a leadership vacuum and a movement to curb busing exacerbated a budget crisis.

Hot School

By the 1990s, Schenley had fully shaken its stigma and was not only viable, but also hip. The school enjoyed a six-page spread in *Seventeen* magazine, a visit from Jesse Jackson (who called it "a little [United Nations]"), and a growing reputation for academic rigor.[1] In 1997, 83 percent of graduates were college-bound, and the International Baccalaureate (IB) magnet was so renowned—churning out Ivy Leaguers, National Merit Scholars, and the 2000 national debate champions—that it was adopted at affluent suburban schools, including Upper St. Clair and Vincentian.[2]

News of these credentials was well-traveled. Lee Scott—a native of rural Butler County who met several Schenley alumni at Carnegie Mellon—"grew up thinking Schenley was a prep school."[3] Private school families were also impressed, and Schenley received transfers from Shady Side Academy, The Ellis School, The Linsly School, Central Catholic, and Oakland Catholic.[4] One such transfer, Knoxville's Carmen Bruce '02, had enjoyed Winchester Thurston but found it unrealistic. "Life isn't a private school," Bruce said, "it's a city school!"[5]

Demand for Schenley's magnets exceeded capacity, and each program had racial quotas. International Studies (IS) reserved seats for those continuing from Frick, leaving long odds for new applicants. In 1995, thirty-three white students entered a lottery for four IS seats.[6] Others got in through less orthodox means, such as one Pittsburgh Ballet Theatre

(PBT) student, who asked not to be named, from suburban Ross Township. Despite dropping dance after her junior year, the student felt so ingrained in Schenley that she paid tuition to stay.[7]

"A Huge Fraternity"

Schenley's new popularity prompted a magnet expansion, and enrollment surged 45.5 percent between the 1991–92 and 2004–5 school years, up to 1,516 students.[8] Accordingly, Robert Nicklos '55, principal from 1995 to 2000, dubbed Schenley the "school of choice."[9] Newcomers brought the most racial balance since the 1960s, with a 56.1 percent to 43.9 percent black majority in 1994–95.[10] Although the District still counted all nonblacks as "other," a yearbook audit indicates that Asian (6.5 percent), Jewish (3.8 percent), Arab (2.3 percent), and Latino (1.6 percent) students were proportionally greater at Schenley than in the region at large.[11] Socioeconomic diversity also proliferated, with wealthier students attending alongside the 57 percent receiving free or reduced-cost lunches, and 20 percent receiving public assistance.[12]

Notably, class began to transcend race, as working-class whites and middle-class blacks, who had fled the school in the late 1960s, returned in significant numbers. Most such whites came from feeder areas, such as Bloomfield, Lawrenceville, and Polish Hill.[13] However, some working-class whites came from the South Hills—despite that area's lingering prejudice—for the High Technology (High Tech) magnet. James Porco '96 said his Bon Avon neighbors laughed that he was a white minority, but Porco liked Schenley's cosmopolitan vibe and that many classmates had "hippie, professor" parents.[14] Significantly, the renewed middle-class black presence was illuminating for both black and white students, as it defied latent stereotypes about race and class.[15]

Competitive admissions bumped spirit up to zeal, as the public school suddenly felt exclusive.[16] Outsiders compared the school to "a huge fraternity," and according to Jesse Andrews '00—who set his Sundance-winning film, *Me and Earl and the Dying Girl,* at Schenley—most students were happily aware that it was odd to enjoy high school. "We know that you're looking at it and not getting it," said Andrews, "and that makes us even prouder."[17] While spirit was certainly not universal, it was pervasive and sometimes manifested in graffiti (e.g., "Schenley High On a Rise" scrawled in a stairwell in 1999).[18]

To be sure, the era brought much to celebrate: academic achievements, the musicals' many Gene Kelly Awards, a rapidly rising brand, and the basketball program was again a power. The Spartans appeared in three

state title games in seven seasons—winning one—and claimed eighty consecutive league victories between 2004 and 2009.[19] Despite this success in sports, many athletes made a point of celebrating their classmates' scholastic and artistic achievements.[20]

This school unity was strengthened by language, as distinctive Hill District slang became ubiquitous across social strata. The foremost expression, "nephs," began as a veracity oath "on [one's] dead homies," and dubious claims were often met with a challenge to "say nephs" that the statement was true. Notably, the word was not used in other Pittsburgh neighborhoods, and as usage grew decidedly casual (e.g., "nephs, I'm hungry"), it became symbolic of Schenley identity—appearing on banners, the backs of athletic jerseys, and even in academic assignments.[21]

In addition to the school's popularity, morale was high because students felt accepted and free to float between "ballerinas, basketball players, theater nerds, band geeks, and hackers."[22] According to Carmen Bruce '02, the lunchroom—where, unlike at many high schools,[23] "everybody sat with everybody"—epitomized the clique-free atmosphere. "I had friends that were in the IB program that were headed to Harvard, and I had friends in Spartan Classics that didn't go to college," said Bruce, who thought this social fusion "was the coolest thing!"[24]

Cooper Miller '00 tested this tolerance in ninth grade when his father went public as Wendi, a transgender woman. After five years of secrecy, Wendi came out on *Ricki Lake*, a television tabloid then attempting a more serious format. Miller also appeared on the show in support of Wendi, as he said producers wanted to show "a kid who's lived with a transgender parent and is okay." The day after the episode aired, a classmate recognized Miller and gushed with questions. Miller recalled, "A black girl said, 'Oh my God! I saw you on TV! It was amazing! How was Ricki? Is she fat in person?' Suddenly it didn't matter why I'd been on [TV]. I was on it! Another girl asked why I was on [*Ricki Lake*], and the first girl said, 'You had to see it.' She was totally protecting me! It was amazing that I went from total anxiety to total support—which is a very Schenley thing."[25]

Not all students were initially so accepting. "I am ashamed to admit it," said Bloomfield's Laura (Sirbaugh) Ratica '97, "but I guess you could say I was a little racist before I went to Schenley." At Immaculate Conception Elementary, classmates told Ratica that blacks were thieves and rapists, while a teacher warned that public school girls became "pregnant, drug addicted, dropout[s] living in the ghetto." Ratica begged her mother not to send her to Schenley and was anxious on her first day. When Toni Edwards '97, a black student, extended a lunch invitation to Ratica, she accepted begrudgingly but quickly felt so welcomed by Edwards and her friends that she "wonder[ed] if the nuns had it wrong." Ratica began attending services with Protestant and Jewish classmates, and made gay friends, whom she supported when the District banned same-sex prom couples. The gay students arrived with opposite-sex dates, Ratica recalled, but "once at prom, we all stood proud with them as they danced with their actual partners."[26]

One gay student, Leland Scruby '99, said his sexual orientation was a burden before coming out in tenth grade. Word quickly spread throughout Schenley, where, to Scruby's surprise, he was "never once" bullied and even became a novelty. Many teachers were protective, and classmates across social strata were supportive, inquisitive, or indifferent at worst. "I got really lucky being at [Schenley]," said Scruby, who imagined a much worse fate at his neighborhood school, Allderdice.[27]

Teen parents were also fortunate. In 1972, the Infant-Toddler Center made Schenley one of the nation's first high schools with on-site child-care services. The Laboratory Nursery School, which gave academic credit for training in early child care, opened in 1985.[28] Moreover, students seemed atypically accepting of pregnant classmates. Rachel Ombres '03, who came to Schenley from Shady Side Academy, was initially shocked to see an ultrasound photo in a student's locker but appreciated that supportive girlfriends surrounded the expecting student. Taboo "appeared to not exist" at Schenley, thought Ombres, and in fact, shaming behaviors were largely seen as unacceptable.[29] For many students, initial fascination with the child-care centers quickly dissipated, as they became "so matter-of-fact, so normal."[30]

This culture of empathy was invaluable when trauma rocked Schenley. In 1997, recent alumna Robin Little '96 was murdered by her husband. Five years later, Jason Griffin '02 and Darren "Deedle" Dolby '02 were both gunned down in the Hill District within a five-month span.[31] Griffin, a college-bound IS student, had just been voted the most popular senior, but according to his homeroom teacher, had difficulty straddling scholars courses and the streets.[32] The school also grappled with mental illness: five IB students attempted suicide between 1995 and 1997, while others struggled publicly with schizophrenia and autism.[33]

Teaching Empathy

This uncommon empathy was not completely organic, as many instructors made it part of their lesson plans. When his predominantly black Spartan Classics Academy (SCA) students said "offensive things" about Jews, Barak Naveh (social studies)—who is Jewish—responded by highlighting parallels in the black and Jewish experiences. Eight months later, on the second leg of a field trip to the Frederick Douglass and Holocaust Memorial Museums, Chris Prince '99—a strapping, stoic football player—hugged a Holocaust survivor, and many other pupils were also moved by the experience.[34]

Even IB students, who considered themselves open-minded, said Naveh challenged them to "question the dominant narrative" of the Cold War and Arab-Israeli conflict.[35] "IB stresses seeing multiple perspectives," Naveh said, "and I always try to teach as if all sides are in the room."[36] Sara Lieber '99 was a quick study, and when US senator Rick Santorum came to Schenley for a Social Security forum, she questioned his math, calculator in hand, and his plan's equitability.[37]

Many teachers stressed plurality of perspective—such as Evelyn King (black history) and Walt Moser (theory of knowledge)—and, against the backdrop of Schenley's mélange, students became unusually discerning.[38] After Dan Chetlin '96 achieved a perfect SAT score, he quipped that the test only measured "one's ability to think like white males from New Jersey."[39] Still, other instructors taught empathy by example. Susan (Baclawski) Jeffers '97 recalled teachers' sensitivity and attention to students with mental illness, as well as those "who were on drugs" and "probably weren't going to graduate."[40] Even Schenley's security guard—Denise

Harrell—was invested, talking Melissa Gatto '99 out of quitting school during a routine bathroom-smoking bust. "She wasn't a teacher and had really nothing to gain or lose with any of us," said Gatto, who ultimately finished both high school and college, "but she did care."[41]

Out of Africa, and Suburbia

This spirit of empathy made Schenley well suited for nontraditional students, such as those in the English as a Second Language (ESL) and PBT programs. Somalia's Haji Muya, an ESL student, spent most of his first thirteen years in a Kenyan refugee camp, with little food and rampant sexual abuse. In 2004, his family arrived in the Homewood neighborhood, where they were startled by squalor. "Even my five-year-old niece said, 'This must be part of Africa,'" recalled Muya. He was much more impressed by Schenley, which "didn't look like a school," but "a United States monument."[42]

Muya largely found acceptance at Schenley. One Hill District classmate bought him clothes and gave him money. Members of the state champion basketball team—namely, future NBA players DeJuan Blair '07 and D. J. Kennedy '07—were especially kind to him. Muya also cultivated community through soccer, as the varsity team bonded at an overnight training camp. "We got real close," he said of the squad that featured ESL students from thirteen countries. Muya was one of many new Somalis at Schenley; some experienced bullying, prompting a 2006 legal settlement between the District and Somali families. Yet, the incurably positive Muya said abuse was mild and exclusively verbal—"African booty scratcher," "Go back to Africa"—and felt that the bullies, who were blacks in the SCA program, were jealous of the school's investment in ESL students.[43]

Another ESL student, Ali Alibeji '01, grew up in Najaf, Iraq, where "very terrifying" bombings punctuated the Gulf War. After immigrating to Pittsburgh in 1994, Alibeji tested out of the ESL program after two years at Frick, allowing him to enter Schenley's High Tech program. Still, he felt "a bond between ESL kids" at Schenley, as sectarian problems were rare. Alibeji experienced some teasing for his outdated clothes but felt the few ethnic-based gibes resulted from ignorance, and said several students and teachers showed a positive interest in his background. A conservative Shi'i Muslim, Alibeji was initially shocked by the school's eccentric set, such as a girl who abruptly shaved her head. "Nobody was afraid to express themselves," he laughed.[44]

Many American students valued their ESL counterparts, especially those from international families. Abass Kamara '95 and Ayo Adisa '02,

FIG. 35 Members of the 1997–98 girls' soccer team smiling before a game. *Journal*, 1998, 4.

FIG. 36 Erin Halloran, a member of the ballet cooperative's first class, performs as Pittsburgh Ballet Theatre's principal dancer in 2008. Courtesy of the Pittsburgh Ballet Theatre. Photo: Rich Sofranko.

with parents from Sierra Leone and Nigeria, respectively, enjoyed this pocket of diversity in an otherwise homogeneous city.[45] "Even though I wasn't in ESL classes, it was cool just knowing [ESL students and I] could connect with each other in an international sense," said Adisa.[46] R. Daniel Lavelle '95, whose family has had a long history in the Hill District, took great interest in foreign students and built friendships with classmates from Egypt and England.[47]

Like ESL students, PBTs also became better integrated during the program's second decade at Schenley. However, Gabrielle Riswold '02, a self-described "type A" "bunhead" "bitch," initially alienated classmates. Riswold came from a small Christian school in Riverside, California, and was "highly judgmental" of Schenley's freewheeling urban culture. She was shocked by the raucous "hootin' and hollerin'" at a pep rally, the dance team's overtly sexual routine, and a classmate named Turquoise's verbal abuse of biology teacher Charlotte Atwood. "It was straight out of a movie," said Riswold, who felt like "Michelle Pfeiffer in *Dangerous Minds*."[48]

Riswold's icy hyperfocus on dance "would've taken [her] to [her] ballet dreams," but in spite of herself, Schenley melted it. In tenth grade, she begrudgingly began to socialize, "fell in love with" hip hop, and started eating in the lunchroom, where PBT students had long been "too scared" to go. Most importantly, Riswold developed an understanding of and empathy for classmates with difficult lives, such as a boy who carried a knife for protection. She even kept her cool when she noticed that a bloodstain on the lunchroom floor—leftover from a student fight—went untouched for several days. "That's just Schenley," she said lovingly in 2014, and is grateful for how the experience "opened [her] mind." "I would never trade Schenley for Brentwood School," said Riswold, who insisted she never seriously considered leaving.[49]

A few dancers did leave Schenley due to the demanding lifestyle and relative social isolation.[50] Katie McGuire Gaines '01 never had a boyfriend, joined a club, or went on a field trip during high school, and grew tired of classmates asking if she could do a split.[51] Unhappy PBT students were more likely to self-segregate—eating lunch in the activities office and only interacting with dancers.[52]

However, some ballerinas, such as Eva Trapp '01, relished the environment. Trapp was "thrilled" with Schenley's realism after her affluent, all-white school in Oakland County, Michigan. "[I]t was so different from the vanilla that I was living," she said, and felt the diversity reflected "what life was going to be like." Trapp was shocked but ultimately impressed by the rawness of Schenley's dance team. "We should've taken real advantage of [the ballet-versus-hip hop motif]," she joked, "and had dance-offs down the hallways."[53]

Despite Trapp's good humor, she scarcely let fun interfere with rehearsals. This dedication helped win her a prominent part in the company's June 2001 show—a rare honor for students. However, the performance was scheduled for the day after prom, and as rehearsal ran late on prom day, PBT forbade Trapp from leaving. Faced with a public, impromptu ultimatum, the wunderkind walked out on the company.

> I was not allowed to perform the part in the show the next day because I left and went to prom . . . I was at a point where I had given up so much, and prom was like a once in a lifetime thing. I made a call, and it was hard. But I went to the show anyway, and I had to watch someone else do my part. . . . It was totally worth it. I don't have a regret at all. [PBT] thought I was a loose cannon for years after that, but I had to take a stand. When a kid is giving up so much, sometimes you have to be human.

The choice could have derailed her professional career, but it didn't. Years later, Trapp became PBT's star, with her likeness on billboards and Port Authority buses.[54]

Living History

In the mid-1990s, Schenley's cohesion was tested by current events, namely, the O. J. Simpson trial. When the verdict was read at 1:10 P.M. on October 3, 1995, Principal Robert Nicklos '55 shared the news through the public address system.[55] Jamel McKelvia '97, a black student in the IB program, was changing for gym class at the time. She said the girls around her—all black and in the SCA program—were elated, while other students seemed subdued or neutral. A confrontation ensued when one reveler taunted a white female gym teacher, shouting, "He got off!" in the teacher's face. The teacher grew visibly angry and red and shouted back that Simpson "did it." McKelvia was ambivalent but felt pressure to embrace a symbolic black triumph, irrespective of Simpson's "actual guilt or innocence."[56]

Many students watched the verdict live in teacher Wilhelmina Fennel's home economics class, which filled with students who had snuck down from the lunchroom. Laura (Sirbaugh) Ratica '97 was there and noted a precise racial split, with black cheers, white groans, and pointed anger from Jews. No fights occurred, Ratica reported, but some friends stopped speaking for several days.[57] Jeff Novelly '98 concurred that race relations were briefly strained but had no fear of violence.[58] The North Side's Denise (Guthrie) Argote '99, a white IB student also in the locker room at the time of the verdict, remembered the day differently. "The student body was overjoyed," said Argote, counting herself among the large, happy majority who thought the prosecution was racially motivated.[59]

Nine days after the Simpson verdict, the region confronted the death of Jonny Gammage. The black motorist was asphyxiated during a struggle with five white suburban police officers, and though three were charged with involuntary manslaughter, none were convicted.[60] The black community was outraged.[61] However, tension at Schenley was not between black and white students, but instead student activists and staff. Schenley's Black Action Society—a student group led by Aisha Taylor '97—organized a walkout and coordinated with chapters from Peabody and Westinghouse High Schools. Flojaune Griffin '00 called the walkout "the original Black Lives Matter movement." Principal Nicklos heard of the plans and "lightly threatened" would-be demonstrators with an implied graduation ban. Many black students were angry with Nicklos and believed that as a black man, he should have been supportive. One administrator called to warn McKelvia's mother but "got upset that my mother wasn't upset," McKelvia recalled.

Notably, Cyril Wecht—a key prosecution witness in the Gammage trials—could relate to the climate at Schenley. A famed forensic pathologist, Wecht had grown up on the edge of the Hill District and been embraced at Fifth Avenue High, which was then two-thirds black. "A lot of white cops have had no relationship with black communities," said Wecht, a Jew, who, as Allegheny County coroner, often recommended criminal charges against white police involved in black citizens' deaths.[62]

The Columbine massacre also resonated powerfully at Schenley, despite lacking a racial dimension and being the eleventh mass school shooting in four years.[63] As details emerged about the killers' motives—revenge for a jock-centric caste system that tormented unpopular students—many schools asked if it could happen to them.[64] "It would totally happen tomorrow at Fox Chapel [Area High School]," thought Megan Stanton, then a junior, of her school's pervasive bullying. Despite living in the city, Stanton attended suburban Fox Chapel and felt Columbine reinforced the value of Schenley, where even her quirkiest Highland Park neighbors felt accepted.[65] As at Columbine, Schenley's disaffected students had long worn black trench coats. Yet at Schenley these students were mostly left alone.[66] "Columbine made us glad that we didn't have a strong in-and-out dynamic," said Griffin. Lauren (Wilharm) Walker '00 stressed that Schenley's "'popular' kids were actually nice, which is probably why they were popular." Students were so troubled by Columbine that the *Journal* theme in 2000, "Different Shades of the Same Color," was a conscious rejection of the polarized American high school.[67]

A District on the Decline

Schenley's popularity dealt a critical blow to successful neighborhood high schools, such as Carrick, Peabody, and Langley, ranked second, third, and fourth, respectively, in the District when the Teacher Center opened.[68] Thus, these schools' stakeholders resented Schenley's reboot.[69] In the two decades that followed, Carrick fell to the middle of the pack as many local honors students opted for Schenley. In fact, Carrick teachers asked the District for a moratorium on students from their feeder pattern enrolling at Schenley.[70] Yet, it was the Carrick neighborhood's aversion to outsiders that precluded a local magnet program and hastened the high school's downturn.[71]

Similarly, in the mid-1990s, Langley's poor reputation drove dozens of West End eighth graders to nearby Catholic schools, although some opted for magnet programs at Brashear and Perry High Schools. Langley's low standing was deserved, said Chris Roth, a 2001 graduate, who coasted through its honors courses yet was ill-prepared for college.[72] However, Peabody fell furthest and had an "atmosphere of hopelessness" by the mid-1990s. The combined eleventh and twelfth grade Advanced Placement (AP) English class enrolled only three students in 2005, the same year that only 4.5 percent of students were proficient or advanced on state math assessments.[73] Changing East End demographics hastened Peabody's demise, but Vincent Carr, the school's principal from 1988 to 1993, said the District did little to slow scholars from "bleeding off" to Schenley.[74] "Peabody was ignored," lamented Carr, who felt the school's Public Safety magnet—established six years after Schenley's renaissance—was insufficient to compete with academic-based programs.[75]

Other high schools suffered from Pittsburgh's early 1990s gang crisis, even Allderdice.[76] The District's top performer for decades, Allderdice experienced a surge in violence—much of it sensational—including a student who died from a sucker-punch; another who had his earlobe bitten off; and an "all-out riot" that stemmed from "KKK" graffiti. The school also endured a cheating scandal that made national news.[77]

Throughout the 1990s, individual schools' hardships were exacerbated by financial instability. The District faced annual budget deficits—sometimes exceeding $30 million—from reductions in the city's tax base and state funding.[78] However, the school board was loath to close schools or raise taxes; a 1992 millage increase cost three board members reelection. Instead, it cut programs (and hundreds of personnel) and "raided" its reserves.[79] Neighborhood schools advocates seized on the District's desperation and argued that busing was too costly to continue.[80] In 1995, Pittsburgh mayor Tom Murphy joined a chorus of local politicians who called for an end to forced busing and privately urged the school board to defy the Pennsylvania Human Relations Commission (PHRC).[81] "Busing has outlived its usefulness," said North Side city councilman Dan Onorato, who claimed constituents were leaving the city when their children finished fifth grade.[82] East End families stayed, but more than half of white students assigned to nonmagnet middle schools—Reizenstein, Arsenal, Milliones, and Gladstone—chose private schools instead.[83]

In 1996, the District acquiesced, and Superintendent Louise Brennen proposed eliminating busing in feeder patterns. The scheme would create nine geographic clusters, with each feeding into the same elementary, middle, and high schools.[84] Students in the all-black Lower Hill District, then assigned to Brashear, would be diverted to Schenley, while Central and Upper Lawrenceville, then overwhelmingly white, would go to Peabody instead of Schenley.[85] Black elected officials and many Schenley parents, such as PTA head Valerie Njie, protested the plan as an attempt to "resegregate the schools."[86] Public hearings were contentious, mirroring those in the 1970s, and the board ultimately passed a scaled-back plan that retained most busing but created four new middle schools in working-class white neighborhoods.[87]

The move effectively segregated Milliones Middle School, which went from 65.4 percent black in the 1995–96 school term to 90.6 percent black the following year.[88] Thus, many Hill District students had few white classmates before attending Schenley. Weeks after the board approved the plan, South Hills state legislators passed a bill stripping the PHRC of its power to impose school assignments.[89] Symbolically, Governor Tom Ridge signed the bill in a ceremony at Carrick's Concord Elementary and called busing a "well-intentioned but failed experiment." Eleven locally elected officials—all white men—flanked Ridge.[90] By 2003, only 39 percent of District students attended integrated schools, down from 61 percent in 1986.[91]

Puzzlingly, the 1996 redistricting plan was even more expensive than retaining the status quo. While the original proposal would have cut costs considerably—$3.8 million the first year and $1.6 million in each subsequent year—the new arrangement would increase the budget nearly $10 million in the first three years.[92] In 1998, another neighborhood-oriented reshuffling promised $22 million in future savings, but it cost $32 million to implement.[93] Between the 1992–93 and 1998–99 school years, the District opened fifteen new schools, despite a 2.1 percent enrollment drop and growing budget deficits.[94] This precarious agenda was due partly to a leadership vacuum—Pittsburgh had four superintendents during the 1990s, including three in two years.[95]

In February 2000, the District hired John W. Thompson, the city's first permanent black superintendent, who quickly moved to raise taxes and close schools—mostly under-capacity elementary schools in white neighborhoods.[96] "For five years, you had the same problems with deficits, and you continued to open schools," the superintendent chided the board.[97] The proposal passed, 5–4, despite emotional opposition from board member Jean Fink, who accused Thompson of having "disdain for Pittsburgh."[98] Mayor Tom Murphy criticized the school closings as "unsettling" and urged Thompson to instead cut staff. In 2001, the mayor helped Fink's conservative bloc win a board majority.[99] As promised, the new board reopened three closed schools, but also frequently obstructed Thompson.[100] By 2002, the board's two factions were so acrimonious that three foundations withheld grants, prompting a *New York Times* story and national embarrassment. "They hired me to balance the budget and get rid of the deficit, and we've done that," Thompson told the *Times*. "But in closing schools, I had to close some that some people didn't want closed, including the mayor and several legislators."[101]

Still, Thompson had success in spite of board dysfunction. He improved test scores, added curricular innovations, and met the board's primary objective of "stabilizing" its finances.[102] The 2003 election created a 5–4 pro-Thompson majority, but the superintendent's leadership style—perceived as standoffish at best and dictatorial at worst—slowly eroded support.[103] "He's better at clearing paths than building consensus," admitted Patrick Dowd, a Thompson ally.[104] In January 2005, Dowd reluctantly joined conservatives in voting, 5–4, to terminate Thompson. Black parents interrupted the meeting, shouting and chanting accusations of racism. In light of threats, police were posted at Dowd's home.[105] The board's three black members were also angry and largely boycotted the search for Thompson's successor.[106]

The new superintendent would inherit this renewed racial strife and face yet more school closings. State funding had again been pared, and forty-four of the District's eighty-six schools were under capacity.[107]

10 | Closing Time
Mark Roosevelt, Asbestos, and the "Save Schenley" Movement

In 2005, new superintendent Mark Roosevelt proposed closing Schenley, citing the need for tens of millions of dollars in asbestos-related repairs. The community was blindsided and angered by the superintendent's move to replace Schenley with separate, specialized schools for its high- and low-track students. For the next thirty months, the battle for Schenley dominated the local media, until 2008, when a bitterly divided school board voted to close the building.

Beginning of the End

In the summer of 2005, the school board hired Mark Roosevelt to be the District's next superintendent.[1] Roosevelt, the charismatic great-grandson of President Theodore Roosevelt, had never worked in education, but his selection followed a national trend of urban superintendents with unorthodox credentials.[2] The new schools chief held a Harvard law degree and brought eight years of experience from the Massachusetts legislature—where he chaired the education committee and co-authored a "landmark" education reform law. His appointment met mostly with optimism, especially from professional East End parents.[3]

On November 9, 2005, Roosevelt released a "right-sizing" plan that would close eighteen of the District's eighty school buildings, including Schenley.[4] The plan meant to target low-performing, undercapacity schools, but Schenley had been a national model of integration and achievement and was actually over capacity.[5] Still, the superintendent cited the need for millions of dollars in repairs at Schenley and proposed moving the school, with its diverse programs intact, to the Reizenstein Middle School building in Shadyside.[6]

Schenley's fatal flaw was asbestos, which is dangerous when airborne, but was safely contained in the plaster. The building had always had asbestos, but problems arose when the District sought to replace the electrical, plumbing, and heating systems. "We're talking about paying an asbestos-abatement contractor to tear out all the plaster in the building to get to the pipes and electrical lines, which is quite an expensive undertaking," said Richard Fellers, the District facilities director.[7]

Schenley supporters quickly mobilized, poking holes in the District's data: namely, the anomalies in two separate repair estimates of $55.7 million and $86.9 million, the latter of which earmarked $500,000 to refurbish the school's pipe organ. Startled by the backlash and rumors of a conspiracy to sell the building to the University of Pittsburgh Medical Center (UPMC), Roosevelt appointed a task force—which included a Schenley parent, the school principal, and the Hill District's board representative—to determine whether the building could be saved.[8] The task force obtained new estimates showing that Schenley could be made safe for as little as $37.8 million, a bargain considering the District's planned $15 million conversion of Reizenstein into a high school.[9] After the new figures were made public, the superintendent pulled Schenley from the chopping block in February 2006 and conceded that it had never belonged in the right-sizing plan.[10]

Task Force Report, District Inaction

In June 2006, the task force submitted a proposal to rehab Schenley for a net cost of $15,544,160. After considering four renovation options from L. D. Astorino & Associates, the task force endorsed "Scope 3B." This project entailed replacing the electrical, plumbing, and heating systems, "minimal asbestos remediation," as well as the addition of air conditioning, as Schenley had no ventilation system. While the work would actually cost $42.4 million, the task force deducted $26.9 million from savings in unnecessary Reizenstein renovations, proceeds from that building's sale, and historic building rehabilitation tax credits.[11] Although the task force included District facilities staff, Roosevelt took no action to repair Schenley. "He kicked that can down the road," said Lisa Fischetti, the superintendent's chief of staff.[12]

In July 2007—more than a year after the task force recommendation——the Post-Gazette reported a ceiling collapse at Schenley, rekindling fears about the building's condition.[13] While "ceiling collapse" was a gross exaggeration—the District assured parents that only "a small piece of plaster on the ceiling" had fallen—it was true that some plaster had begun to delaminate, or peel, which could have released asbestos into the air. The District moved summer school to Peabody High, spent $750,000 on

FIG. 37   A stairwell where sections of plaster had been replaced, 2010. From Matthew Christopher, *Abandoned America: Dismantling the Dream* ([UK]: Carpet Bombing Culture, 2016). Photo: Matthew Christopher.

10,000 plaster patches, and paid $10,000 per month to monitor the air.[14] The building reopened in the fall, but Roosevelt agonized about its decline and asked four construction firms to assess the asbestos threat.[15] The Astorino firm concluded that plaster delamination, although not unusual after ninety-one years, had been accelerated by record high summer temperatures, moisture-trapping windows, and lack of ventilation.[16]

"God Preserve Thee": Round 2

On October 31, 2007, Roosevelt again proposed shuttering Schenley. Instead of merely closing the building, as he had planned in 2005, Roosevelt now wanted to divide Schenley's curricular programs into new schools. The International Studies (IS) program would become an elite, magnet-only International Baccalaureate (IB) school at Reizenstein, tentatively named "IB World."[17] Spartan Classics Academy (SCA) would be diverted to the remedial "University Prep," where a partnership with the University of Pittsburgh's School of Education would devote "a laser focus" to underserved students. Sited for the Upper Hill District's Milliones Middle School building, University Prep was pitched as "a national center for excellence in public education and a model for school district/

university partnerships."[18] The Robotics program, formerly High Technology (High Tech), would be integrated into Peabody High School in East Liberty.[19]

As a consolation, Schenley's ninth through eleventh grade students could remain together at Reizenstein—which they would share with the distinct IB World—until the last class graduated in 2011. At that time, the school would be dissolved. Students and parents panned the proposal as "resegregation" and argued that diversity provided essential life preparation. "It's getting us prepared for the workforce," said the Hill District's Sean Thomas '09. "We're not going to be working with all black people or all white people."[20]

Schenley supporters again organized: rallying outside District headquarters (with the marching band), giving impassioned testimony at board meetings, and holding frequent strategy sessions.[21] The renewed debate was more adversarial. At a November 2007 public forum, 125 Schenley backers booed, interrupted, and shouted down Derrick Lopez, the District's chief of high school reform, as he tried to justify the move. "We didn't anticipate the reaction," said Roosevelt, who thought parents would be more alarmed by the asbestos risk.[22]

Finding a Way to Pay for Schenley

The superintendent insisted he was loath to close the building, and added, "If anybody had been able to tell me that we could've renovated Schenley, to a condition that we would've been proud of, for an amount of money that we could've afforded, we would've done it. And it just never came close."[23] Accordingly, a formidable team of Schenley supporters— six professional parents, former local NAACP president Tim Stevens '63, and architectural experts Vivian Loftness and Rob Pfaffmann—spent the winter brainstorming creative solutions.

Team member Annette Werner, an attorney, consultant, and Schenley parent, seized on a proposal to finance repairs through the sale of and tax revenue generated by the Reizenstein property.[24] Reizenstein's stock was soaring, as its neighbor across Penn Avenue, the blighted former Nabisco factory, was being converted into Bakery Square—a high-end mixed-use development.[25] In March 2008, Werner presented the plan to Roosevelt, who rejected it on the grounds that tax revenues were too speculative.[26]

However, then city councilman Bill Peduto loved the model, having occasionally coordinated with Werner's team throughout the winter. A group from Carnegie Mellon University helped Peduto retool Werner's proposal, and two weeks before the vote to close Schenley, the councilman presented a sale-and-leaseback plan. Under Peduto's version, a for-profit entity would temporarily buy Schenley, finance a $40 million renovation, and then lease it back to the District until the tab was paid over a twenty-year period. To settle its debt, the District would sell Reizenstein for high-end development, creating annual property tax revenues just under $1.9 million, or $37.9 million over twenty years. (The former Allegheny County Jail was renovated under a similar arrangement in 1998.)[27]

Roosevelt again dismissed the idea, telling the *Post-Gazette* it was "a package of inaccurate information and unworkable ideas." Privately, the superintendent excoriated Peduto, who was by then in Turkey on an interfaith peace mission. "It was shocking," said Peduto of Roosevelt's diatribe "laced with profanities."[28]

The Deciders

Despite protests, public hearings, and sparring in the press, the real battle happened behind the scenes, where both sides courted a majority of the nine-member school board. When the superintendent announced his intentions in October 2007, he had six votes in favor of closing Schenley— Theresa Colaizzi, Patrick Dowd, Jean Fink, Bill Isler, Floyd McCrea, and Daniel Romaniello Sr.—but the count quickly fell to four. Six days later, Romaniello lost his reelection bid to Beechview's Sherry Hazuda, and Dowd would soon be replaced by Heather Arnet, as he had not sought a second term.[29]

Schenley backers had reliable nay votes from the board's three black members—Mark Brentley, Randall Taylor, and Thomas Sumpter '68. Brentley and Taylor usually opposed the superintendent—the former often obstructed seemingly reasonable initiatives with racial rhetoric— and were incensed by what they perceived as the dismantling of the District's most successful black school.[30] Although Sumpter frequently sided with Roosevelt, he was the third in four generations of Schenley alumni. Moreover, Sumpter was critical of the superintendent's rush to hire contractors for Reizenstein and Milliones only two weeks after the proposal was announced.[31]

At four votes to three in favor of closing, Schenley's fate rested with Hazuda and Arnet, who had been in office fewer than ninety days by the February vote. Hazuda was expressly ambivalent on the issue, and although Arnet refrained from decisive public comment, she had been elected with the help of Kathy Fine, an enthusiastic Schenley parent, and those close to Arnet believed she would vote to save the school.[32]

The Seven Votes that Killed Schenley

Despite preoccupation with the vote to close the Schenley building, the school's demise also came through six other votes on separate but interrelated proposals. By early 2008, Roosevelt's top priority was the creation of new high schools, which would necessarily exhaust Schenley's resources. In addition to taking students and programs, IB World and University Prep would divert considerable capital from a prospective Schenley renovation. The District would pay $21.85 million to simply reopen the Reizenstein and Milliones buildings, which had been closed since 2006. A third school, Science and Technology Academy ("Sci-Tech"), required a $12.98 million makeover of the Frick building.[33] "I contend that you cannot vote for Schenley renovation at the same time you are voting for tens of millions of dollars at Milliones and at Frick," said Taylor.[34]

Votes on Schenley and its successor schools were scheduled for February 27, 2008, but in late January, the superintendent delayed the question of permanent closure. "We think [Schenley] merits a couple of more months of evaluations," he said, but cautioned against false hope.[35] Thus, the February agenda only included the following items:

- Item 46: whether to move the Robotics program to Peabody beginning with the 2008–9 school year;
- Item 48: whether to move Schenley students to Reizenstein to establish Schenley High at Reizenstein, a grades 10–12 school, beginning with the 2008–9 school year; and
- Item 49: whether to establish University Prep at Milliones, beginning with grade 9 in the 2008–9 school year.[36]

Taylor objected to this bifurcated process and argued that all related issues should wait until a final recommendation on the building.[37]

The board ignored Taylor's plea, and Items 46 and 49 passed 7–2, with Brentley and Taylor dissenting.[38] Debate of Item 48 was more pointed. Sumpter insisted the move was "necessary" but "not permanent," before voting in the affirmative. Arnet asked Roosevelt for clarification on permanency and then voted against student relocation.[39] Hazuda expressed pained ambivalence, speaking reverently of the school's spirit and suggesting that allowing Schenley parents to fundraise independently would "make a national statement." She ultimately tendered a yea vote, and Item 48 was adopted, 6–3, with Brentley and Taylor joining Arnet in dissent.[40]

The February meeting made it difficult to gauge support for the remaining Schenley items, which would be decided in June. The equivocations of Sumpter, Arnet, and Hazuda indicated that they might vote to save the building. Yet, given their unqualified support for Item 49, the three seemed resigned to split up the school's tracks. This divided position mirrored Roosevelt's, who said he agonized over the facility but was convinced that severing Schenley's programs would improve outcomes for all students.[41]

The superintendent's stance was confirmed by an April 11, 2008, conversation with Jill Weiss, a parent from the professional team, in which the building seemingly won a reprieve. Weiss described the meeting in an e-mail to the team:

> I had a good conversation with Mark Roosevelt today and things are looking very well[!] He felt that [architect] Al [Filoni] had done a convincing job of proving that Schenley would be the building to renovate as opposed to Reizenstein. He told me he had our document and asked if I had previously sent it to him. I told him that we had agreed that it was to go to MCF. He said he will look at all of the paperwork in the next few days.
>
> The Executive Committee was very concerned about the projected enrollment for high schools for 2014, and that one of the 3 members felt (at least today) that the students should go to an already closed or underused building, but [the] logistics of that are not possible, if the district doesn't want to lose even more students. He also would still like to see Schenley as the home of the Sci Tech and a Health Careers high school, but acknowledges that probably won't happen—and there was an announcement today of 183 positions being cut. So, he is walking a thin line. . . .
>
> But. . . . Schenley is going to be renovated!!!!!! It is almost a sure thing, but we still have to be cautious. Mark will still need to convince the board, but he told the 3 he met with today that he will make that recommendation. And, of course, it won't be the school that some of us remember, but hopefully, the building will inspire a wonderful school with wonder things happening in it. Mark says that the PG editorial board will have to be convinced (he did a good job convincing them otherwise, but I told him that I have connections!). I also re-emphasized that there would be foundation and other funding available if the building was made even greener than it is.
>
> So, thank you everyone for the jobs that you did and are still doing. Even if some of you were not as actively involved as others, your concern and advice has always been encouraging for all of us. Saying that, our work is not done!

Annette and Linda, please tell those on the building and finance committees, whom you feel is appropriate. We all still need to be careful with this information.[42]

Roosevelt's abrupt about-face was only known to a handful of supporters, but it pacified much of the organized movement at a critical juncture.[43]

Significantly, Al Filoni, the superintendent's most trusted architect, was a Schenley proponent and made the building's case to Roosevelt throughout the spring. In mid-May, Filoni's firm—MacLachlan, Cornelius & Filoni—estimated that a partial renovation could be done for $61 million and stressed that the building was "worth the investment." However, a few days later, the superintendent recommended closing Schenley.[44]

At its June 25, 2008, meeting, the board faced the remaining items:

- Item 63: whether to establish Sci-Tech at Frick, beginning with grades 6–9 for the 2009–10 school year;
- Item 64: whether to establish IB World at Reizenstein, beginning with grades 6–10 for the 2009–10 school year;
- Item 65: whether to close the Schenley facility for use as a school effective June 30, 2008; and
- Item 66: whether to establish Pittsburgh Schenley as a grades 10–12 school at the Reizenstein facility beginning with the 2008–9 school year. "The Pittsburgh Schenley school will be reduced by one grade per year and remain at the Reizenstein facility until its last class graduates in 2010–11."[45]

Tensions were high, as the issue had dominated local media for months, and Roosevelt was believed to have four votes (Colaizzi, Fink, Isler,

TABLE 6 High School Reform Vote Roll Call

February 27, 2008
   Item 46: Move Schenley Robotics program to Peabody
   Item 48: Move Schenley to Reizenstein
   Item 49: Create a University Prep 6–12 school at Milliones

June 25, 2008
   Item 63: Create a Sci-Tech 6–12 school at Frick
   Item 64: Create an IB 6–12 school at Reizenstein
   Item 65: Permanently close the Schenley building
   Item 66: Move Schenley to Reizenstein before dissolving in 2011

	Item 46	Item 48	Item 49	Item 63	Item 64	Item 65	Item 66
Arnet	Y	N	Y	Y	Y	Y	Y
Brentley	N	N	N	N	N	N	N
Colaizzi	Y	Y	Y	Y	Y	Y	Y
Fink	Y	Y	Y	Y	Y	Y	Y
Hazuda	Y	Y	Y	N	N	N	N
Isler	Y	Y	Y	Y	Y	Y	Y*
McCrea	Y	Y	Y	Y	Y	Y	Y
Sumpter	Y	Y	Y	N	Y	N	Y
Taylor	N	N	N	N	N	N	N
	Y 7–2	Y 6–3	Y 7–2	Y 5–4	Y 6–3	Y 5–4	Y 6–3

Sources: Pittsburgh Board of Public Education, *Meeting Agenda, February 27, 2008* (Pittsburgh: 2008), 554–55; Pittsburgh Board of Education, *Transcript, Board of Education Legislative Meeting, February 27, 2008,* (Pittsburgh: 2008), 60–62; Pittsburgh Board of Education, *Meeting Agenda, June 25, 2008* (Pittsburgh: 2008), 1710–12; Pittsburgh Board of Education, *Transcript, Board of Education Legislative Meeting, June 25, 2008* (Pittsburgh: 2008), 118–20.

McCrea) to Schenley's three (Arnet, Brentley, Taylor). Thus, saving the building required help from Hazuda and Sumpter, who, given their February votes, were seen to lean toward closure.[46]

On Item 65, the roll call raised eyebrows, even if the outcome did not. While Schenley picked off both Hazuda and Sumpter, supporters were surprised when Arnet cast the deciding vote to close the building. The measure passed, 5–4.[47] Arnet's vote came with an amendment that the board create a committee to "pursue several long-term options for use, investment and/or renovation of this historic landmark." Arnet's amendment passed, 6–3.[48]

Items 63 and 64 also passed, 5–4 and 6–3, respectively, with Sumpter joining Brentley, Hazuda, and Taylor in dissent of the former.[49] In regard to Item 66, Brentley and Taylor begged their colleagues to continue the school's legacy, even if in a different building.[50] "African-Americans are catching hell all over the place," said Brentley, "but we're closing the one where they're doing very well."[51] Item 66 passed, 6–3, with Brentley, Hazuda, and Taylor voting nay.[52]

Taylor, a Peabody graduate, was heartbroken:

> [T]he closing and the destruction of Schenley High School, the public's not going to forget this one. They're not going to forget this. They're not going to forget this, and it did not have to happen, and it certainly didn't have to happen the way that it did happen. So my apologies as a [b]oard member to Schenley families, to our students, to those most wonderful teachers who make out a wonderful program, to Mr. Rich Wallace who spoke this morning about the proudest achievement that he had was . . . turning Schenley into one of our finer schools.[53]

Dormancy, Point Count, and Sale

The Schenley building sat vacant for years despite supporters' prompting to reconsider renovation.[54] Arnet's resolution never came to fruition in light of her abrupt resignation a year later, and the superintendent, too, left his post early at the end of 2010.[55] Roosevelt became president of the defunct Antioch College, charged with reopening a school that had been closed on June 30, 2008—the same day as Schenley's closure.[56] "The irony is not lost on me," he said.[57] Still Schenley sat dormant.

In June 2012, four years after the Schenley building was shuttered, it was revealed that its "plaster contained only trace amounts of asbestos." Dan Davis, who had tested plaster samples as a Kimball & Associates engineer in 2009, made the passive mention during an otherwise benign radio interview with the local NPR affiliate.[58] Kimball's test revealed that only 2 of the 476 plaster samples contained at least 1 percent asbestos—the threshold that triggers most environmental regulations—considerably less than the 6 percent AGX discovered in 2002.[59] "The estimated cost to remove and dispose of [Schenley's asbestos-containing materials] is $1,060,590," opined the Kimball report.[60]

AGX "didn't do anything wrong," Davis explained to the *Pittsburgh City Paper*, but merely employed a bulk analysis—a cheaper, less precise method than the point count, which Kimball had used. Notably, Astorino had recommended a point count in 2006, arguing that the analysis might reveal less asbestos and thus a reduced remediation cost. The District

FIG. 39 A science classroom more than six years after the building was closed, 2014. Photo: Cooper Miller.

declined to follow that recommendation. "Some people may feel that it's not important to know what [the level of asbestos] is," said AGX owner Dan Winkle.[61] Although the Kimball report was dated August 2009, the District's IB World site selection committee, which convened a few months later, was "not allowed" to consider the Schenley building.[62]

News of the lower count infuriated Schenley supporters, who questioned why the District sat on the data for three years. Barbara Daly Danko, a county councilwoman and Schenley parent, compared the discrepancy to the Iraq War's phantom weapons of mass destruction.[63] Taylor had never been told about the new count and blasted off an angry letter to his board colleagues.[64] Lisa Fischetti, Roosevelt's chief of staff, was also "furious" when the news broke, but for different reasons.

> We didn't have that document. I wondered at that point, had somebody, like—where was that? Mark told everyone, "I want every document out there!" Why did that document only appear years later? When that document appeared, I had to say, "I'm sorry," and I went back and put that document on the website. We didn't wash it under the rug and say it was always there. So I have no idea where that document was. That was infuriating, because one of the things that we prided ourselves on was complete transparency. To this day,

I don't understand where that document was, and why it wasn't put out to the public. . . . It was infuriating, because then the whole conspiracy thing came out again.[65]

Isler insisted the report was immaterial and that "a series of issues" had prompted Schenley's closure.[66]

By the fall of 2012, the District was seeking bids to sell Schenley.[67] Supporters organized yet again and successfully petitioned the board to obtain new estimates in January 2013. Thus, bids for sale rolled in while supporters sought an estimate low enough to entice the board to renovate. In mid-February, architecture and engineering firms HHSDR and Astorino submitted estimates of $53.1 million and $59.3 million, respectively. The figures were too high for Superintendent Linda Lane, who pressed forward with the sale. "[W]e must balance the need to resolve a very concerning financial future in the context of our need to accelerate the academic achievement of all students," said Lane.[68]

The District proceeded to sale and received four bids: PMC Property Group ($5.2 million), who would turn the building into luxury apartments; Kossman Development Company ($4.6 million), for use as both a charter school and housing units; alumni Edward Alexei '88, Liz Berlin '88, and David Tinker '89 ($4.1 million), who would create a private or charter visual arts school named for Andy Warhol; and alumnus Ralph Falbo '55 ($4 million), who would create apartments.[69] Each bid contained renovation estimates that ranged from $15,446,424 to $32,234,061—all a fraction of those the District obtained.[70] "The question is sell or sell out," said Sumpter, who opposed the sale. On February 27, 2013, the board voted 5–4 to sell Schenley to PMC, with nay votes from the board's four black members—Brentley, Sumpter, Regina Holley, and Sharene Shealey.[71]

Hindsight Not 20/20

More than eight years after the building was closed, stakeholders agree on little, as the Roosevelt era has become even muddier. "In a lot of cases, hindsight is 20/20," said Hazuda in 2011. "In this, it isn't."[72] This is true in part because Schenley's successor schools have produced mixed results.

University Prep has thus far proved a disappointment, with few of the promised curricular innovations and no material improvement from the same population's outcomes at Schenley. "I think you'd be hard-pressed to find anyone who thinks it lived up to the original vision," said Carey Harris, executive director of A+ Schools, an independent watchdog organization.[73] IB World—later renamed Barack Obama International

Studies Academy—has fared well academically. However, the school lacks the diversity Schenley enjoyed—students are predominantly poor and black—and has underscored the District's difficulty in managing real estate.[74] After Peabody High was closed in 2011, Obama Academy moved into the larger, better-equipped Peabody building, which was later learned to have "essentially the same asbestos plaster situation as Schenley."[75] Obama Academy's former home, Reizenstein, was sold to the Bakery Square developers for a modest $5.4 million. The sale represented a loss for the District, which had invested $6.27 million in the property since 2008.[76]

Crucially, Roosevelt's high school reforms seemed to exacerbate the District's enrollment crisis. The new schools proved to be less attractive than their predecessor, especially to middle-class families and whites.[77] In the 2013–14 school year, University Prep and Obama Academy averaged a combined 205.6 students per grade, compared with Schenley's 310.8 in the 2007–8 school year.[78] While Sci-Tech likely absorbed some Schenley-bound pupils, others left the District altogether—choosing private, charter, or suburban alternatives.[79] Between 2007 and 2013, District enrollment dropped at nine times the rate that the city lost population.[80] "We made a lot of progress with K-8 schools, but not a lot of progress in high school," admitted Roosevelt.[81]

Fuzzy Math

Initial doubts about closing Schenley were aggravated by inconsistencies in the District's financial logic. Alexei—one of the alumni who attempted to buy the building—insists that the board had the money to repair Schenley, claiming $800 million in unused credit and $50 million in cash on hand in 2013.[82] Roosevelt said that the cash-strapped District should fund academic programs rather than construction, but spent a combined $31.4 million on projects at Colfax and Concord Elementary Schools the year Schenley closed. Even dissolving Schenley was expensive: the District paid $37.43 million to reopen or reconfigure the four buildings impacted by its reorganization.[83]

District officials blamed these high construction costs on erratic estimates and frequent change orders. "Mark was frustrated, because he felt like he could never get a straight answer," said Fischetti, who added that "[t]rying to find the reason behind any number was complete frustration."[84] Schenley renovation estimates, which ranged from $37 million to $86.9 million, rarely trended in a consistent direction.[85] Moreover, the estimates procured before critical votes in May 2008 and February

2013 went far beyond the scope of safety—calling for full refurbishments, classroom reconfigurations, and miscellaneous gym and auditorium improvements.[86] Even the $37 million estimate, described as a partial renovation, would have been broad in scope, according to Vivian Loftness, a Carnegie Mellon architecture professor. "Asbestos removal would never have been $37 million," she said, "so they were doing far more than asbestos to ever even get that high."[87]

Others took issue with the process. Bill Peduto, who became Pittsburgh's mayor in 2014, was stung by the superintendent's unwillingness to engage Schenley supporters.

> The most disappointing part of it—the part that left so many people who had the highest hopes for Mr. Roosevelt so completely disappointed in him—was there was never an opportunity to have a real dialogue. . . . You had a blue ribbon panel of people who came together on their own and were willing to volunteer their own time and services and expertise in order to be able to come up with an alternative. If that report had gone right into the garbage can, it would've been treated a heck of a lot better than the way it was treated. . . . [E]very time we had a number, the District would move the goalposts.

Sitting in the mayor's office in 2015, Peduto called Schenley's closing a "fait accompli," and lamented that process deficiencies undermined Roosevelt's agenda. "That's where doubt comes from," Peduto said, "that's what feeds conspiracy."[88]

Indeed, the District's process, much more so than the outcome, created suspicion among many. Annette Werner, a parent from the professional team, believes Schenley was treated differently than other schools with asbestos, and cited hundreds of pages of District reports on Peabody, Miller (formerly McKelvey), Vann, and Woolslair schools. Moreover, a 2007 letter from Kimball stated that "large sections of plaster began falling from ceilings, walls, and banister walls throughout the buildings," but emergency plaster records revealed no such event.[89] Although rumors of a deal with UPMC or Carnegie Mellon were never substantiated, the District fueled distrust by discussing Schenley's marketability with developers before announcing the building would close.[90] Jet Lafean, an engineer and Schenley supporter, denied that any asbestos "crisis" existed and accused the District of lying.[91]

Most supporters eschewed conspiracy theories and instead believed the District simply reached a bad conclusion from its own straw-man

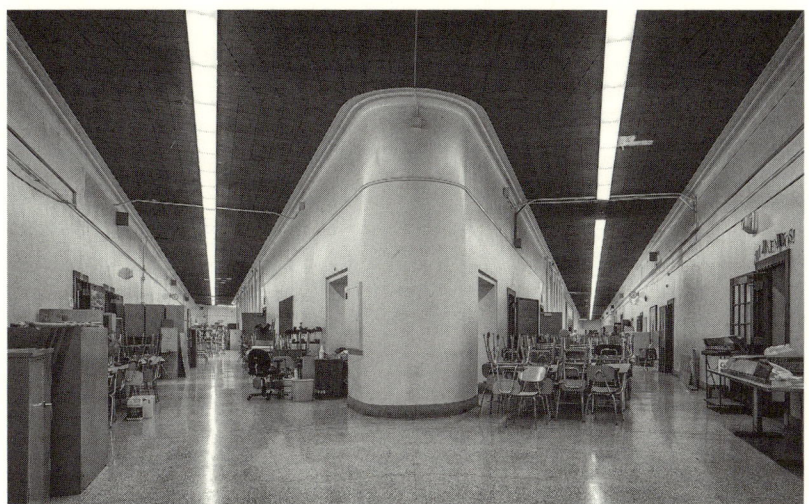

FIG. 40 Schenley's spacious triangular corridors, 2010. From Matthew Christopher, *Abandoned America: Dismantling the Dream* ([UK]: Carpet Bombing Culture, 2016). Photo: Matthew Christopher.

logic. The District argued that it could not justify such a large sum to rehab a single building. However, the question was not whether Schenley was worth the money, said Loftness, but whether it was preferable to invest in a beautifully crafted building with a history of excellence in education or spend that capital on several smaller, poor-quality buildings. Loftness called Schenley a "[g]reen building ahead of its time," praising its ideal location and abundance of natural light. "Why didn't you just make Schenley the showcase and make it the centerpiece?" Loftness argued. "Environmentally, those buildings were designed before electric lighting and air conditioning. They are resilient buildings, where you could survive without air conditioning, and you could continue to teach if the lights went out. As a city, we should be investing in those buildings and not throwing money into Reizenstein where we're barely making things work." A refurbished Schenley could last another century, Filoni advised Roosevelt in May 2008, while Loftness gave Reizenstein and Milliones another two decades.[92]

Roosevelt in Retrospect

While Roosevelt's tenure was controversial, it was also boldly ambitious. In his first two years, he overhauled the training and accountability standards for principals, developed new curriculum in grades K-8, and introduced merit-based pay. Roosevelt also brought in grants, with awards of $40 million and $37.4 million, from the Gates Foundation and US Department of Education, respectively.[93] His crowning achievement was the Pittsburgh Promise: a scholarship program launched in 2006 that within six years offered qualified District graduates a maximum of $40,000 toward college.[94] Carey Harris, executive director of A+ Schools from 2004 to 2016, credited Roosevelt with getting the District "focused on its outcomes," while board member Jean Fink felt "[h]e's moved us light years forward."[95]

Still, Schenley clouds Roosevelt's legacy, and speaking in the fall of 2014—his fourth year at Antioch—he remained baffled by notions that he was eager to close the school. "That one mystifies me," said Roosevelt, who remembered thinking, "I need this like I need a hole in my head," and ranked the episode among his life's low points. The former superintendent said he often "veer[ed] emotionally" toward renovation until "facilities people" could "get him to see reality."[96] Roosevelt, a confirmed history buff, found his ignorance of the region to be an asset when closing schools. "If I had known all the history . . . all of the love that people developed for that kind of institution, a school, it would have been paralyzing."[97]

While Roosevelt regrets that the building had to close, he is unapologetic about dismantling the school inside. "The data that we had showed us that Allderdice, and Schenley in particular, were very apartheid schools," Roosevelt said. "If you got in [scholars courses], it was successful. If you didn't, it was no better than Perry or Brashear." Even so, the former superintendent insists he "wouldn't have made any move to close Schenley based on the data." However, the building's maintenance issues presented an opportunity to see if smaller, specialized schools could better serve both populations, while enhancing choice beyond the comprehensive school model.

Roosevelt was admittedly ineffective at selling this vision and, in this attempt, unwittingly hastened backlash.[98] The decision to split Schenley students—however well-intentioned—prompted concerns about resegregation. In response, the District incensed supporters by contending that Schenley's diversity was not only illusory but also detrimental to poor black students. "Schenley itself was segregated by the magnet and non-magnet student populations," said Derrick Lopez, Roosevelt's high school reform chief, in January 2008. "[T]he underachievement of [non-magnet] students was shrouded by the overachievement of the students in the IB/IS program."[99]

Even some Roosevelt fans were critical of his execution. Tina Calabro, who has long covered education and disability issues for Pittsburgh publications, said Roosevelt "largely did a very good job," and that closing Schenley was probably necessary. However, Calabro felt that Roosevelt's style—excitable, argumentative, and "unyielding about his numbers"—was detrimental to convincing the public.[100] The superintendent's penchant for nuance was also problematic, admitted Lisa Fischetti, his District chief of staff. If he gave a definitive answer, she said, "you remembered it." Despite her boss's communication deficit, Fischetti insists he was a stickler for transparency and often had her locate old facilities reports to appease Schenley parents.[101]

Ann (Sharpe) Haley '59 resents that the SCA program, of which she was an architect and director, was made a scapegoat in Schenley's demise. The program's first decade was largely successful, she said, but was neutered by reduced funding from the District. Haley was frustrated that Roosevelt criticized the SCA program without knowledge of its features or history and that he proposed pouring resources into a vastly similar enterprise at Milliones. "Roosevelt had never been inside of a classroom, and he was a superintendent giving out orders," said Haley.[102] The former superintendent admitted, "We didn't handle the process even close to perfectly."

Throughout his tenure, Roosevelt found it difficult to establish trust with the black community, in whom he perceived "a large sense of being scammed." He understood disagreements about which schools to close, but was shocked by a poll showing a large number of black Pittsburghers did not think any closings were necessary. Roosevelt was frequently opposed by black board members and occasionally excoriated by the *New Pittsburgh Courier* and local NAACP. However, he still doesn't "accept the proposition" that he lacked black support, and cited his good relationships with the Urban League, black ministers, and elected officials. Roosevelt also insists that the racial composition of his school board coalition "was far more complex" than it appeared. "The hostility that I got on Schenley was vast majority from white people," said Roosevelt, who was uncomfortable with the alliance between white parents and board member Brentley. "[T]he parental community knew that [Brentley] was an irresponsible participant in the high school reform debate."[103]

The Schenley battle was more difficult for Roosevelt than most realized. According to filmmaker Elizabeth Seamans, who became friendly with her subject after shooting *Mark Roosevelt: In Uncharted Waters*, the superintendent felt battered by the vitriol and said he even received a death threat.[104] Roosevelt never mentioned the death threat publicly, but recalled a time he was driving with his wife when "someone I knew from the Schenley movement was behind me, and honked and flashed the finger repeatedly."[105] Undoubtedly, Schenley supporters could be truculent, and

Roosevelt withstood "three or four minutes" of boos at a graduation at the Civic Arena, said Darrick Suber '89. "[I]t was the appropriate thing to do," said Suber, who respected the superintendent for attending the ceremony. "It was as classy a way to boo someone as there could be."[106] At public hearings, the school's partisans were like hungry wolves, joked Howard Bullard, the former principal who was head of secondary schools when the Schenley building closed. "And, not to call Schenley graduates wolves," Bullard qualified, "but they're passionate."[107]

Roosevelt was admittedly ill-suited for the fight, saying, "I nurse people's wounding comments. I do not have thick skin. In the five-and-a-half years I was in Pittsburgh, I don't know how many nights I woke up without some level of stress. Maybe fifty or 100. . . . In a personal way, you know when you've just had it, and Schenley became a personal thing. I just couldn't go on. I started planning my exit." He left Pittsburgh at the end of 2010, and thus Schenley ended Roosevelt's tenure just as Roosevelt had ended Schenley.[108]

11 | After Oakland
Reizenstein, University Prep, and Obama Academy

The final months in Oakland were marked by activism and, eventually, mourning. Students were aggressive in the fight to save their school and were doubly wounded by the District's seeming indifference to their pleas. The school's lineage remained through 2011, allowing underclassmen to graduate as Spartans. However, the last three years were uncomfortable and often humiliating, as Schenley was eventually reduced to occupying an upstairs corner of the Reizenstein building. Still, Schenley's spirit persists through its heirs: University Prep and Obama Academy.

Shouting at No One

The Schenley marching band played down Bellefield Avenue in the dark with 100 protesters in tow. The throng, mostly students, chanted and waved hand-made signs that read "Save Schenley," "Remain Diverse, Do Not Disperse," and "Forces That Divide We Will Not Abide." This November 2007 rally outside the Board of Education building accented the public hearing inside, where most of the 100 speakers gave impassioned pro-Schenley testimony.[1] A rally two weeks earlier had drawn 250 supporters.[2] "The effort to save Schenley was massive, unprecedented," said Bullard.[3]

While adults had greater political agency, students were a considerable force in the effort to save their school. Activists were merely being good students, said parent Geneva Taylor, in reference to Be the Change!—a new, District-wide civics course designed to inspire civic engagement.[4] However, students said their most enduring lesson resulted from feeling unheard. "I learned a lot about the power of money that year," said Teressa LaGamba '09, who felt empty when her classmates' "trembling, passionate" speeches were ignored.[5] "No matter what we did, it didn't seem to make a difference," said Greg Galuska '08, who sensed the board had "their minds made up from the beginning."[6]

The 2007–8 school year ended with the building still in limbo—the formal vote would take place two weeks after classes ended. A funereal

FIG. 41 Students rally to save Schenley outside the Board of Education building, 2007. *Pittsburgh Post-Gazette*, November 28, 2007, A-7. Photo: John Heller. Copyright © *Pittsburgh Post-Gazette*, 2016, all rights reserved. Reprinted with permission.

feeling dominated the final days in the Schenley building. After *All Shook Up*'s curtain call, director Kelly McKrell '95 defiantly declared that Schenley musicals would continue, "even if they have to be performed on the street."[7] An alumni couple in their late sixties came from Kansas to reclaim the wife's cheerleading uniform and megaphone, which she had loaned for display.[8] Some students from peripheral neighborhoods agonized about their long commute to Reizenstein.[9]

On June 10, 2008, the building closed to students. The *Pittsburgh Tribune-Review* documented the day: "As the last bell sounded at 11:10 A.M. Tuesday, freshmen, sophomores, and juniors hugged each other, snapped photos in the hallway, and said good-bye. Seniors had their last day of class Friday. In tribute, they scattered [ninety-two] roses—one for each year of the school's existence—on its front steps. . . . One sign on the floor said, 'Schenley we'll miss you' . . . When the final bell rang, some students whooped their approval. Then they trudged down the steps past the wilted roses." Morningside's Luke Trout '09 wanted "something to remember Schenley" and swiped a framed picture of a rocket from the cafeteria. "What are they going to do?" he asked,

FIG. 42   The Roger Babusci Auditorium had been renovated in 2006. From Matthew Christopher, *Abandoned America: Dismantling the Dream* ([UK]: Carpet Bombing Culture, 2016). Photo: Matthew Christopher.

"suspend me?" In a room filled with props from musicals past, McKrell was more plaintive. "I don't know how I'm going to walk out," she told the *Tribune-Review*.[10]

Alumni around the country mourned with students and staff, and many filled Internet forums with their heartbreak and fury.[11] April Weitzel '91 was one of the lucky ones who got a chance to say good-bye to the school during a private tour from Nina Sacco—a friend and Schenley vice principal. Sacco joked that she owed her life to Schenley, as her grandparents were students when they met in the auditorium. "I cried that day as she walked with me through those halls one last time," said Weitzel, who emphasized that despite having different experiences at the school, she and Sacco reached the same conclusion. "Something special occurred there," she said. "There was magic in that building."[12]

Schenley High School at Reizenstein

On August 28, 2008, sophomores, juniors, and seniors moved into the Shadyside building that the District rebranded "Schenley High School at Reizenstein." The plain, squat structure had opened in 1975 and served as a middle school named for civil rights leader Florence Reizenstein until its closure in 2006.[13] The move to Reizenstein was "devastating," said LaGamba, who noted that the "depressingly sterile" facility was a daily reminder of their lost treasure in Oakland.[14] Deficiencies included few windows; an abundance of headache-inducing fluorescent lights; paper-thin walls that did not reach the ceiling (Fred Quinn '09 offered a "bless you" after hearing a sneeze in the adjacent classroom); purple walls and orange pillars; inadequate numbers of restrooms and science labs; narrower hallways and stairwells; and the absence of an auditorium.

The disappointing new digs left students "feeling like second-class citizens," and Molly Tonsor '09 reported "a lot of palpable anger and resentment in the students."[15] James Hill '11, who had practically grown up in the Oakland building where his uncle, Fred Lucas, held weekend track practices, said, "Walking up to [Reizenstein] almost seemed like a joke." Although District staff hung red and black banners at the entrance and painted Clark Winter's W-shaped *Celebration* sculpture red, "it wasn't real" to Hill.[16] Sarah Dolby '09 resigned to "just cope" with feeling like a disoriented freshman during her senior year.[17] Reizenstein had some amenities Schenley lacked—air conditioning and on-campus venues for baseball, soccer, and tennis—and the District invested $5 million in new carpets, furniture, lighting, and paint.[18] Still, the space felt like "it could be broken down tomorrow," said Minrose Straussman '09. "It doesn't feel like home."[19]

With a Whimper

"It was pretty sad at Reizenstein," said Jeff Dugan '00, who coached boys' soccer from 2004 to 2010 and taught at Schenley from 2007 to 2010. "The school just had no energy. There were times when I felt like, 'What the hell am I doing here?'"[20] Many students wondered the same, and enrollment plunged each year. Schenley averaged 310.8 students per grade in its final Oakland term before dipping to 259.7 students in the 2008–9 school year, 228.5 students in 2009–10, and just 177 graduates in 2011.[21] This drop in enrollment was partly due to inconvenience, as the longer commute required some South Hills, West End, and North Side students to leave home before 6 A.M.

Actors and athletes also had challenges. The musical was performed at nearby Peabody High, as Reizenstein had no stage, and students were shuttled back and forth between buildings for rehearsals and set construction.[22] Varsity teams continued to compete under the Schenley banner but were drawn from a four-school cooperative, with students from Schenley, IB World, University Prep, and Sci-Tech. All teams were based out of

Reizenstein, except for football, which continued to practice at Schenley Field, adjacent to University Prep in the Upper Hill District. "It's going to be almost impossible to run a sports program from four schools," said basketball coach Kevin Reid in June 2008. John Tokarski '09 feared that his sister Leeza, a rising ninth grader at Frick—where future IB World students were temporarily housed during the 2008–9 school term—would have difficulty bonding with her soccer teammates, who mostly inhabited Reizenstein.[23]

The school also lost programs in the transition, despite the promise that Schenley would stay intact. While it was known that the Robotics program would be moved to Peabody and that the District would transport Schenley students, "no one was willing to make those daily trips," said Hill, "especially in the winter."[24] The English as a Second Language (ESL) program was detached altogether and moved to Allderdice High. "I was very disappointed," said Haji Muya, a Somali civil war refugee. "I had no choice but to go to Allderdice," moped the soccer player, who joked that he was forced to join Schenley's rival.[25]

No Room of One's Own

The Reizenstein experience was more difficult the second year, 2009–10, when Schenley's remaining juniors and seniors were forced to share the building with the new IB high school. The two schools were organizationally distinct, physically separate, and, according to Hill, unequal. Schenley was relegated to a corner on the second floor and progressively "made less important."[26] To this end, the District even advertised IB World by using profiles of Schenley alumni. However, the profiles never mentioned Schenley, despite naming alumni's elementary schools, middle schools, and colleges.[27] "It's been really sad," said Nubia Williams '11 in May 2011. "We're in a corner, literally. We see the same people. I don't feel like we really got the whole high school experience."[28]

Several top Schenley teachers followed job security downstairs to IB World, exacerbating the sense of deprivation. Students felt like intruders when visiting Peabody for play practice or certain elective courses, a feeling compounded by long-standing tensions between teens from East Liberty and the Hill District. After a Peabody student accosted a Schenley student outside an East Liberty convenience store, Schenley pupils, who traditionally wore jerseys on game days, were told not to do so at Peabody. By the end, being a "Schenley kid" was almost a source of embarrassment, according to Hill. "At that point we didn't have a school anymore."[29]

Still Like a Family

Despite the inconveniences and indignities of Reizenstein, the shrinking Schenley High School retained its close community. Staying together was worth it, students said unequivocally.[30] "Everyone was a family," recalled Erin McMahon '11, a Pittsburgh Ballet Theatre (PBT) student from Houston, who was welcomed into the fold despite arriving at Schenley in its final year.[31] Natalie Sorce '11 bragged that the school had no cliques, which social studies teacher Barak Naveh called "so unique to Schenley." Naveh said that returning alumni usually reported that "[i]n college, the black kids hang out with the black kids."[32] Moreover, the school had zero incidents based on violence, weapons, or controlled substances in the 2009–10 school year, according to District records.[33] "Bullying wasn't a thing," explained Hannah Guy '11, while LaGamba described "one big team always fighting for the same thing."[34]

The team's last captain, Principal Sophia Facaros, led Schenley from 2006 to 2011.[35] Also an Oakmont borough councilwoman, Facaros was only one year on the job when she was blindsided by the school's closure. Her mouth "dropped open" when she got the call, but she was ultimately inspired by students' efforts to save their school. "These kids learned hard lessons at young ages about politics and tough choices," she said.[36] Facaros even stayed upbeat throughout the Reizenstein move and insisted, "What the heart of Schenley is has never changed."[37]

Strong teachers continued to define the learning environment in the school's final years. Mario Iasella (physics)—who left a career in civil engineering to be a teacher—"inadvertently" made students love physics, while Joe Ehman (social studies), the unfailingly positive activities director, became essential to diverse facets of campus life.[38] Pete Vitti (social studies) used charisma and humor to make coursework relatable, but demanded that students respect him and themselves. "He was one of those teachers who you didn't want to let down," said Sorce.[39] These instructors helped Schenley remain academically strong despite anger over the move. The school awarded nineteen IB diplomas in 2008 and twelve in 2010, and sent graduates to Stanford, the University of Chicago, Carnegie Mellon, and Haverford.[40]

University Prep and Obama Academy

As Schenley dwindled, its successor in the Upper Hill struggled to replicate its record. Officially named the University Preparatory School at Margaret Millones, the school opened in 2008 and was founded on the promise of "incredible innovations."[41] Plans included Pitt's Center for Urban Education on site, a take-home laptop for every student, and an extended school day. However, the school board failed to fund much of Superintendent Mark Roosevelt's vision. The Pitt partnership and laptop access were initially effective, but both were later limited by budget constraints. The extended school day was never adopted, as the board winced at its cost—an extra $2,100 per teacher annually.[42] University Prep spent $8,895 per student in the 2013–14 school year, the most of any District high school, yet achievement has been low.[43]

In the 2013–14 and 2014–15 school terms, fewer than half of the students scored proficient in reading or math—40 percent and 30 percent, respectively. Only 39.5 percent were eligible for the Pittsburgh Promise scholarship, which meant that the rest had an unweighted GPA under 2.5. A mere 35 percent of graduates enrolled in college or trade school, and only 54 percent of the school's teachers found it "a good place to work and learn."[44] With at least one "serious" fight per week in the 2015–16 school year, including a thirty-girl brawl that lasted over thirty minutes and made international news, safety is also an issue.[45] "This is a school where you gotta fight," said Amina Morris, a ninth grader attacked in the melee.[46] Community leaders have blamed the District for mixing rival neighborhoods without a plan to defuse tensions, and former city councilman Sala (Samuel Howze) Udin even mocked the school's name. "It is not preparatory for university," said Udin, "as much as it's preparatory for the penitentiary."[47]

However, Chris Horne, the school's principal since 2015, fiercely defends his students, many of whom have issues more urgent than homework. "Kids come hungry," said Horne, whose office is stocked with snacks. Pupils also have high rates of abuse, neglect, and exposure to trauma, yet Horne—a former Schenley teacher with deep family roots in the Hill District—is committed to improving outcomes. "I wouldn't be here if I didn't believe we could transform this school and this community," said Horne, who seeks a stronger Pitt partnership and a second on-site social worker. Still, the school touts incremental progress, including an uptick in after-school program participation, a student-organized basketball fundraiser, and an incident-free, school-wide pep rally just two months after the brawl.[48]

Schenley's other heir, the International Baccalaureate (IB) school, opened at Reizenstein in 2009 with "a very serious" identity problem.[49] The school was christened Barack Obama International Studies Academy, as pupils on the naming committee "really wanted a name that they knew" and resisted adults' suggestions, such as Andrew Carnegie or H. J.

Heinz.[50] Despite concerns that the honor was premature, the name was approved out of deference to students. "It sends a message to students that they can effect change if they get involved in the process," said board member Thomas Sumpter '68.[51]

While the student body had chosen to name its new school after Barack Obama—selected over Andy Warhol and Roberto Clemente—many students wanted to remain Schenley and were miffed that District policy purportedly required a name change.[52] Former District officials have vague and conflicting memories of that policy rationale, but parents and students recalled that the new school's principal, Wayne Walters, "was very interested" in creating a distinct entity.[53] "[Walters' attitude] was very much, 'We're not Schenley,'" said Hannah Green, one of several 2013 Obama Academy graduates who wore Schenley attire on picture day. "To sort of put it in their faces," explained Green, "that Schenley never dies."[54]

Branding aside, early Obama Academy students felt robbed of a traditional high school experience. The Class of 2012 spent ninth grade confined to the Frick building's basement, the next two years sharing Reizenstein with Schenley students who "hated" them, and their senior year, still at Reizenstein, amidst the school's plans to thrive at Peabody after they graduated. "We were middle schoolers for four years!" lamented Lewis Thompson, a 2012 graduate, who said classmates remain "really, really pissed."[55]

Beyond early identity and facilities hiccups, Obama Academy has largely performed well. In 2015, it ranked second of Pittsburgh's nine high schools in college or trade school enrollment (70 percent) and third in reading (87.9 percent) and math (76.8 percent) proficiency. Moreover, 69 percent of graduates are eligible for Pittsburgh Promise scholarships. Obama Academy is 73 percent black, and despite a pronounced District-wide achievement gap, it often outperforms Allderdice and Sci-Tech—high-achieving schools with white enrollment pluralities.[56] "Obama is an outlier in the District," said Carey Harris, head of education watchdog A+ Schools from 2004 to 2016, "but they're getting great outcomes for black kids."[57] In Obama Academy's first five years as a full-fledged high school, the musical has received ten Gene Kelly Awards and higher participation per capita than Schenley. However, interest in athletics has waned as few students on the three-school cooperative teams actually attend Obama Academy.[58]

Despite its origins and kinks, Pete Vitti—an Obama Academy teacher who spent seventeen years at Schenley—feels Spartan alumni can be proud of the IB school. Vitti loved Schenley's inclusiveness and "family feel" but thinks Obama Academy is even more unified—a by-product of an intentionally small school (100 students per grade) with a single academic track. Additionally, the "IB-only" format means more low-income and minority students are exposed to high-caliber courses, which also serve to foster more diverse friendships. Though he still calls Schenley's closing "a huge mistake," Vitti considers Obama Academy "a success story," where the racial achievement gap is close to half the District's average, and the IB curriculum challenges all students, regardless of ability or background. "There's a lot to feel good about," insists Vitti, his arms crossed in the gym foyer, where Obama Academy's Wall of Fame is flanked by a trophy case for Schenley and Peabody artifacts. "A lot of Schenley's values are alive here."[59]

Conclusion

On June 12, 2011, Schenley High School succumbed with its final commencement, and most students beamed as they moved in procession toward their diplomas at the Petersen Events Center in Oakland. After the ceremony, at the corner of Terrace and De Soto Streets, Eric Smith '84 showed a KDKA news camera the Spartan tattoo that runs from wrist to elbow. "It's heartbreaking," said Smith, a Hill District native, who faced uphill and squinted into the sunset. "Just to see my alma mater close forever."[1]

Today, more than five years since the last commencement and more than eight years since the Oakland building was shuttered, many Schenley partisans still bounce between anger and grief. Nevenka Kurjakovic, a Yugoslavian immigrant, felt stifled by her own American schooling, but as a mother of eight, she was drawn to the District's dynamic magnets. She sent seven of her children to Schenley, mostly through East Hills and Frick, and—in reference to recent unrest in Ferguson, Missouri, and Baltimore—laments the end of integrated education. "Why do we not have the hate that other cities have?" she shouts between sobs in her Central Oakland kitchen. "Why?" Choking back tears, Kurjakovic recalls Schenley's final concert, where the multiracial chorus sang "He's Got the Whole World in His Hands" in the style of Mahalia Jackson—her "all-time, all-time favorite" singer. She closes her eyes and hums a few bars. "We were gonna change the world," she says, wiping her cheek dry. "It was the end of all we stood in line for."[2]

For most of its ninety-five-year existence, Schenley reflected the vision of its first principal, James Noble Rule. Principal Rule believed the modern secondary school should foster community and "functional equality" across social strata. A century later, scholars cite "a mounting body of evidence" that integrated schools create "profound benefits for all children." Such schools enhance diversity of perspective, the ability to communicate across cultural lines, and minority student achievement. Pluralistic education also renders students of all races more inclined to seek out integrated environments later in life—such as colleges, workplaces, and neighborhoods. "It is not [Schenley's primary function] to prepare girls and boys for college or business," said Principal Rule in 1919, but "for life here and now," and "to live and to work in happy, effective co-operation."[3]

Schenley is gone, and four of the District's nine current high schools are segregated by race and class, but still Rule's cooperation goes on.[4] In a corner cafe in downtown Washington, DC, Bill Mitchell '85 and Diane Thompson '85 distill the last three decades into one long lunch. Mitchell is black and grew up in the projects, but went from Schenley to Harvard to a US Navy commission. Thompson is white and from the Shadyside neighborhood—with tranquil, tree-lined streets and upscale boutiques—but spent thirteen years serving hardscrabble East St. Louis as a legal aid attorney. They talk career, family, and dessert, but mostly laugh recalling life within those three walls.[5]

Back on Pittsburgh's South Side on a sticky August night, the Class of 1965 mingles on a riverfront patio. There are kisses, hugs, and enthusiastic backslaps before the doe-eyed freshmen from the fall of '61 talk retirement and travel, and pull out iPhones to show off photos of grandchildren. A half century ago, they lapped the triangle looking for classrooms, slow danced in the musty basement gym, and dreamed out into Oakland from the chorus room windows while the world around them. It burned at Ole Miss; in Havana and at the Kremlin; in the schoolhouse door; in Birmingham; in Dallas; in the Gulf of Tonkin; and at the Edmund Pettus Bridge. They were black and white—though many are now gray—and the class president still floats between tables, reviving impressions of teachers and long-dormant nicknames.

Tonight there is cheesecake, a slideshow, and a DJ—but no numbers. There are no budget deficits or achievement gaps; no court orders or construction estimates; and no government agency counting pupils by race. Tonight there is the Electric Slide and shrill, unapologetic laughter. Tonight under the Monongahela sky, four dozen middle-aged kids are gliding around the dance floor in happy, effective coordination.

Appendix A

Notable Central High Alumni

Names are followed by the year of graduation. No graduation year appears if the alumnus (1) dropped out of high school altogether, (2) left Central/Schenley and graduated from a different high school, or (3) is believed to have graduated from Central/Schenley, but the specific year is unknown.

Students

Barchfeld, Andrew Jackson. A physician and hospital executive who served in Congress and on Pittsburgh's Common council. Jackson died in the Knickerbocker Theater disaster.[1]

Cooper, Alexander. 1913. An Allegheny County (PA) Common Pleas Court judge.[2]

Friedman, William F. 1909. An army cryptographer who led the team that cracked Japan's Purple code in World War II. Friedman earned the Medal of Merit and the National Security Award.[3]

Glick, Frank. 1912. An All-American quarterback and three-sport athlete at Princeton, Glick was also Lehigh's head football coach, and later, a US Army officer. He married literary mogul Virginia Kirkus.[4]

Mazet, Robert. 1875. A New York state legislator who chaired a special committee to investigate Tammany Hall corruption at the direction of Governor Theodore Roosevelt.[5]

McClelland, William "Doc." 1914. A dentist by trade, he served Pennsylvania as state boxing commissioner, Allegheny County (PA) as commissioner and coroner, and Pittsburgh as City Court magistrate. McClelland was also a Pitt football star.[6]

McCloskey, Manus. 1894. A US Army brigadier general who distinguished himself in the Spanish-American War, the Boxer Rebellion, and World War I.[7]

Mitchell, H. Walton. An Allegheny County (PA) Orphans' Court judge.[8]

Rauh, Bertha (Florsheim). 1884. The first female member of an American mayoral cabinet, she headed Pittsburgh's Department of Welfare in the 1920s but was best known as an activist and reformer. Rauh successfully pushed for the creation of the Mayview psychiatric hospital, anti-pollution legislation, and reduced-cost school lunches. She also helped establish more than a dozen civic and philanthropic organizations.[9]

Schultz, Albert L. 1871. A prominent civil engineer, he founded the Schultz Bridge and Iron Company, which built the Schenley Park and Brady Street bridges, and many others.[10]

Soffel, Sara M. 1904. Pennsylvania's first female judge, she served Allegheny County (PA) on the County and Common Pleas courts. She taught at Central while attending law school in the evenings and continued to teach at Schenley when—despite graduating with highest honors—no law firm would hire her because of her gender.[11]

Stanton, William H. 1891. Among the first black attorneys in Western Pennsylvania, and according to the *Post*, Stanton ranked with the area's best, irrespective of color. He successfully defended eighty-one of eighty-three homicide cases.[12]

Turfley, George G. 1876. Turfley is believed to be the first registered black physician in Allegheny County (PA).[13]

Staff

Cather, Willa. A Pulitzer Prize-winning author, she taught Latin and English at Central for approximately twenty-nine months, from 1901 to 1903. The school figured prominently in her 1905 short story, "Paul's Case."[14]

Gelbert, Charlie. A college football Hall of Famer who coached Central's football team in 1899.[15]

Thompson, Joseph H. A college football Hall of Famer, Pennsylvania state senator, and attorney, Thompson won the Congressional Medal of Honor for his service in World War I. He coached Central's undefeated football team in 1906.[16]

Appendix B:
Notable Schenley High Alumni

Students

Abrams, Solomon. 1931. He founded two synagogues, earned four post-graduate degrees from Pitt, served on the Pittsburgh Board of Education, and was director of Pittsburgh's Hebrew Institute.[1]

Allen, Cheryl Lynn. 1965. The first and only black woman elected to the Pennsylvania Superior Court, she was also an Allegheny County (PA) Common Pleas Court judge.[2]

Andrews, Jesse. 2000. Author of *Me and Earl and the Dying Girl*—a novel-turned-motion picture set at Schenley, with some scenes filmed inside the school—which won the Sundance Film Festival's grand jury and audience awards.[3]

Baer, Howard. 1924. An internationally known artist, with paintings in the Metropolitan Museum of Art's permanent collection and illustrations published in *The New Yorker* and *Saturday Evening Post*. He was also a World War II artist-correspondent in Asia and a professor at Parsons.[4]

Balfour, Stanton. 1924. Director of the Pittsburgh Foundation and the Pittsburgh Symphony Society, Balfour was a trustee, board member, or consultant to numerous regional philanthropic organizations.[5]

Bell, Derrick. 1948. The first black tenured Harvard law professor and a critical race theory pioneer, Bell advised the legal team that integrated the University of Mississippi, and was, according to Barack Obama, "the Rosa Parks of legal education." He quit the US Department of Justice when asked to leave the NAACP and resigned dean and professor posts at the University of Oregon and Harvard law schools, respectively, when each failed to hire a woman of color. At Schenley, Bell was vice president of a class that was 71 percent white.[6]

Berlin, Liz. 1988. A founding member of alternative rock band Rusted Root, whose 1994 album, *When I Woke*, was certified platinum.[7]

Blair, DeJuan. 2007. He played seven NBA seasons for San Antonio, Dallas, and Washington, and was an All-American forward at Pitt.[8]

Braemer, Samuel D. 1923. A Fayette County (PA) Common Pleas Court judge.[9]

Brown, Byrd R. 1947. A civil rights attorney who helped force integration at Duquesne Light and worked for race-related reforms in the Pittsburgh Public Schools. He earned his bachelor's and law degrees at Yale and was president of Pittsburgh's NAACP chapter.[10]

Brown, Jason. 1989. At age 12, Brown wrote *Tender Places*, which was staged Off-Broadway to rave reviews in the *New York Times*, and also adapted into a CBS television special starring Jean Stapleton.[11]

Brown, Larry. 1965. The 1972 NFL Most Valuable Player and a four-time All-Pro, Brown led Washington to Super Bowl VII.[12]

Brown, Ray. 1944. He discovered the jazz bass in high school, when Schenley's orchestra already had twenty-six pianists. Brown became a Grammy-award winner—playing on over 2,000 recordings, with stars like Dizzy Gillespie, Oscar Peterson, and Charlie Parker. He also accompanied famous singers, including Frank Sinatra and Ella Fitzgerald, and married the latter.[13]

Buncher, Jack. 1929. He turned a "scrap business into a multimillion-dollar real estate empire," wrote the *Post-Gazette*, adding that his Buncher Co. accumulated "one of the largest real estate portfolios ever" in Pittsburgh. Buncher studied medicine and law at Duquesne before the Depression forced him into the workforce.[14]

Cenci, Nick. 1949. He produced top 10 singles for Lou Christie ("Two Faces Have I") and The Vogues ("You're the One" and "Five O'Clock World") and revived Tommy James and the Shondells's career.[15]

Curto, Frank. 1927. A horticulturalist for the National Parks Service, Pittsburgh's parks department, and Phipps Conservatory. He was also an instructor at Carnegie Mellon and Buhl Planetarium, and is the namesake of the Strip District's sculpture-filled Frank Curto Park.[16]

Dallas, Cynthia "Cindy." 1998. An actress with over a dozen television credits, including *Days of Our Lives* and *2 Broke Girls*. Before her acting career, Dallas was drafted by the WNBA's San Antonio Silver Stars after thrice leading the Big Ten Conference in rebounds at the University of Illinois.[17]

Daniels, Marc. 1929. A three-time Emmy nominee who directed *I Love Lucy*, *Star Trek*, *Gunsmoke*, *Bonanza*, and *Hogan's Heroes*, Daniels pioneered the use of three cameras in filming.[18]

Davis, Lew. 1923. A Tucson, Arizona, mayor who the cast tie-breaking vote to pass a nondiscrimination public accommodations ordinance. He was also a pharmacist and real estate investor.[19]

Dinkins, Darnell. 1995. He played eight NFL seasons for Baltimore, Cleveland, New Orleans, and the New York Giants, and was later a Tampa Bay assistant coach.[20]

Dobrin, Milton B. 1932. A leading geophysicist who wrote the field's seminal textbook, Dobrin also helped perfect a then-state-of-the-art scanning technique for petroleum prospecting.[21]

Durrett, Kenny. 1967. The NBA's fourth overall in draft pick in 1971, he played four seasons for Cincinnati, Kansas City-Omaha, and Philadelphia. He was also an All-American forward at La Salle.[22]

Falk, Leon Jr. A business mogul whose largesse helped Jews escape Nazi Germany. He also created Pitt's Falk Medical Fund, Falk Clinic, and Falk School.[23]

Gainsford, Ronald. 1948. West Virginia University's head swimming coach and a three-time All-American at Pitt.[24]

Getting, Ivan. 1929. A GPS cocreator and Draper Prize-winner ("the Nobel of engineering"), Getting earned Edison and Rhodes scholarships to MIT and Oxford, respectively. During World War II, he led military research and was a consultant to US War Secretary Henry Stimson. As a child, his family moved to

Pittsburgh, where his father was the Czechoslovak consul. Getting was Schenley's class president.[25]

Glancy, Harry. An International Swimming Hall of Famer and two-time Olympian, Glancy won gold in the 800-meter freestyle relay in 1924.[26]

Glinn, Burt. 1943. An award-winning Cold War photojournalist and president of the Magnum photo agency.[27]

Hammon, William. 1922. He collaborated on the polio vaccine, although he was initially Jonas Salk's rival. Hammon developed the first feline panleukopenia vaccine and was a World War II tropical diseases consultant to the United States. He also headed epidemiology and microbiology departments at Pitt for twenty-three years, and earned Harvard medical and doctoral degrees.[28]

Harper, Walt. 1944. An internationally known jazz musician who recorded eight albums and an Emmy-nominated PBS special, *Walt Harper at Fallingwater*.[29]

Hershkovitz, Philip. 1927. A leading mammalogist and curator at Chicago's Field Museum of Natural History for more than forty years.[30]

Hines, Earl "Fatha." The "father of modern jazz piano," Hines "revolutionized" the genre with Louis Armstrong in the 1920s, wrote the *New York Times*.[31]

Kaufman, Louis L. 1921. He balanced careers as a popular KDKA radio host and an attorney for nearly thirty years before becoming an Allegheny County (PA) County Court judge.[32]

Lavine, Stan. 1946. An orthopedic surgeon, he was head physician for the NBA's Washington Bullets, the NFL's Washington, DC, franchise, and the University of Maryland's twenty-four varsity teams. Lavine was also a college athlete, playing quarterback and leading Maryland to a Gator Bowl title.[33]

Lucas, Maurice. 1971. A four-time NBA All-Star, Lucas helped Portland win the 1977 NBA title, and was named to the ABA's All-Time team based on two seasons in that league. He was also an All-American forward at Marquette and an NBA assistant coach for Portland.[34]

McSorley, John Jr. McSorley played football and hockey at Notre Dame, served as Pitt's head hockey coach, and was also a minor league hockey referee. He was later president of Sterling Land Co., which developed Pittsburgh's King Edward, Royal York, and Wellington apartments.[35]

Moore, Donald "Dudey." 1928. A two-time college basketball Coach of the Year, he guided Duquesne to the 1955 National Invitation Tournament (NIT) title and four consecutive NIT semifinal appearances.[36]

Moore, Joe. 1951. The "best line coach in college football," wrote *Sports Illustrated*. Moore was an assistant coach at Pitt, Temple, and Notre Dame—where he won a national title and later, an age discrimination lawsuit.[37]

Moriarty, Richard. 1957. The father of Mr. Yuk stickers and the National Poison Center Network. He was also Pittsburgh Children's Hospital's chief pediatric resident and director of the Pittsburgh Poison Center.[38]

Mosley, Robert. 1946. A pioneering black opera singer whose career spanned six decades, Mosley sang lead in the Metropolitan Opera's *Porgy and Bess*.[39]

Mosteller, Frederick. 1934. The only person to chair four Harvard academic departments, including statistics, which he founded.[40]

Noszka, Stanley. 1938. A Pennsylvania state senator who played four professional basketball seasons in the leagues that became the NBA.[41]

Nunn, Bill. 1970. Nunn acted in more than forty films, including *Do the Right Thing* (Radio Raheem), *Sister Act* (Lt. Eddie Souther), and Sam Raimi's *Spider-Man* trilogy (Robbie Robertson). Active in student council and orchestra at Schenley, Nunn stumbled into acting at Morehouse College, where he became friends with Samuel L. Jackson.[42]

O'Toole, Joe. 1942. He earned three World Series rings in four decades in the Pittsburgh Pirates front office, including a stint as co-general manager.[43]

Peay, Francis. 1962. He played nine NFL seasons for Green Bay, Kansas City, and the New York Giants. Peay was also an All-American tackle at Missouri, and later, Northwestern's head coach.[44]

Poole, Cecil F. 1932. The first black US Ninth Circuit Court of Appeals judge, he was also a federal trial court judge, a US attorney, Harvard Law alum, and US Army officer. During high school, Poole befriended future jazz legend Billy Eckstine, when the two worked on a garbage truck.[45]

Prince, Bob. 1934. A sports media Hall of Famer and Ford C. Frick Award-winner, Prince was a Pittsburgh Pirates broadcaster for twenty-eight seasons. He attended seventeen high schools before Schenley, and was mischievous—once renting a hearse for a swim meet at heavily favored Carrick. He lettered in swimming at Pitt and the University of Oklahoma, spent two years at Harvard Law School, and also called Steelers, Penguins, and Penn State games.[46]

Rakow, Ed. He pitched seven Major League Baseball seasons for Detroit, Atlanta, the Los Angeles Dodgers, and Kansas City Athletics.[47]

Reed, Vivian. 1963. The two-time Tony Award nominee and one-time Drama Desk Award winner had a four-decade Broadway career and is best known for her work in *Bubbling Brown Sugar*. Reed was the "backbone" of Schenley's soprano section before going to Juilliard. She has also performed in four films, on *The Merv Griffin Show*, and at the Apollo Theater.[48]

Ritchey, Dahlen K. 1927. An architect who designed the Civic Arena, Three Rivers Stadium, Mellon Square, Allegheny Center, as well as several schools, universities, and hospitals. Ritchey's Schenley art teacher suggested he study architecture, and he later trained at Carnegie Tech and Harvard.[49]

Robinson, William R. 1960. A Pennsylvania state representative, Allegheny County (PA) councilman, and Pittsburgh city councilman.[50]

Rothschild, Jacob "Jack." 1927. A civil rights rabbi and Martin Luther King Jr. confidant, his Atlanta synagogue was bombed because of his activism. When Atlanta's elites were reticent to honor King's Nobel Prize, Rothschild organized and emceed a sold out, integrated banquet. "[I]t really was 'black and white together,'" said Coretta Scott King.[51]

Sammartino, Bruno. 1955. A pro wrestling Hall of Famer, Sammatino held the WWE title for more than eleven years and sold out Madison Square Garden 187 times—each a record. He was bullied at Schenley before taking up bodybuilding, but classmates recall him as imposing. "If they teased him, they did it running away," said Richard Nicklos '57. Schenley had no wrestling team, but Sammartino was invited to practice with Pitt, who offered him an athletic scholarship.[52]

Schmitt, Gladys. 1927. She published twenty short stories and eleven novels, including *David the King* and *Rembrandt*, and founded Carnegie Mellon's creative writing program.[53]

Shull, Clifford G. 1933. Shull won the Nobel Prize in physics for developing neutron scattering—a molecular probing technique—and "helped answer the question of where atoms 'are.'" A math and science "wizard," recalled Schenley classmates, Shull worked at what is now Oak Ridge

National Laboratory and also taught at MIT for thirty-one years.[54]

Sowell, Arnold. 1953. He captured multiple middle-distance track and field world records, fourth place at the Olympics, and a gold medal at the Pan-Am Games. Sowell also won two NCAA titles and was a US Army lieutenant colonel.[55]

Stepien, Ted. 1943. An advertising mogul who briefly owned the NBA's Cleveland Cavaliers, he made headlines for racially insensitive remarks. His mismanagement led to poor play, paltry attendance, and the "Stepien Rule"—barring teams from trading future first-round draft picks in consecutive years. At Schenley, Stepien was a football and basketball star who led all Pittsburgh City League scorers in the latter.[56]

Tatar, Benjamin. 1948. He acted in at least twenty films, including *Battle of the Bulge* and *Patton*. He was also Jackie Gleason's personal assistant and Ava Gardner's live-in companion.[57]

Trawick, Herbert. 1939. The first black player in the Canadian Football League, where he was a Hall of Famer and seven-time All-Star. Living in Montreal, Trawick "sought out and befriended every" black player on the newly integrated Royals baseball club. He was later an NFL scout for Denver.[58]

Turner, Oliver E. 1929. He was Allegheny County (PA)'s Director of Public Health, a public health policy leader, and a diabetes researcher. Turner was also personal physician to Pennsylvania governor Jim Duff and Steelers owner Art Rooney Sr.[59]

Turrentine, Stanley. A jazz saxophonist and four-time Grammy nominee, he produced more than thirty-five albums, including *Sugar*. He frequently played with fellow Hill District native George Benson, who did not attend Schenley, despite popular myth.[60]

Warhol, Andy. 1945. Among the most famous and influential artists of his era, his *Campbell's Soup Cans* and *Marilyn Diptych* are iconic. Warhol was serious, shy, and "a total outsider," said Schenley classmates, yet he was close with a group of Jewish girls, including Mina (Serbin) Kavaler '47. Warhol dunked her long pigtails in the ink well, said Kavaler, who called him "very sweet," but a "kook." He was inspired by art teacher Joseph Fitzpatrick, and students would huddle near his desk to watch him sketch.[61]

Watkins, Richard T. 1965. A television producer, he won Emmy and Alfred E. duPont-Columbia University Awards.[62]

Watson, Robert. 1973. An Allegheny County (PA) Common Pleas Court judge.[63]

Staff

Cantini, Virgil. See chapter 5.

Kerr, Andy. A college football Hall of Famer, Kerr coached Central's football, basketball, and track teams to regional titles. He later coached the same sports at Pitt—although only as an assistant in football—but remained a full-time Schenley math teacher. After helping Pop Warner win three national football titles, he left to become Stanford's head coach. His 1932 Colgate football team was undefeated and unscored upon, yet controversially excluded from the Rose Bowl.[64]

Rule, James Noble. See chapter 3.

Appendix C
Athletics

Venues followed by an asterisk no longer exist, and their locations are approximate, reflecting present-day street configurations.

Baseball, boys

Seasons: 93 (1918–44, '46–2011)
City titles: 8 (1925, '27–'31, '92, '99)
Notable alumni: Joseph "Ziggy" Kahn '17 (minor leagues); Vic Harris (Negro leagues); Harold Tinker '23 (Negro leagues); George C. M. Susce '27 (St. Bonaventure; 5 MLB teams); John W. Moore '28 (Negro leagues); George Hornyak (Georgetown); Regis Smith '28 (Penn State); John Balquist '28 (Columbia); Joe Kielb '41 (Pitt); Ed Korpa '44 (minor leagues); Fred Armbruster '46 (minor leagues); Bobby Lewis '47 (Pitt); Josh Gibson Jr. '48 (Negro leagues; minor leagues); George D. Susce '48 (2 MLB teams); Paul Susce (Auburn; minor leagues); Ed Rakow (4 MLB teams); Alex Perinis '53 (minor leagues); Nick Kartsonas '56 (Pitt); Louis DeMar '61 (minor leagues); Marvin Randall '92 (West Virginia); Jon Smith '00 (Duquesne); Keith Meyer '04 (Duquesne; minor leagues)

Baseball/softball, girls

Seasons: 36 (1923, '77–2011)

Basketball, boys

Seasons: 95 (1917–2011)
City titles: 20 (1917, '26–'27, '31–'32, '65–'67, '70–'71, '74, '78–'79, '91, '96–'97, 2005–8)
WPIAL titles: 1 (1917)
State titles: 5 (1966, '71, '75, '78, 2007)
Notable alumni: Joseph "Ziggy" Kahn '17 (US pro teams); Meyer Gefsky '17 (US pro teams); Bernard "Buck" Sandomire '17 (US pro teams); Elmer Lissfelt '21 (Pitt); Bill James '21 (Pitt); Ben Jones '22 (Pitt); Nathan "Johnny" Serbin '22 (Duquesne); Jacob "Jock" Rosenberg '23 (Duquesne); Donald "Dudey" Moore '28 (Duquesne); Art Hyatt '33 (NBL Detroit); Parry Thomas '36 (Duquesne); Stanley Noszka '38 (Duquesne; 2 BAA teams; NBL Youngstown); Saul Chosky '43 (Pitt); Eugene Harris '58 (Penn State); Marvin Snowden '66 (West Virginia); Kenny Durrett '67 (La Salle; 3 NBA teams); Ed "Petie" Gibson '67 (New Mexico); Bob Evans '69 (Columbia); Clarence Hopson '70 (St. Francis [PA]); Maurice Lucas '71 (Marquette; 6 NBA teams; 2 ABA teams); Ricky Coleman '71 (Jacksonville); Tom Thornton '72 (Detroit); Robert "Jeep" Kelley '73 (UNLV/Hawaii); Kelvin Smith '75 (Pitt); Wayne Williams '75 (Pitt); Nathan "Sonny" Lewis '76 (Pitt); Harvey Daniels '76 (Kent State); Jamie Smith '78 (Wisconsin/Indiana State); David Thornton '78 (George Washington/Eastern Kentucky); Tim Curges (Niagara); Calvin Kane '79 (Lamar); Larry Anderson '79 (UNLV); Mark Halsel '80 (Northeastern); Norris Thompson '83 (St. Francis [PA]); Darrick Suber '89 (Rider); Samba Johnson '91 (Robert Morris); Naron Jackson '97 (Robert Morris); Brian Carroll '97 (Loyola [MD]); Chaz McCrommon '00 (Robert Morris); Jack Higgins '01 (Cleveland State/Duquesne); Nate Gerwig '01 (Kent State; US, Europe pro teams); Shawn Hawkins '01 (Long Beach State; US, Europe, Asia pro teams); DeJuan Blair '07 (Pitt; 3 NBA teams); D. J. Kennedy '07 (St. John's; NBA Cleveland); DeAndre Kane '08 (Marshall/Iowa State; Europe pro teams)

Seasons

Term	League	Division	Finish	Record	Postseason
1916–17	WPIAL	City Lg.	1st of 6	21–3 (10–0)	W WPIAL final Game 1 (Braddock) 30–28 (OT) W WPIAL final Game 2 (Braddock) 32–29
1917–18	WPIAL	City Lg.	4th of 7	6–9 (6–6)	
1918–19	WPIAL	City Lg.	T4th of 7	11–5 (5–7)	
1919–20	WPIAL	City Lg.	3rd of 7	13–9 (7–5)	
1920–21	WPIAL	City Lg.	T1st of 7	8–3 (5–1)	L City tie-breaker (Fifth Avenue) 26–21
1921–22	WPIAL	City Lg.	3rd of 7	11–6 (4–2)	
1922–23	WPIAL	City Lg.	4th of 7	4–9 (2–3)	
1923–24	WPIAL	City Lg.	4th of 7	8–8 (6–6)	
1924–25	WPIAL	City Lg.	3rd of 8	11–4 (10–4)	
1925–26	City Lg.	Sec. I	T1st of 5	13–5 (7–1)	W Sec. I tie-breaker (Westinghouse) 24–12 L City final Game 1 (South Hills) 30–25 W City final Game 2 (South Hills) 31–24 W City final Game 3 (South Hills) 39–9
1926–27	City Lg.	Sec. I	1st of 5	14–3 (7–1)	L City final Game 1 (Allegheny) 21–20 W City final Game 2 (Allegheny) 21–18 W City final Game 3 (Allegheny) 31–18
1927–28	City Lg.	Sec. I	2nd of 5	14–2 (6–2)	
1928–29	City Lg.	Sec. I	2nd of 6	8–5 (7–3)	
1929–30	City Lg.	Sec. I	T2nd of 7	10–5 (9–3)	
1930–31	City Lg.	Sec. I	T1st of 7	15–3 (10–2)	W Sec. I tie-breaker (Westinghouse) 22–19 W City final Game 1 (South Hills) 28–14 W City final Game 2 (South Hills) 25–20
1931–32	City Lg.	Sec. I	T1st of 7	13–5 (9–3)	W Sec. I tie-breaker (Fifth Avenue) 22–19 L City final Game 1 (Allegheny) 22–20 W City final Game 2 (Allegheny) 31–9 W City final Game 3 (Allegheny) 31–18
1932–33	City Lg.	Sec. I	2nd of 7	12–5 (8–4)	
1933–34	City Lg.	Sec. I	3rd of 7	10–5 (7–5)	
1934–35	City Lg.	Sec. I	T3rd of 7	9–6 (6–6)	

Term	League	Division	Finish	Record	Postseason
1935–36	City Lg.	Sec. I	4th of 7	10–6 (7–5)	
1936–37	City Lg.	Sec. I	T6th of 7	3–14 (2–10)	
1937–38	City Lg.	Sec. I	T2nd of 8	13–4 (11–3)	
1938–39	City Lg.	Sec. I	T3rd of 7	7–9 (7–5)	
1939–40	City Lg.	Sec. I	T5th of 8	10–9 (7–7)	
1940–41	City Lg.	Sec. I	7th of 8	4–11 (4–10)	
1941–42	City Lg.	Sec. I	6th of 8	5–12 (4–10)	
1942–43	City Lg.	Sec. I	2nd of 8	14–2 (12–2)	
1943–44	City Lg.	Sec. I	3rd of 8	12–4 (10–4)	
1944–45	City Lg.	Sec. I	7th of 8	4–13 (4–10)	
1945–46	City Lg.	Sec. I	4th of 8	7–7 (4–3)	
1946–47	City Lg.	Sec. I	3rd of 8	10–8 (7–7)	
1947–48	City Lg.	Sec. I	6th of 8	8–9 (6–8)	
1948–49	City Lg.	Sec. I	8th of 8	1–17 (1–13)	
1949–50	City Lg.	Sec. I	T6th of 8	5–14 (3–11)	
1950–51	City Lg.	Sec. I	T4th of 8	7–10 (6–8)	
1951–52	City Lg.	Sec. I	T2nd of 8	10–7 (9–5)	
1952–53	City Lg.	Sec. I	T7th of 8	4–13 (2–12)	
1953–54	City Lg.	Sec. I	7th of 8	3–12 (3–11)	
1954–55	City Lg.	Sec. I	6th of 8	7–9 (5–9)	
1955–56	City Lg.	Sec. I	5th of 8	5–11 (5–9)	
1956–57	City Lg.	Sec. I	T3rd of 8	11–7 (9–5)	
1957–58	City Lg.	Sec. I	T4th of 8	9–8 (7–7)	
1958–59	City Lg.	Sec. I	T4th of 8	11–8 (8–6)	

Term	League	Division	Finish	Record	Postseason
1959–60	City Lg.	Sec. I	3rd of 8	12–7 (9–5)	
1960–61	City Lg.	Sec. I	T4th of 8	10–7 (8–6)	
1961–62	City Lg.	Sec. I	T4th of 8	9–9 (7–7)	
1962–63	City Lg.	Sec. I	7th of 8	2–16 (2–12)	
1963–64	City Lg.	Sec. I	T3rd of 8	9–10 (8–6)	
1964–65	City Lg.	Sec. I	1st of 8	19–3 (13–1)	W City final (South Hills) 77–45 W State first round (Brookville) 93–54 W State quarterfinal (Erie Strong Vincent) 74–48 L State semifinal (Midland) 76–62
1965–66	City Lg.	Sec. I	1st of 7	19–2 (12–0)	W City final (Allegheny) 87–52 W State quarterfinal (Punxsutawney) 98–56 W State semifinal (Uniontown) 71–67 W State final (Chester) 74–64
1966–67	City Lg.	Sec. I	1st of 7	20–3 (12–0)	W City title (South Hills) 65–49 W State first round (Hickory) 79–58 W State quarterfinal (Bradford) 77–36 L State semifinal (Ambridge) 68–50
1967–68	City Lg.	Sec. I	1st of 7	15–4 (12–0)	L City final (Allegheny) 70–67
1968–69	City Lg.	Sec. I	T1st of 7	16–4 (11–1)	L Sec. I tie-breaker (Fifth Avenue) 92–69
1969–70	City Lg.	Sec. I	T1st of 6	19–3 (9–1)	W Sec. I tie-breaker (Fifth Avenue) 78–63 W City final (Carrick) 88–76 W State first round (Erie Strong Vincent) 81–53 W State quarterfinal (Bradford) 69–62 L State semifinal (Beaver Falls) 87–83
1970–71	City Lg.	Sec. I	1st of 6	24–3 (10–0)	W City final (South Hills) 66–48 W State first round (Bradford) 88–63 W State quarterfinal (Erie McDowell) 67–51 W State semifinal (Farrell) 74–63 W State final (Norristown) 77–60
1971–72	City Lg.	Sec. I	2nd of 6	11–13 (7–3)	W City runner-up game (Carrick) 72–59 L State play-in round (Allegheny) 63–53
1972–73	City Lg.	Sec. I	2nd of 6	12–11 (8–2)	L City runner-up game (Oliver) 68–61
1973–74	City Lg.	Sec. I	1st of 6	19–7 (9–1)	W City final (Oliver) 65–42 W State first round (Jersey Shore) 77–45 W State second round (South Hills Catholic) 64–60 L State quarterfinal (Peabody) 67–62

Term	League	Division	Finish	Record	Postseason
1974–75	City Lg.	Sec. I	2nd of 7	26–3 (10–2)	W City runner-up game (Perry) 83–47 W State first round (Jersey Shore) 65–44 W State second round (Erie Cathedral Prep) 76–48 W State quarterfinal (Uniontown) 92–77 W State semifinal (Fifth Avenue) 78–63 W State final (Abington) 65–64
1975–76	City Lg.	Sec. I	2nd of 6	12–4 (8–2)	W City runner-up game (Oliver) 91–53 W State first round (Johnstown) 59–52 W State second round (Monessen) 107–88 L State quarterfinal (Farrell) 69–50
1976–77	City Lg.	Sec. I	3rd of 6	11–9 (6–4)	
1977–78	City Lg.	Sec. I	1st of 6	27–3 (9–1)	W City final (South Hills) 74–70 W State first round (Wilkinsburg) 62–61 W State second round (Norwin) 58–48 W State quarterfinal (Allderdice) 61–58 W State semifinal (Erie Cathedral Prep) 67–66 W State final (Lebanon) 51–50
1978–79	City Lg.	Sec. I	1st of 6	26–2 (10–0)	W City final (South Hills) 52–48 W State first round (Bradford) 94–59 W State second round (Erie Strong Vincent) 66–63 L State quarterfinal (Valley) 75–45
1979–80	City Lg.	Sec. I	3rd of 6	14–9 (6–4)	
1980–81	City Lg.	Sec. I	4th of 6	10–13 (6–4)	
1981–82	City Lg.	Sec. I	T3rd of 6	10–14 (5–5)	
1982–83	City Lg.	Sec. I	1st of 6	12–14 (8–2)	L City final (Langley) 74–61 L State first round (Farrell) 66–54
1983–84	City Lg.	Sec. I	3rd of 6	9–15 (5–5)	
1984–85	City Lg.	Sec. I	2nd of 6	13–11 (8–2)	W City semifinal (Perry) 67–62 L City final (Brashear) 72–69 L State first round (Blackhawk) 75–63
1985–86	City Lg.	Sec. I	5th of 6	7–15 (3–7)	
1986–87	City Lg.	Sec. I	2nd of 5	17–8 (6–2)	W City 4A semifinal (Langley) 72–70 L City 4A final (Allderdice) 63–43 L State first round (Moon) 63–52
1987–88	City Lg.	Sec. I	2nd of 5	17–11 (5–3)	W City 4A tie–breaker (Brashear) 73–64 W City 4A semifinal (Carrick) 82–59 L City 4A final (Allderdice) 55–44 L State first round (Uniontown) 81–74

Term	League	Division	Finish	Record	Postseason
1988–89	City Lg.	Sec. I	T4th of 5	12–16 (2–6)	W City 3A first round (Langley) 68–54 W City 3A semifinal (South) 59–57 L City 3A final (Perry) 65–62 L State first round (Blackhawk) 73–67
1989–90	City Lg.	Sec. II	T1st of 5	17–9 (6–2)	W City 3A semifinal (Langley) 69–66 L City 3A final (Perry) 64–53 L State first round (West Mifflin) 73–59
1990–91	City Lg.	Sec. II	3rd of 5	23–5 (4–4)	W City 3A semifinal (Westinghouse) 51–38 W City 3A final (Perry) 67–62 W State first round (Knoch) 65-54 W State second round (Aliquippa) 59-43 L State quarterfinal (Blackhawk) 61-60
1991–92	City Lg.	Sec. II	1st of 5	19–7 (8–0)	W City 4A semifinal (Langley) 70–56 L City 4A final (Brashear) 52–38 L State first round (Penn-Trafford) 75–62
1992–93	City Lg.	Sec. II	T2nd of 5	9–12 (3–5)	L City 3A first round (Westinghouse) 56–46
1993–94	City Lg.	Sec. II	T2nd of 5	16–9 (5–3)	W City 3A semifinal (Westinghouse) 53–33 L City 3A final (Perry) 71–68 L State first round Seton LaSalle 54–52
1994–95	City Lg.		T1st of 10	22–4 (16–2)	W City quarterfinal (South) 62–42 L City semifinal (Oliver) 85–77 (OT)
1995–96	City Lg.		3rd of 10	25–5 (14–3)	W City quarterfinal (Oliver) 46–20 W City semifinal (Perry) 43–39 W City final (Westinghouse) 59–52 W State first round (Butler) 52–47 W State second round (Central Catholic) 63–52 L State quarterfinal (Erie Cathedral Prep) 60–44
1996–97	City Lg.		2nd of 10	25–5 (15–3)	W City quarterfinal (South) 62–48 W City semifinal (Peabody) 57–50 W City final (Perry) 60–49 W State first round (Albert Gallatin) 68–46 W State second round (Erie Cathedral Prep) 36–33 L State quarterfinal (Franklin Regional) 60–56
1997–98	City Lg.		7th of 10	11–15 (8–10)	W City first round (Carrick) 73–37 L City quarterfinal (Peabody) 57–50 (OT)
1998–99	City Lg.		T3rd of 10	18–7 (12–6)	L City quarterfinal (Westinghouse) 49–47
1999–2000	City Lg.		1st of 10	26–2 (18–0)	W City quarterfinal (Allderdice) 85–61 W City semifinal (Oliver) 70–53 L City final (Peabody) 62–54 L State first round (Uniontown) 71–70 (OT)

Term	League	Division	Finish	Record	Postseason
2000–2001	City Lg.		1st of 10	29–3 (18–0)	W City quarterfinal (Brashear) 74–42 W City semifinal (Perry) 64–42 L City final (Peabody) 39–38 W State first round (New Castle) 59–44 W State second round (Erie Central) 71–42 W State quarterfinal (Central Catholic) 66–58 W State semifinal (George Jr. Republic) 83–77 (OT) L State final (Coatesville) 70–57
2001–2	City Lg.		3rd of 10	18–10 (13–5)	W City quarterfinal (Carrick) 74–53 W City semifinal (Oliver) 59–53 L City final (Peabody) 43–42 W State first round (North Hills) 68–52 L State second round (Erie Cathedral Prep) 57–49
2002–3	City Lg.		T5th of 10	10–15 (9–9)	L City quarterfinal (Peabody) 53–41
2003–4	City Lg.		3rd of 10	19–8 (14–4)	W City quarterfinal (Langley) 51–47 W City semifinal (Peabody) 45–39 L City final (Perry) 42–37 L State first round (Penn Hills) 69–58
2004–5	City Lg.		1st of 9	25–5 (16–0)	W City quarterfinal (Westinghouse) 72–42 W City semifinal (Allderdice) 40–25 W City final (Oliver) 73–50 W State first round (Chartiers Valley) 46–37 W State second round (Upper St. Clair) 59–49 L State quarterfinal (Erie Cathedral Prep) 53–49
2005–6	City Lg.		1st of 9	30–2 (16–0)	W City quarterfinal (Langley) 93–28 W City semifinal (Oliver) 81–54 W City final (Allderdice) 82–46 W State first round (Bethel Park) 77–64 W State second round (Chartiers Valley) 45–23 W State quarterfinal (McKeesport) 70–58 W State semifinal (Harrisburg) 66–46 L State final (Lower Merion) 60–58
2006–7	City Lg.		1st of 9	29–3 (16–0)	W City quarterfinal (Carrick) 83–43 W City semifinal (Perry) 69–57 W City final (Oliver) 56–49 W State first round (Fox Chapel) 71–48 W State second round (Mt. Lebanon) 80–41 W State quarterfinal (Moon) 73–59 W State semifinal (Harrisburg) 85–62 W State final (Chester) 78–71

Term	League	Division	Finish	Record	Postseason
2007–8	City Lg.		1st of 9	25–3 (16–0)	W City quarterfinal (Langley) 100–53 W City semifinal (Carrick) 67–51 W City final (Brashear) 72–63 L State first round (McKeesport) 59–49
2008–9	City Lg.		4th of 9	12–13 (10–6)	W City quarterfinal (Brashear) 65–61 L City semifinal (Allderdice) 64–53 L State first round (North Hills) 66–50
2009–10	City Lg.		T7th of 9	6–16 (4–12)	L City quarterfinal (Oliver) 54–38
2010–11	City Lg.		3rd of 9	15–10 (11–5)	W City quarterfinal (Oliver) 55–39 L City semifinal (Allderdice) 88–71 L State first round (Mt. Lebanon) 78–61

Coaches

Name	Seasons	Record	Titles
Merle C. Knapp	1 (1917)	21–3 (10–0)	1 City (1917) 1 WPIAL (1917)
R. H. McLean	1 (1918)	6–9 (6–6)	
Fred E. Foertsch	6 (1919–24)	55–40 (29–24)	
R. R. Zahniser	1 (1925)	11–4 (10–4)	
Walter S. Gross	33 (1926–58)	287–260 (207–201)	4 City (1926–27, '31–'32)
Fred Cupples	1 (1959)	11–8 (8–6)	
Willard Fisher	9 (1960–68)	115–61 (83–37)	3 City (1965–67) 1 State (1966)
Spencer Watkins	8 (1969–76)	139–48 (72–12)	3 City (1970–71, '74) 2 State (1971, '75)
Fred Yee	6 (1977–82)	98–50 (42–18)	2 City (1978–79) 1 State (1978)
Ed Fullum	1 (1983)	12–14 (8–2)	
Fred Skrocki	24 (1984–2007)	446–202 (240–81)	6 City (1991, '96–'97, 2005–7) 1 State (2007)
Kevin Reid	4 (2008–11)	58–42 (41–23)	1 City (2008)

Home courts

Venue	Location	Seasons
Schenley boys' gym	4101 Bigelow Blvd., Oakland	53 (1917–69)
East Liberty YMCA	S. Whitfield & Mignonette Sts., East Liberty	1 (1917)
Trees Gym*	Allequippa & Brackenridge Sts., Terrace Village	1 (1917)
Pitt Stadium*	Terrace & De Soto Sts., Oakland	1 (1928)
Pitt Field House	Allequippa & Darragh Sts., Oakland	5 (1965–69)
West Penn Recreation Center	30th & Paulowna Sts., Polish Hill	16 (1970–76, '78–'86)
Civic Arena*	Centre Ave. & Washington Pl., Downtown	1 (1970)
Herron Hill School	3117 Centre Ave., Upper Hill District	1 (1977)
Schenley gym II	4101 Bigelow Blvd., Oakland	22 (1987–2008)
Reizenstein School*	Penn Ave. & E. Liberty Blvd., Shadyside	3 (2009–11)

Basketball, girls

Seasons: 53 (1917–31, '74–2011)
City titles: 6 (1998–2000, '02, '04–'05)
Notable alumni: Mary Myers (Kansas); Robbin (Smith) Capers '79 (Kansas); Cynthia "Cindy" Dallas '98 (Illinois); Traci Bankston '00 (Robert Morris); Carmen Bruce '02 (Georgetown/Duquesne); Dominique Duck '05 (Western Kentucky); Markel Walker '09 (UCLA; US, Australia pro teams)

Seasons

Term	League	Division	Finish	Record	Postseason
1916–17	City Lg.		2nd of 6	9–4 (7–3)	
1917–18	City Lg.		3rd of 7	10–6 (8–4)	
1918–19	City Lg.		3rd of 7	10–5 (6–3)	
1919–20	City Lg.		3rd of 7	10–5 (7–5)	
1920–21	City Lg.		T4th of 7	5–5 (3–3)	
1921–22	City Lg.		N/A	4–7 (3–3)	
1922–23	City Lg.		N/A	4–6 (3–3)	
1923–24	City Lg.		2nd of 8	7–2 (6–1)	
1924–25	City Lg.		T2nd of 8	8–2–1 (5–2)	
1925–26	City Lg.	Sec. I	3rd of 3	2–6 (0–4)	
1926–27	City Lg.	Sec. I	3rd of 4	3–7 (2–4)	
1927–28	City Lg.	Sec. I	T3rd of 4	3–5 (1–5)	
1928–29				0–5	
1929–30				2–0	
1930–31				1–0	
1931–73	No girls' varsity basketball team				
1973–75	No information available for these seasons				
1975–76	City Lg.	Sec. I	5th of 6	2–8 (2–8)	
1976–80	No information available for these seasons				
1980–81	City Lg.	Sec. I	6th of 6	2–18 (1–9)	
1981–82	City Lg.	Sec. I	5th of 6	2–18 (2–8)	
1982–83	City Lg.	Sec. I	T5th of 6	2–20 (2–8)	
1983–84	City Lg.	Sec. I	6th of 6	7–14 (1–9)	

Term	League	Division	Finish	Record	Postseason
1984–85	City Lg.	Sec. I	5th of 6	4–15 (2–8)	
1985–86	City Lg.	Sec. I	T4th of 6	5–12 (2–8)	
1986–87	City Lg.	Sec. I	5th of 5	7–15 (1–7)	
1987–88	City Lg.	Sec. I	5th of 5	7–14 (0–8)	
1988–89	City Lg.	Sec. I	5th of 5	5–18 (0–8)	L City 3A first round (Langley) 57–55
1989–90	City Lg.	Sec. II	T3rd of 5	4–19 (3–5)	L City 3A semifinal (Perry) 54–40
1990–91	City Lg.	Sec. II	4th of 5	5–16 (3–5)	L City 3A semifinal (Westinghouse) 53–40
1991–92	City Lg.	Sec. II	3rd of 5	8–13 (5–3)	L City 4A semifinal (Carrick) 34–28
1992–93	City Lg.	Sec. II	3rd of 5	10–11 (4–4)	W City 4A first round (Peabody) 48–47 L City 4A semifinal (Allderdice) 54–48
1993–94	City Lg.	Sec. II	3rd of 5	8–13 (4–4)	L City 4A first round (Brashear) 49–38
1994–95	City Lg.		4th of 10	14–12 (11–7)	W City quarterfinal (Brashear) 37–29 L City semifinal (Westinghouse) 72–59
1995–96	City Lg.		4th of 10	16–11 (12–6)	W City quarterfinal (Carrick) 59–47 L City semifinal (Westinghouse) 61–49 L State first round (Oakland Catholic) 55–37
1996–97	City Lg.	Sec. I	1st of 5	21–6 (13–0)	W City quarterfinal (Peabody) 63–26 L City semifinal (Perry) 52–48 L State first round (Woodland Hills) 73–47
1997–98	City Lg.	Sec. I	1st of 5	25–3 (13–0)	W City quarterfinal (Langley) 71–21 W City semifinal (Allderdice) 49–33 W City final (Westinghouse) 69–53 L State first round (Upper St. Clair) 57–37
1998–99	City Lg.	Sec. I	2nd of 5	18–10 (10–3)	W City quarterfinal (Carrick) 56–26 W City semifinal (Peabody) 56–20 W City final (Westinghouse) 54–51 L State first round (Hempfield) 58–56
1999–2000	City Lg.	Sec. I	1st of 5	23–5 (13–0)	W City quarterfinal (Oliver) 69–34 W City semifinal (Allderdice) 64–36 W City final (Westinghouse) 64–54 L State first round (Seneca Valley) 54–52
2000–2001	City Lg.	Sec. I	1st of 5	19–9 (13–0)	W City quarterfinal (Oliver) 57–9 W City semifinal (Allderdice) 66–36 L City final (Westinghouse) 56–48 (OT) L State first round (Mt. Lebanon) 43–39

Term	League	Division	Finish	Record	Postseason
2001–2	City Lg.	Sec. I	1st of 5	24–6 (13–0)	W City quarterfinal (South) 65–14 W City semifinal (Allderdice) 62–29 W City final (Westinghouse) 66–59 W State first round (Plum) 49–31 W State second round (Hempfield) 65–59 (OT) L State quarterfinal (Oakland Catholic) 56–42
2002–3	City Lg.	Sec. I	1st of 5	23–6 (12–0)	W City quarterfinal (Langley) 61–21 W City semifinal (Allderdice) 64–20 L City final (Westinghouse) 34–32 (OT) W State first round (McKeesport) 50–48 L State second round (Oakland Catholic) 64–40
2003–4	City Lg.	Sec. I	1st of 5	24–4 (13–0)	W City quarterfinal (Langley) 70–10 W City semifinal (Carrick) 61–18 W City final (Westinghouse) 46–32 L State first round (Trinity) 63–52
2004–5	City Lg.	Sec. I	1st of 5	22–4 (12–0)	W City quarterfinal (Oliver) 69–16 W City semifinal (Allderdice) 52–33 W City final (Westinghouse) 43–27 L State first round (Gateway) 43–41
2005–6	City Lg.		4th of 9	12–14 (10–6)	W City quarterfinal (Langley) 48–22 L City semifinal (Westinghouse) 43–35
2006–7	City Lg.		3rd of 9	15–12 (11–5)	W City quarterfinal (Carrick) 49–32 L City semifinal (Allderdice) 37–12 L State play-in round (Norwin) 51–39
2007–8	City Lg.		T1st of 9	24–5 (15–1)	W City quarterfinal (Peabody) 71–27 W City semifinal (Perry) 79–27 L City final (Westinghouse) 52–51 W State first round (Oakland Catholic) 42–36 W State second round (Peters Township) 49–45 L State quarterfinal (Mt. Lebanon) 74–42
2008–9	City Lg.		T1st of 9	21–5 (15–1)	W City quarterfinal (Brashear) 84–39 W City semifinal (Perry) 47–42 L City final (Westinghouse) 56–50 L State first round (Fox Chapel) 64–52
2009–10	City Lg.		4th of 9	12–13 (10–6)	W City quarterfinal (Brashear) 46–30 L City semifinal (Perry) 74–55 L State play-in round (Bethel Park) 57–31
2010–11	City Lg.		5th of 9	8–15 (7–9)	W City quarterfinal (Perry) 36–29 L City semifinal (Allderdice) 52–23

Coaches

Name	Seasons	Record	Titles
Jeannette Lawrence	1 (1917)	9–4 (7–3)	
Marion Roberts	4 (1918–21)	35–21 (24–15)	
Roberta Saunders	1 (1922)	4–7 (3–3)	
Margaret Mitchell	2 (1923-24)	11–8 (9–4)	
Sigrid S. Topp	3 (1925–27)	13–15–1 (7–10)	
Elizabeth Webb	1 (1928)	3–5 (1–5)	
Lucille McClellan	1 (1929)	0–5	
Helen McNaugher	1 (1930)	2–0	
Deborah Wells	1 (1976)	2–8 (2–8)	
Deborah Horwitz	1 (1981)	2–18 (1–9)	
Florence May	2 (1982–83)	4–38 (4–16)	
Kathy Olesak	19 (1984–2002)	230–222 (123–85)	4 City (1998–2000, '02)
Debbie Lewis	9 (2003–11)	161–78 (105–28)	2 City (2004–5)

Home courts

Venue	Location	Seasons
Schenley girls' gym	4101 Bigelow Blvd., Oakland	15 (1917–31)
West Penn Recreation Center	30th & Paulowna Sts., Polish Hill	6 (1981–86)
Schenley gym II	4101 Bigelow Blvd., Oakland	22 (1987–2008)
Reizenstein School*	Penn Ave. & E. Liberty Blvd., Shadyside	3 (2009–11)

Cross country, boys

Seasons: 71 (1929–44, '46, '48–'49, '59–2010)
City titles: 8 (1929–31, '37, '39, '61, '65, '94)

Notable alumni: John Mackrell Jr. '32 (Pitt); Arnold Sowell '53 (Pitt)

Cross country, girls

Seasons: 33 (1976–79, '82–2010)

City titles: 3 (1991–92, '98)

Football

Seasons: 95 (1916–2010)
City titles: 8 (1924–26, '29, '43, '50, '99, 2009)
Notable alumni: Bernard "Buck" Sandomire '17 (Pitt); Tommy Elias '18 (Pitt); Harry "Red" Seidelson '19 (Pitt; 2 NFL teams); Ulhard "Hank" Hangartner '21 (Pitt); Tom Murdoch '21 (Pitt); Ben Jones '22 (Pitt); John McSorley Jr. (Notre Dame); Bucky Wagner '27 (Pitt); John W. Moore '28 (US pro teams); Abe Marcovsky '29 (Michigan); Art Sekay '29 (Pitt); William "Buck" McKee '30 (Penn State); Tommy Slusser '30 (Penn State); Pete Rembert '31 (US pro teams); Johnny Economos '33 (Penn State); Johnny Patrick '34 (Penn State); Andrew Brunski '36 (Temple; NFL Philadelphia-Pittsburgh); Herb Trawick '39 (CFL Montreal); Gabe Patterson '39 (CFL Saskatchewan); James Antonelli '39 (Pitt); Lawrence Klotz '39 (Pitt); Jack Banbury '40 (Penn State); Joe Kielb '41 (Pitt); Stan Lavine '46 (Maryland); Bill Robinson '48 (2 NFL teams); Henry Ford '51 (Pitt; 2 NFL teams); Joe Moore '51 (Tennessee/Penn State); James Dalrymple '51 (Maryland);

Bernie Eisen '51 (Pitt); John Cenci '52 (Pitt; NFL Pittsburgh); Irvin "Chappie" Hill '52 (Penn State); James O'Mahoney '59 (Miami [FL]; AFL New York); Francis Peay '62 (Missouri; 3 NFL teams); Larry Brown '65 (Kansas State; NFL Washington); Lamont Patterson '79 (Cincinnati); Orvell Johns '81 (Ohio); Miles Brandon '82 (Ohio); Anthony Williams '82 (Ohio); George Germany '94 (Akron); Ahmad Peterson '94 (Akron); Darnell Dinkins '95 (Pitt; 4 NFL teams); Troy Davidson '95 (Maryland); David Dinkins '97 (US, Europe pro teams); Patrick Body '00 (Toledo; NFL Cincinnati); Keith Hill '00 (Pitt); Greg Blair '08 (Cincinnati); Manny Bell '09 (Toledo)

Seasons

Term	League	Division	Finish	Record	Postseason
1916–17	WPIAL			1–4–1	
1917–18	WPIAL	City Lg.	4th of 6	2–3–2 (1–2–2)	
1918–19				1–3–0	
1919–20	WPIAL	City Lg.	3rd of 7	4–3–2 (3–1–1)	
1920–21	WPIAL	City Lg.	T3rd of 7	3–3–1 (3–3–0)	
1921–22	WPIAL	City Lg.	3rd of 7	5–2–1 (4–2–0)	
1922–23	WPIAL	City Lg.	2nd of 7	5–1–2 (4–1–1)	
1923–24	WPIAL	City Lg.	T2nd of 8	5–4–0 (5–2–0)	
1924–25	WPIAL	City Lg.	1st of 8	7–1–0 (7–0–0)	
1925–26	City Lg.		1st of 9	8–0–1 (8–0–0)	
1926–27	City Lg.	Sec. I	1st of 4	8–0–0 (3–0–0)	W City final (South Hills) 19–0
1927–28	City Lg.	Sec. I	2nd of 5	5–2–0 (3–1–0)	
1928–29	City Lg.	Sec. I	3rd of 5	3–4–1 (2–2–0)	
1929–30	City Lg.	Sec. I	1st of 5	7–1–1 (3–0–1)	W City final (South Hills) 15–0
1930–31	City Lg.	Sec. I	T3rd of 6	5–2–1 (2–2–1)	
1931–32	City Lg.	Sec. I	1st of 6	5–3–1 (4–0–1)	L City final (South Hills) 7–0
1932–33	City Lg.	Sec. I	5th of 6	2–4–2 (1–3–1)	
1933–34	City Lg.	Sec. I	T4th of 6	1–5–2 (1–2–2)	
1934–35	City Lg.	Sec. I	T4th of 6	1–7–0 (1–4–0)	
1935–36	City Lg.	Sec. I	5th of 6	2–5–1 (1–3–1)	
1936–37	City Lg.	Sec. I	T4th of 6	3–4–1 (1–3–1)	

Term	League	Division	Finish	Record	Postseason
1937–38	City Lg.	Sec. I	3rd of 6	4–3–0 (3–2–0)	
1938–39	City Lg.		2nd of 12	6–2–0 (5–1–0)	
1939–40	City Lg.		5th of 12	4–4–0 (4–2–0)	
1940–41	City Lg.	Sec. I	T3rd of 6	2–4–1 (2–2–1)	
1941–42	City Lg.	Sec. I	T2nd of 6	3–4–1 (3–1–1)	
1942–43	City Lg.	Sec. I	2nd of 6	4–4–0 (4–1–0)	
1943–44	City Lg.	Sec. I	1st of 6	6–2–1 (5–0–0)	W City final (Allegheny) 21–7
1944–45	City Lg.	Sec. I	5th of 6	3–5–1 (1–3–1)	
1945–46	City Lg.	Sec. I	T2nd of 6	3–5–0 (3–2–0)	
1946–47	City Lg.	Sec. I	3rd of 6	3–5–0 (3–2–0)	
1947–48	City Lg.	Sec. I	3rd of 6	3–4–0 (3–2–0)	
1948–49	City Lg.	Sec. I	T4th of 6	3–4–0 (2–3–0)	
1949–50	City Lg.	Sec. I	4th of 6	2–6–0 (2–3–0)	
1950–51	City Lg.	Sec. I	1st of 6	9–0–0 (5–0–0)	W City final (Carrick) 6–0
1951–52	City Lg.	Sec. I	T3rd of 6	2–6–0 (2–3–0)	
1952–53	City Lg.	Sec. I	5th of 6	1–6–1 (1–4–0)	
1953–54	City Lg.	Sec. I	6th of 6	0–8–0 (0–5–0)	
1954–55	City Lg.	Sec. I	4th of 6	2–6–0 (2–3–0)	
1955–56	City Lg.	Sec. I	3rd of 6	3–5–0 (3–2–0)	
1956–57	City Lg.	Sec. I	T3rd of 6	2–6–0 (2–3–0)	
1957–58	City Lg.	Sec. I	5th of 6	1–7–0 (1–4–0)	
1958–59	City Lg.	Sec. I	6th of 6	0–7–1 (0–4–1)	
1959–60	City Lg.	Sec. I	6th of 6	0–8–0 (0–5–0)	
1960–61	City Lg.	Sec. I	T3rd of 6	2–5–1 (2–2–1)	

Term	League	Division	Finish	Record	Postseason
1961–62	City Lg.	Sec. I	2nd of 6	4–4–0 (4–1–0)	
1962–63	City Lg.	Sec. I	6th of 6	0–8–0 (0–5–0)	
1963–64	City Lg.	Sec. I	6th of 6	0–8–0 (0–5–0)	
1964–65	City Lg.	Sec. I	T5th of 6	0–7–1 (0–4–1)	
1965–66	City Lg.	Sec. I	T2nd of 6	3–4–0 (3–2–0)	
1966–67	City Lg.	Sec. I	5th of 6	1–5–0 (1–4–0)	
1967–68	City Lg.		T4th of 13	6–2–0 (6–2–0)	
1968–69	City Lg.		T7th of 13	4–4–0 (4–4–0)	
1969–70	City Lg.		T11th of 13	1–7–0 (1–7–0)	
1970–71	City Lg.		6th of 13	4–3–1 (4–3–1)	
1971–72	City Lg.		T6th of 13	3–4–1 (3–4–1)	
1972–73	City Lg.		T9th of 13	2–6–0 (2–6–0)	
1973–74	City Lg.		T6th of 13	4–3–1 (4–3–1)	
1974–75	City Lg.		T5th of 13	3–3–2 (3–3–2)	
1975–76	City Lg.		T11th of 13	1–7–0 (1–7–0)	
1976–77	City Lg.		6th of 12	3–4–1 (3–4–1)	
1977–78	City Lg.		8th of 12	3–4–1 (3–4–1)	
1978–79	City Lg.		T3rd of 12	6–2–0 (6–2–0)	
1979–80	City Lg.		3rd of 12	5–2–1 (5–2–1)	
1980–81	City Lg.		8th of 12	2–6–1 (2–5–1)	
1981–82	City Lg.		4th of 12	5–4–0 (5–3–0)	
1982–83	City Lg.		T5th of 11	3–5–0 (3–4–0)	
1983–84	City Lg.		T10th of 11	1–7–0 (1–6–0)	
1984–85	City Lg.		T10th of 11	0–9–0 (0–7–0)	
1985–86	City Lg.		5th of 10	3–5–0 (3–3–0)	

Term	League	Division	Finish	Record	Postseason
1986–87	City Lg.		8th of 10	2–7–1 (2–6–1)	
1987–88	City Lg.		T7th of 10	2–7–0 (2–7–0)	
1988–89	City Lg.		T8th of 10	1–6–2 (1–6–2)	
1989–90	City Lg.		10th of 10	0–9–0 (0–9–0)	
1990–91	City Lg.		5th of 10	5–5–0 (5–4–0)	
1991–92	City Lg.		T4th of 10	5–4–2 (5–2–2)	L City semifinal (Westinghouse) 13–0
1992–93	City Lg.		T4th of 10	4–5–1 (4–4–1)	L City semifinal (Westinghouse) 56–0
1993–94	City Lg.		T1st of 10	8–2–0 (8–1–0)	L City semifinal (Perry) 20–14 (OT)
1994–95	City Lg.		2nd of 10	9–3–0 (8–1–0)	W City semifinal (Perry) 21–14 L City final (Peabody) 8–7 L State first round (Erie Central) 25–0
1995–96	City Lg.		T2nd of 10	7–4 (7–2)	L City semifinal (Westinghouse) 14–0 L State first round (Erie McDowell) 42–6
1996–97	City Lg.		T4th of 10	5–6 (5–4)	L City semifinal (Peabody) 14–12 L State first round (Erie McDowell) 25–6
1997–98	City Lg.		2nd of 10	9–3 (8–1)	W City semifinal (Westinghouse) 33–28 L City final (Perry) 34–6 L State first round (Erie McDowell) 45–12
1998–99	City Lg.		1st of 10	10–2 (9–0)	W City semifinal (Brashear) 34–14 L City final (Perry) 26–6 L State first round (Erie Cathedral Prep) 36–0
1999–2000	City Lg.		1st of 10	11–1 (9–0)	W City semifinal (Brashear) 24–21 W City final (Oliver) 41–27 L State first round (Erie Cathedral Prep) 70–0
2000–2001	City Lg.		T3rd of 10	6–3 (6–3)	
2001–2	City Lg.		8th of 10	3–6 (3–6)	
2002–3	City Lg.		4th of 10	6–4 (6–3)	L City semifinal (Perry) 54–0
2003–4	City Lg.		4th of 10	6–4 (6–3)	L City semifinal (Brashear) 40–0
2004–5	City Lg.		T6th of 9	2–7 (2–6)	
2005–6	City Lg.		T3rd of 9	5–4 (5–3)	

Term	League	Division	Finish	Record	Postseason
2006–7	City Lg.		T4th of 9	5–6 (5–3)	L City semifinal (Oliver) 23–0
2007–8	City Lg.		T2nd of 9	7–4 (6–2)	L City semifinal (Allderdice) 16–15
2008–9	City Lg.		3rd of 9	6–4 (6–2)	L City semifinal (Perry) 14–0
2009–10	City Lg.		T1st of 9	10–2 (7–1)	W City semifinal (Brashear) 14–2 W City final (Oliver) 34–32 (2OT) W State play-in round (Punxsutawney) 54–0 L State first round (Erie Cathedral Prep) 44–12
2010–11	City Lg.		T3rd of 9	5–5 (5–3)	L City semifinal (Perry) 29–8

Coaches

Name	Seasons	Record	Titles
Merle C. Knapp	1 (1916)	1–4–1	
R. H. McLean	1 (1917)	2–3–2 (1–2–2)	
George T. Newman	1 (1918)	1–3–0	
Fred E. Foertsch	7 (1919–25)	37–14–7 (34–9–2)	2 City (1924–25)
Walter S. Gross	32 (1926–57)	108–133–15 (75–66–11)	4 City (1926, '29, '43, '50)
Fred Cupples	1 (1958)	0–7–1 (0–4–1)	
Willard Fisher	12 (1959–70)	25–65–3 (25–44–3)	
Tom Moul	12 (1971–82)	40–50–8 (40–47–8)	
Jim Trent	25 (1983–2007)	122–123–6 (116–92–6)	1 City (1999)
Jason Bell	3 (2008–10)	21–11 (18–6)	1 City (2009)

Home fields

Venue	Location	Seasons
Exposition Park III*	Tony Dorsett Dr. & W. Gen. Robinson St., North Shore	2 (1916–17)
Carnegie Tech Field*	Margaret Morrison & Tech Sts., Squirrel Hill	3 (1918–20)
Trees Field	Vera St. & Robinson St. Ext., Terrace Village	3 (1921–23)
Duquesne Field*	Shingiss & Locust Sts., Uptown	2 (1922–23)
Schenley Field	Shawnee & Camp Sts., Upper Hill District	34 (1924–52, '67–'71)
Pitt Stadium*	Terrace & De Soto Sts., Oakland	3 (1950–52)
Cupples Stadium	S. 9th & E. Carson Sts., South Side Flats	33 (1953–54, '72, '81–2010)
Monument Hill Field*	Ridge Ave. & Brighton Rd., Allegheny West	1 (1954)
Arsenal Field	Butler & 40th Sts., Lawrenceville	21 (1955–66, '72–'80)

Golf

Seasons: 33 (1977–2008, '10)
City titles: 1 (1994)

Gymnastics

Seasons: 25 (1918–21, '24–'43)
City titles: 2 (1933, '43)
Note: Schenley had two 1924 seasons, as gymnastics moved from spring to fall in the 1924-25 term.

Ice hockey

Seasons: 7 (1917–21, '24–'25)
City titles: 3 (1920–21, '25)
Notable alumni: Shirley Austin '20 (Dartmouth); Frank McSorley '21 (Notre Dame); John McSorley Jr. (Notre Dame)

Life saving

Seasons: 11 (1924–33, '55)
Regional titles: 5 (1924, '26–'27, '29, '32)
National titles: 1 (1929)

Rugby, boys

Seasons: 2 (2001–2)

Rugby, girls

Seasons: 5 (2000–2004)

Soccer, boys

Seasons: 23 (1988–2010)
City titles: 3 (2002, '05, '09)

Soccer, girls

Seasons: 22 (1989–2010)
City titles: 8 (2000–2003, '07–'10)
Notable alumni: Mandela Schumacher-Hodge '03 (North Carolina State); Marisha Schumacher-Hodge '05 (Boston University; US, Europe pro teams)

Swimming, boys

Seasons: 95 (1917–2011)
City titles: 11 (1917–18, '20, '22, '25–'26, '29, '32, '50, '57, 2010)
Regional titles: 6 (1917–18, '20–'21, '25–'26)
Notable alumni: Alan Kistler '19 (Pitt); Harry Glancy (Olympics); Bill McQuillan '33 (Pitt); Bob Prince '34 (Pitt/Oklahoma State); Ronald Gainsford '48 (Pitt); Harry Piwowarski '50 (Pitt); Paul Ostfield '51 (Pitt); Bob Stratiff '51 (Florida State); Sheldon "Skip" Monsein '52 (Pitt); Harry Castelucci '53 (Pitt); Robert Levine '60 (Pitt); Ron Levine '60 (Pitt)

Swimming, girls

Seasons: 59 (1917–31, '33–'34, '36–'37, '72–'77, '79–2011)
City titles: 10 (1917–25)
Notable alumni: Frances Taylor '22 (Olympics); Jacqueline Zivic '45 (Penn State); Lauren McElroy '03 (Pitt)
Note: Schenley had two 1923 seasons, as girls' swimming moved from spring to fall in the 1923-24 term, and no 1978 season, as it moved from fall to winter in the 1978–79 term.

Tennis, boys

Seasons: 56 (1917, '20–'22, '25–'42, '76–2011)
Notable alumni: Robert Madden '33 (Pitt; Grand Slam tournaments)
Note: Boys' tennis was, at various times, contested in fall (1917, '20); both fall and spring, counted as a single season (1921–22, '25–'36); and spring (1937–'42, '76–2011).

Tennis, girls

Seasons: 48 (1920–'21, '25, '28, '30, '32–'33, '35–'36, '73–2010)
City titles: 2 (1994–95)

Note: Schenley had two 1975 seasons, as girls' tennis moved from spring to fall in the 1975–76 term.

Track, boys

Seasons: 94 (1917–44, '46–2011)
City titles: 16 (1919–20, '22–'25, '95, '98, 2001, '04–'07, '09–'11)
City Relays titles: 11 (1998, 2001–7, '09-'11)
WPIAL titles: 1 (1920)
Notable alumni: Gerald Allen '17 (Pitt); Bill James '21 (Pitt); Tom Murdoch '21 (Pitt); Ben Jones '22 (Pitt); Marshall Lewis '28 (Pitt); James S. Robinson Jr. '29 (Pitt); Arnold Sowell '53 (Pitt; Olympics); Paul Thrash '54 (Pitt); Rodney Brown '01 (Kent State)

Track, girls

Seasons: 55 (1917–32, '73–2011)
City titles: 18 (1918, '25–'26, '92–'96, 2001–6, '08–'11)

City Relays titles: 14 (1993–96, 2001–7, '09–'11)
Notable alumni: Kim Martin '94 (Minnesota); Samara Parr '96 (Pitt); Kaetlyn Brown '06 (Pitt); Ashley Berfield '08 (North Carolina State)

Volleyball, boys

Seasons: 61 (1924–32, '60–2011)
City titles: 8 (1930, '32, 2006–11)
Regional titles: 1 (1930)

Volleyball, girls

Seasons: 47 (1924–31, '58, '73, '75–2010)
City titles: 4 (1975, 2008–10)
Note: Schenley had two 1984 seasons, as girls' volleyball moved from spring to fall in the 1984–85 term.

Wrestling

Seasons: 23 (1989–2011)

Appendix D
Theater

From 1917 through 1964, Schenley graduated two classes per year—in February (F) and June (J)—which staged separate class plays through 1950.

Class Plays

Class	Play	Leads
1917 (F)	*A Thousand Years Ago*	Dora Breskin, Carl Reisman
1917 (J)	Canceled because of World War I	
1918 (F)	*Their Green Stockings*	Mary Grauer, Ira Deitrick
1918 (J)	*The Passing of the Third Floor Back*	Margaret Henius, Emmanuel Rosenthal
1919 (F)	Canceled because of influenza outbreak	
1919 (J)	*The Quest for Happiness*	Louise Miller, Robert Litchfield
1920 (F)	*Of Mice and Men*	Jean Newell, Robert Braun
1920 (J)	*Are You a Mason?*	Maurice Claster, Helen Brooks
1921 (F)	*The Maker of Dreams* *The Play-Goers* *The Arch Fear*	Richard Fleck, Rosalind Davidson Richard Fleck, Hortense Florsheim Erna Knorr, Charles Stewart
1921 (J)	*The Lottery Man*	Ulhard "Hank" Hangartner, Freda Wechsler
1922 (F)	*A Midsummer Night's Dream*	Joseph Heatley, Grace Israel
1922 (J)	*Quality Street*	Doris Rigby, Sylvia Siljander
1923 (F)	*Twelfth Night*	Edward Gordon, Anna Grabert
1923 (J)	*The Importance of Being Earnest*	Allan Nern, Maurice Arnd
1924 (F)	*She Stoops to Conquer*	Thelma Tanner, Harry Kramer
1924 (J)	*Mr. Pim Passes By*	Elizabeth Carnes, Harvey Bott
1925 (F)	*The Doctor in Spite of Himself*	Geraldine Guarino, Carl Williams
1925 (J)	*You Never Can Tell*	Leila Earhart, Morley Jubelirer
1926 (F)	*The Romancer* *Beauty and the Jacobin*	Mildred Baxendall, Walter Sickles Kenneth Dyer, Ruth Cadwallader
1926 (J)	*The Goose Hangs High*	Patterson Covert, Marie Descalzi
1927 (F)	*Grumpy*	D. C. Edwards
1927 (J)	*So This Is London*	Barbara Egleston, Robert Levin
1928 (F)	*The Admirable Crichton*	Thomas McFarland, Harry Olson
1928 (J)	*Bab*	Anna Hoop
1929 (F)	*Merton of the Movies*	William Ruckel, Bernice Green
1929 (J)	*The Farmer's Wife*	Norman Wolken, Elaine Moskowitz
1930 (F)	*The Show Off*	Karl Weber
1930 (J)	*The Rivals*	Elaine Blauvelt, William Mosenson
1931 (F)	*The Lion and the Mouse*	Hyman Paransky, Rhea Colker
1931 (J)	*Miss Lulu Bett*	Patti Littell
1932 (F)	*Trelawny of the "Wells"*	Florence Vernon, Arthur Owens

Class	Play	Leads
1932 (J)	The Nut Farm	Jack Challinor, Water Donaldson, William Gordon, Alice Kruckewitt
1933 (F)	The New Poor	Ruth Cohen, June Robinson
1933 (J)	Once There Was a Princess	Ruth Earhart, Edward Geiger
1934 (F)	Peg O' My Heart	Virginia Osterman, William Ewing
1934 (J)	Rollo's Wild Oat	Alfred Voyer
1935 (F)	The Whole Town Is Talking	Edward Brandau, Anne Tomko
1935 (J)	Growing Pains	Betty Yoho, David Blaustein
1936 (F)	Skidding	Helen Manson, Stanley Pearle
1936 (J)	The Rivals	Rosa Longenecker, Parry Thomas
1937 (F)	Shirt Sleeves	Beatrice Eisenstat, Abe Lederman
1937 (J)	The Bridal Chorus	Blanche Covaleski, Lillian Davis
1938 (F)	The Adorable Spendthrift	Jeannette Caplan, Kenneth Robinson
1938 (J)	Charm School	Herman Routh
1939 (F)	Captain Applejack	George Wukitch, Ellen McCaul
1939 (J)	Growing Pains	Arnold Stern, Edythe Morris
1940 (F)	Headed for Eden	Grace Evans, Louis Lautman
1940 (J)	Young April	Edward Foster, Herb Nicholas
1941 (F)	American Passport	Warren Spryer, Irene Waichler
1941 (J)	June Mad	Florence Becker, Sabina Rutkowski, Paul Begler
1942 (F)	Sky Road	Marshall Pitler, Jean Lederman
1942 (J)	Mr. and Mrs. North	Milton Hammerman, Gertrude Beamon
1943 (F)	Ever Since Eve	Rita Spardy
1943 (J)	Plane Crazy	Fred Obley, Eleanor Zusinas
1944 (F)	Kitty Foyle	Peggy Bailey, Sidney Baker
1944 (J)	Stage Door	Peggy Bailey, Sidney Baker
1945 (F)	Nine Girls	Jacqueline Zivic, Stella Arvanitas
1945 (J)	Double Exposure	Edwin Kremer, Robert Ricci
1946 (F)	The Patsy	Irma Kalet, Gerald Rubin
1946 (J)	Seven Sisters	Helena Crawford, Frank Sweer
1947 (F)	Brother Goose	Jack Amplas
1947 (J)	Kind Lady	Benjamin Tatar, Pegee Kremer
1948 (F)	The Fighting Littles	Katherine Rose, Benjamin Tatar
1948 (J)	Meet Arizona	Norma Labovitz, Jean Mestelman, James Tsikerdamos, Richard LaFean
1949 (F)	Dear Ruth	LaVerne Zahn
1949 (J)	Stage Door	Shirli Hathaway, Charles Sciulli
1950 (F)	Kitty Foyle	Marilyn Masamed, Jordan Haller
1950 (J)	The Rivals	Jim Fisher, Trudy Fuhs
1951	Headed for Eden	Orvetta Martorelli, Tom Montgomery
1952–61	Class plays were replaced with operettas	
1962	The Jury Room	N/A
1963–71	Class plays were discontinued	
1972	Five on the Black Hand Side	Michael Hayes, Cecilia Rivers

Class	Play	Leads
1973	*To Be Young, Gifted and Black*	Arletta Lawrence, Kim Jackson, Carolyn Beasley, Phylis Brown
1974	*Tambourines to Glory*	Dennis Jones, Sheryl Strothers
1975	*Purlie*	Lynn Burke, Gladys Jelks
1976	*Guys and Dolls*	Marty Threatt, William Booker, Sandy Herron, Denise Hilton
1977	*The Pajama Game*	Yvonne Walden, Neal Harp, Reggie Long
1978	*Bye, Bye, Birdie*	Glenn Brown, Donna Lee, William Campbell, Carolyn Brown
1979	*Pippin*	Harlan Williams, Glenn Brown
1980	*The Wiz*	Terri Rucker, Sara Dalton, Harold Simmons, Harlan Williams
1981	*Bubbling Brown Sugar*	Daryl Matthews, Robin Brock, Roland Howze, Kevin Byrd
1982	*West Side Story*	Kim Cobbs, Shuron Flowers
1983	*Ain't Misbehavin'*	Tony Dixon, Selene West, Adrian Toliver
1984	*Barnum*	Tony Dixon
1985	*Grease*	Ron Pratt, Ronelle Thomas
1986	*Anything Goes*	Ronelle Thomas, Chris Barnhill
1987	*Leader of the Pack*	Alphonso Hyman, Karla White, Alison Babusci
1988	*The Wiz*	Karla White, Tiffany Ellis, Jason Brown, Brian McDaniel
1989	*A Chorus Line*	Sloan Wilson, Amy Shaughnessy, Nick Moore, Jason Brown
1990	*Pippin*	Ian Wilson, Nick Moore
1991	*All Night Strut*	Bruce Harris, Sarah Dinmore, Kelly Stuart, Nikki Johnson
1992	*Ain't Misbehavin'*	Bruce Harris,** Kelly Stuart, Jeff Webb, Ben Tinker
1993	*Guys and Dolls*	Brian Salter,* James Moore, Kaycee Mitchell, Devon Wyman
1994	*Once on This Island*	Sabrina Gutierrez,** Kris Storey, Cary Duschl
1995	*Bubbling Brown Sugar*	Jamel McKelvia, Kyle Abraham, Dwayne Moore, Shani Alexander
1996	*West Side Story*	Doug Anderson, Shani Alexander
1997	*Leader of the Pack*	Shani Alexander,* Andy Place,** Kadia Givner**
1998	*Anything Goes*	Andy Place, Kadia Givner
1999	*The Wiz*	Kadia Givner, Adolph Sims, Jonathan Blandino, Gordon Agie
2000	*Once Upon a Mattress*	Angela Machi,* Jeff Minshall, Cordelia Stearns
2001	*Once on This Island*	Mike Wilson, Angela Machi, Derek Steele,* Erika Taylor*
2002	*The Melody Lingers on—The Songs of Irving Berlin*	Mike Wilson,** Angela Machi,** Matt Gormley*
2003	*Lucky in the Rain*	Madeline Seltman, Mike Wilson, Jaimie Finseth**

Class	Play	Leads
2004	*Smokey Joe's Café*	Jaimie Finseth, Amber West, Kerry Allen, Shawn Biggs
2005	*Grease*	Nick Lehane, Jennifer Pogue-Geile
2006	*Joseph and the Amazing Technicolor Dreamcoat*	Sarah Jane Kirkland,* Racquel Khosah, Teressa LaGamba, Will Gasch
2007	*Leader of the Pack*	Sarah Jane Kirkland,* Teressa LaGamba,* Carter Redwood
2008	*All Shook Up*	Sarah Jane Kirkland,* Teressa LaGamba,** Will Gasch
2009	*Return to the Forbidden Planet*	Michael Ellwood,* Teressa LaGamba*, Loni Ben-Zvi*
2010	*You're a Good Man, Charlie Brown*	Tyller Little, Jaslyn Hodge,* Rain Rivera
2011	*Seussical*	Keyanna Taylor-Thomas,* Aman Milliones-Roman, Tyller Little, Fletcher Jones

*Gene Kelly Award nominee
**Gene Kelly Award winner

Directors

Name	Plays directed
Cecil H. Dean	2 (1917 [F], 1922 [F])
Wilmer H. Seawright	7 (1918 [F]–[J], 1919 [J]–1921 [J])
Theodore Viehman	13 (1922 [J]–1928 [J])
J. Russell Clements	20 (1929 [F]–1930 [F], 1943 [F]–1951)
Chester B. Story	25 (1930 [J]–1942 [J])
Robert Berkebile	1 (1962)
Roger Babusci	35 (1972–2006)
Kelly McKrell	5 (2007–2011)

Gene Kelly Awards

Award	Nominations	Awards
Best Musical	17 (1991–94, '96–'97, 2000–6, '08–'11)	9 (1993, '97, 2001–2, '04, '08–'11)
Best Lead Actor	3 (1992–93, 2009)	1 (1992)
Best Lead Actress	6 (1994, '97, 2000, '07–'09)	1 (1994)
Best Supporting Actor	4 (1997, 2001–2)	2 (1997, 2002)
Best Supporting Actress	10 (1997, 2001–3, '06–'11)	4 (1997, 2002–3, '08)
Best Scenic Design	8 (1992, '94–'95, '97, 2001–2, '10–'11)	1 (2002)
Best Costume Design	10 (1992–93, '96, '98, 2000–2002, '06, '10–'11)	2 (1992–93)
Best Lighting Design	9 (1993–94, '96–'97, 2001–2, '04, '10–'11)	2 (1993, 2002)
Best Orchestra	8 (1999–2000, '02–'04, '06, '09–'10)	3 (2002–3, '09)

Award	Nominations	Awards
Best Ensemble	12 (1997, 2000–2006, '08–'11)	6 (1997, 2001–2, '04, '09–'10)
Best Crew	3 (1995, '97, 2010)	0
Best Choreography	16 (1991–94, '96–'97, 2000–2006, '09–'11)	7 (1991, '94, '97, 2001–2, '06, '10)
Best Direction	9 (1994, '97, 2001–2, '04, '06, '09–'11)	2 (1997, 2002)
	115 nominations	40 awards

Note: In 2002, two Schenley students earned Best Supporting Actor nominations.

Appendix E
Pittsburgh Public High Schools Index

Buildings followed by an asterisk no longer exist, and their locations are approximate, reflecting present-day street configurations.

Pittsburgh Central (1855–1916)

Location

Quigg building* (506–508 Smithfield St.), Downtown (1855–1868)

Bank of Commerce Building* (Wood St. & 6th Ave.), Downtown (1868–1871)

1277–1433 Bedford Ave.*, Crawford-Roberts (1871–1916)

Format

City-wide exam/academic (1855–1868, 1896–1916)

City-wide comprehensive (1868–1896)

Notable alumni

See Appendix A

Allegheny (1883–1983)

Location

Allegheny Colored School* (810 Arch St.), Allegheny Center (1883–1889)

Allegheny High I* (810 Arch St.), Allegheny Center (1889–1938)

Allegheny High annex (810 Arch St.), Allegheny Center (1904–1983)

Allegheny High II (810 Arch St.), Allegheny Center (1938-1983)

Format

Allegheny City-wide exam/academic (1883–1889)

Allegheny City-wide comprehensive (1889–1911)

Neighborhood comprehensive (1911–1983)

Notable alumni

Dwight Morrow (politician); Mary Roberts Rinehart (writer); Pete Flaherty (politician); Pete Ladygo (pro football); Dorothy Mae Richardson (activist); Ralph H. Smith Sr. (judge); Steve Swetonic (pro baseball); Walt Framer (radio/television producer); Bob Timmons (college basketball coach)

Fifth Avenue (1896–1976)

Location

1800 Fifth Ave., Uptown

Format

City-wide commercial program (1896–1912)

City-wide normal program (1896–1912)

Neighborhood comprehensive (1912–1976)

Notable alumni

Sam Clancy (pro football), Sophie Masloff (politician), Cyril Wecht (forensic pathologist)

South (1898–2004)

Location

S. 10th & E. Carson Sts., South Side Flats

Format

Neighborhood comprehensive (1898–1985)
Vocational department (1940–1965)
Alternative department (1975–1976)
Law & Public Service magnet (1979–1985)
Journalism & Publishing magnet
(1979–1985)
Vocational-Technical magnet (1982–2004)

Notable alumni

Bill Cullen (game show host), Ed
(Milkovich) Melvin (pro basketball)

Peabody (1911–2011)

Location

Margaretta Street School (E. Liberty Blvd. &
N. Beatty St.), East Liberty

Format

Neighborhood exam/academic (1911–1912)
Neighborhood comprehensive (1912–2011)
Public Safety magnet (1989–2011)

Notable alumni

Romare Bearden (artist), Malcolm Cowley
(writer), Billy Eckstine (musician), Charles
Grodin (actor), Gene Kelly (entertainer),
David Logan (pro football), Edith S.
Sampson (judge), David Tepper (financier),
John Edgar Wideman (writer)

Ralston (1912–1930)

Location

Ralston School* (15th St. & Penn Ave.),
Strip District

Format

Short course business (1912–1916)
Boys' vocational (1916–1930)

Westinghouse (1912–present)

Location

Brushton School No. 3 (Brushton Ave. &
Baxter St.), Homewood (1912–1922)
N. Murtland & Monticello Sts., Homewood
(1922–present)

Format

Neighborhood comprehensive (1912–2011,
2012–present)
Business & Management magnet
(1979–1985)
Engineering & Architecture magnet
(1979–1985)

Single-gender Academies magnet
(2011–2012)

Notable alumni

Chuck Cooper (pro basketball), Erroll
Garner (musician), Tony Liscio (pro
football), Naomi Sims (model), Maurice
Stokes (pro basketball), Billy Strayhorn
(musician)

Business (1916–1933)

Location

Central High* (1277–1433 Bedford Ave.),
Crawford-Roberts

Format

Short course business

Schenley (1916–2011)

Location

4101 Bigelow Blvd., Oakland (1916–2008)
Reizenstein School* (Penn Ave. & E. Liberty
Blvd.), Shadyside (2008–2011)

Format

Neighborhood comprehensive (1916–2011)
Health Careers magnet (1979–1985)
International Studies/Baccalaureate magnet
(1983–2011)
High Technology magnet (1983–2011)

Notable alumni

See Appendix B

South Hills (1917–1986)

Location

125 Ruth St., Mount Washington

Format

Neighborhood comprehensive

Notable alumni

Ralph Cappy (judge), James G. Fulton
(politician), Bob Purkey (pro baseball),
Byrant Salter (pro football)

Langley (1923–2012)

Location

2940 Sheraden Blvd., Sheraden

Format

Neighborhood comprehensive (1923–2012)
Teaching Academy magnet (1989–2012)

Notable alumni

Richard B. Chess (politician), Bobby Howard (pro football), David Lee (pro baseball)

Perry (1923–present)

Location

Perry School (3875 Perrysville Ave.), Perry North

Format

Neighborhood comprehensive (1923–1982, 2012–present)

Traditional Academy magnet (1979–2014)

Math & Science magnet (1979–2014)

Junior ROTC magnet (2012–present)

Notable alumni

Glenn Beckert (pro baseball), Darelle Porter (college basketball coach)

Allegheny Vocational (1924–1965)

Location

Allegheny Vocational School (N. Lincoln & Galveston Aves.), Allegheny West

Format

Boys' vocational

Notable alumni

Josh Gibson (pro baseball); Bill Hill (labor leader)

Carrick (1924–present)

Location

125 Parkfield St., Carrick

Format

Carrick Borough-wide comprehensive (1924–1926)

Neighborhood comprehensive (1927–present)

Business, Finance & Information Technology magnet (2009–2010)

Notable alumni

Tom Atkins (actor), Mike Dawida (politician), Phyllis Hyman (actress/musician), Jack Johnson (pro football), John Wehner (pro baseball)

Oliver (1925–2012)

Location

2323 Brighton Rd., Marshall-Shadeland

Format

Neighborhood comprehensive (1925–2012)

Junior ROTC magnet (1978–2012)

Law & Public Service magnet (1983–2009)

Notable alumni

Bill Strickland (community leader), Ray Zellars (pro football); Bill Hill (labor leader)

Irwin Ave. Girls' Vocational (1926–1961)

Location

Irwin Ave. School* (Brighton Rd. & Wright Way), Perry South

Format

Girls' vocational

Allderdice (1927–present)

Location

Shady & Forward Aves., Squirrel Hill

Format

Neighborhood comprehensive (1927–present)

Pre-engineering magnet (1997–present)

Notable alumni

Myron Cope (journalist/broadcaster), Howard Fineman (journalist), Antoine Fuqua (film director), Wiz Khalifa (musician), Larry Lucchino (baseball executive), Rob Marshall (film director), Curtis Martin (pro football), Gerald Stern (poet), Evan Wolfson (civil rights activist)

Bellefield Girls' Vocational (1928–1957)

Location

Bellefield School* (Fifth Ave. & Bouquet St.), Oakland

Format

Girls' vocational

Connelly Vocational (1930–1968)

Location

Bedford Ave. & Crawford St., Crawford-Roberts

Format

Boys' vocational

Notable alumni

George Benson (musician), August Wilson (playwright)

Washington Vocational (1937–1969)

Location
Washington School (40th St. & Eden Way),
  Lawrenceville
Format
Boys' vocational

Morse Vocational (1939–1950)

Location
Morse School (S. 25th & Sarah Sts.), South
  Side Flats
Format
Girls' vocational

Arsenal Girls' Vocational (1957–1969)

Location
Arsenal School (Butler & 40th Sts.),
  Lawrenceville
Format
Girls' vocational

Gladstone (1958–1976)

Location
Gladstone School (327 Hazelwood Ave.),
  Hazelwood
Format
Neighborhood comprehensive
Notable alumni
August Wilson (playwright)

Educational-Medical (1965–1986)

Location
S. Oakland Community Center (Ward St. &
  Blvd. of the Allies), Oakland (1965–1968)
Health Training Institute (319 Hemlock St.),
  Central Northside (1968–1971)
Roselia Foundling Home (Bedford Ave.
  & Manilla St.), Crawford-Roberts
  (1971–1973)
Letsche School (1530 Cliff St.), Crawford-
  Roberts (1973–1986)
Format
Expectant/new mothers

Letsche Alternative (1973–2004)

Location
South Hills High (125 Ruth St.), Mount
  Washington (1973–1974)
Peabody High (E. Liberty Blvd. & N. Beatty
  St.), East Liberty (1973–1975)
Letsche School (1530 Cliff St.), Crawford-
  Roberts (1975–2004)
Format
Alternative (1973–2004)
Expectant/new mothers (1986–1997)

Brashear (1976–present)

Location
  590 Crane Ave., Beechview
Format
Neighborhood comprehensive
  (1976–present)
Computer Science magnet (1979–2015)
Teaching Academy magnet (2012–present)
Notable alumni
Sam Clancy (pro football), Solomon Page
(pro football)

Pittsburgh Creative & Performing Arts (1979–present)

Location
Baxter School (Brushton Ave. & Baxter St.),
  Homewood (1979–2003)
111 9th St., Downtown (2003–present)
Format
Creative & Performing Arts magnet
Notable alumni
Billy Porter (entertainer)

Secondary Alternative (1994–1997)

Location
Occupational-Vocational-Technical Center
  (Ridge Ave. & Bank St.), Allegheny West
Format
Alternative

Student Achievement Center (2004–present)

Location
Baxter School (Brushton Ave. & Baxter St.),
  Homewood

Format
Alternative

Milliones University Prep (2008–present)

Location
Milliones School (3117 Centre Avenue),
    Upper Hill District
Format
Neighborhood comprehensive
    (2008–present)
University Prep magnet (2008–present)

Science & Technology (2009–present)

Location
Frick School (Fifth Ave. & Thackeray St.),
    Oakland
Format
Science & Technology magnet

Obama (2009–present)

Location
Reizenstein School* (Penn Ave. & E. Liberty
    Blvd.), Shadyside (2009–2012)
Peabody High (E. Liberty Blvd. & N. Beatty
    St.), East Liberty (2012–present)
Format
International Baccalaureate magnet

Notes

Many of the historical sources for *The Schenley Experiment*—school catalogues, early twentieth-century magazines, and course projects, for example—are unpaginated, but page numbers are provided when available.

Abbreviations

Courier	*Pittsburgh Courier*
GT	*Gazette Times*
Journal	*The Journal* (Schenley High School)
P-G	*Pittsburgh Post-Gazette*
Post	*Pittsburgh Post*
Press	*Pittsburgh Press*
Triangle	*The Triangle* (Schenley High School)

Introduction

1. James N. Rule, "The Place of the Modern Secondary School in a Democracy," *Third Yearbook of the National Association of Secondary Principals* (1920): 18–20.

2. Pittsburgh Board of Education, *Meeting Minutes, September 22, 1914* (Pittsburgh, [1915]).

3. John Bigham, *Class Book: The Class of 1880, Pittsburgh Central High School, Academical Department* (Pittsburgh, 1905), 108.

Chapter 1

The epigraph to this chapter is drawn from Percy B. Caley, "Historical, Social and Economic Background of Schenley High School," in *Schenley High School: Prepared for an Evaluation by the Commission on Secondary Schools March 13–16, 1950* (Pittsburgh: Schenley High School, 1950), 1.

1. Richard J. Altenbaugh, *The American People and Their Education: A Social History* (Upper Saddle River, NJ: Merrill/Prentice Hall, 2003), 164; US Bureau of the Census, *Fourteenth Census of the United States 1920*, vol. 1, *Population, Number and Distribution of Inhabitants* (Washington, DC: Government Printing Office, 1921), 81.

2. "The New School Law," *Daily Pittsburgh Gazette*, February 9, 1855.

3. The official name was "the Pittsburgh High School"; see George Thornton Fleming, *My High School Days: Including a Brief History of the Pittsburgh Central High School from 1855 to 1871 and Addenda* (Pittsburgh: Press

of Wm. G. Johnston, 1904), 166, 168. The reason for the Central moniker is unclear, as no other high schools then existed. It is likely that the name identified the school with the Central Board of Education, which, in 1855, succeeded the unmanageable ward-based "mini-boards"; see Sarah Hutchins Killikelly, *The History of Pittsburgh: Its Rise and Progress* (Pittsburgh: B. C. & Gordon Montgomery, 1906), 325–26. According to George Thornton Fleming, an enthusiastic Central alumnus and historian, "The word, Central, readily conveys the impression that some day other high schools not central might and would be established, and they have been,"; see *My High School Days*, 124. For evidence that newspapers transitioned from "the High School" to "Pittsburgh High" and "Central High" in the 1880s, see "Central Board of Education," *Daily Post*, September 13, 1866; "Farewell to School," *Daily Post*, June 15, 1881; and "High School Fun," *Pittsburgh Commercial Gazette*, April 11, 1885, 5. For more information on Central's first day, see "Education in Pittsburgh," *Daily Pittsburgh Gazette*, September 29, 1855; and "The High School," *Daily Pittsburgh Gazette*, September 26, 1855.

4. Ralph Proctor Jr., "Racial Discrimination Against Black Teachers and Black Professionals in the Pittsburgh Public School System, 1834–1973" (PhD diss., University of Pittsburgh, 1979), 32–34; and Edward J. Price Jr., "School Segregation in Nineteenth-Century Pennsylvania," *Pennsylvania History* 43, no. 2 (April 1976): 125. Adjacent to an editorial discussing school integration, the *Daily Post* asked, "Will the Radical Controllers of the High School Admit Colored Children or Would the Parents of White Children Rebel?" *Daily Post*, September 8, 1871.

5. "The Central Board of Education," *Daily Pittsburgh Gazette*, June 21, 1855; and Fleming, *My High School Days*, 11–13, 153.

6. Heppie Wilkins Hamilton, *The Old Central High School (P.C.H.S.): Reminiscences of the Class of 1859 with an Introduction and Addenda* (Pittsburgh: Dean Pupils Association, 1915), 1–2. In the first year, 114 students passed the exam of 198 who attempted; see William D. McCoy, *The Establishment and Development of the Pittsburgh Central High School: Prepared in Commemoration of the One Hundredth Anniversary of the First Graduating Class 1859–1959* (Pittsburgh: Pittsburgh Public Schools, 1959). Pittsburgh Public Schools Records, Detre Library & Archives, Heinz History Center.

7. "The High School," *Post*, July 9, 1859.

8. Fleming, *My High School Days*, 74; S. Trevor Hadley, "Central High School: Pittsburgh's First," *Pittsburgh History* 73, no. 2 (Summer 1990): 72–73; and "The High School," *Daily Pittsburgh Gazette*, September 26, 1855.

9. Fleming, *My High School Days*, 111–12; and "The High School," *Post*, July 9, 1859.

10. Hadley, "Central High," 72; and McCoy, *Establishment and Development*.

11. Hadley, "Central High," 73; Central's average antebellum enrollment (147.4) was nearly identical to that during the war (144.4); see Fleming, *My High School Days*, 222.

12. McCoy, *Establishment and Development*.

13. Fleming, *My High School Days*, 16.

14. Ibid., 20; Ileen A. DeVault, *Sons and Daughters of Labor: Class and Clerical Work in Turn-of-the-Century Pittsburgh* (Ithaca: Cornell University Press, 1990), 29–30; Alina Laó Keebler, *The History and Architecture of the Henry Clay Frick School* (Pittsburgh: Frick ISA, 1996), 16.

15. Fleming, *My High School Days*, 222, 20.

16. David W. Lonich, "Metropolitanism and the Genesis of Municipal Anxiety in Allegheny County," *Pittsburgh History* 76, no. 2 (Summer 1993): 81–82; and Fleming, *My High School Days*, 16, 222.

17. Fleming, *My High School Days*, 16.

18. Ibid., 112.

19. Hadley, "Central High," 73; and "Meeting of the Central Board of Education," *Daily Post*, February 10, 1869.

20. When the building was razed in 1946, it stood immediately west of Connelly Vocational High School; see Leonard Thompson, "The First Hundred Years . . . ," *Sunday Magazine, Press*, August 21, 1955, 23.

21. "Laying of the Corner Stone of the New High School Building," *Pittsburgh Gazette*, October 1, 1869, 1.

22. "Our High School," *Pittsburgh Gazette*, October 14, 1871; Fleming, *My High School Days*, 222; and Hadley, "Central High," 73–74.

23. Altenbaugh, *American People*, 166.

24. Fleming, *My High School Days*, 222.

25. "Our Public Schools," *Daily Post*, December 11, 1878. Beginning in 1837, Pittsburgh's public school district operated "colored schools" in various locations, usually basements of black churches. In 1867, the District christened the Miller Street school—at what is now Miller Street and Forside Place in Crawford-Roberts—which was built specifically for black students. Motivated by a desire to save money, the school board closed Miller in 1874, resulting in legal integration of all Pittsburgh schools; see Proctor, "Racial Discrimination," 31–33 and "The Miller Street School," *Pittsburgh Commercial*, June 29, 1874. For evidence of the move to Franklin School, see "Public School Matters," *Post*, May 11, 1892, 2. For evidence of the move to Fifth Avenue High, see "Central Board Reception," *Pittsburgh Commercial Gazette*, May 1, 1896, 4.

26. Altenbaugh, *American People*, 231.

27. DeVault, *Sons and Daughters of Labor*, 33. One school board member lamented a procedural "rat hole" through which Commercial students could be admitted to the Academic Department; see "High School Examination," *Daily Post*, July 10, 1886.

28. "Pupils Who Passed," *Daily Post*, July 1, 1886; and "Win Their Way Into Pittsburgh High School," *GT*, June 26, 1907, 5.

29. Bigham, *Class Book*, 108.

30. Caley, "Historical, Social and Economic," 9A; and Jake Oresick, "What's in a Namesake?: Mary Schenley," *Western Pennsylvania History* 98, no. 3 (Fall 2015): 31.

31. Alice N. Bailey, "My High School Days," *Journal*, May 1918, 32.

32. Demographic data were not yet collected, but a 1949 survey sought clues by indexing the perceived national origins of surnames from the Class of 1900. Notwithstanding this method's flaws, results were as follows: British 52%, Irish 23%, German 17%, Hebrew 4%, French 3%; see Caley, "Historical, Social and Economic," 13. Harvey Thorpe '13, who attended Central from 1909 to 1913, said, "There were very few black students in the high school"; see interview by Bessie Heymann and Marjorie Silverman, December 20, 1977, National Council of Jewish Women (NCJW), Pittsburgh Section Papers, University of Pittsburgh. For more information on Turfley and Whitson, see "Dr. J. T. Whitson," *Cleveland Gazette*, July 7, 1888, 1. The state school law of 1854, section 24, required districts with at least twenty black students to establish separate schools. "In the absence of separate schools, the regular schools were to admit black children." Section 24 was repealed in 1881; see Price, "School Segregation," 124, 134–35. For an account of the law's effect in Pittsburgh, see Proctor, "Racial Discrimination," 32–39.

33. The first Jewish graduate is believed to be Albert Berkowitz '70, followed by his brother, Henry '72; see Alumni Association of the Pittsburgh High School, *Alumni Register: Pittsburgh High School* (Crafton, PA: Cramer Printing & Publishing, 1905), 25–29; Fleming, *My High School Days*, 101–03, 115; and Malcolm H. Stern, "Early Jews of Fall River, Massachusetts," *Rhode Island Jewish Historical Notes* 5, no. 2 (November 1968): 146.

34. "The anti-Semitism only became more apparent due to the immigration of thousands of Russian, Polish, and Eastern European Jews," Hast continued, revealing intra-Jewish class tensions that persisted in Pittsburgh through at least the 1970s; see interview by Harold Kimball and Ann Faigen, November 22, 1985, National Council of Jewish Women (NCJW), Pittsburgh Section Papers, University of Pittsburgh, and Myrna Katz Frommer and Harvey Frommer, *Growing Up Jewish in America: An Oral History* (Lincoln: University of Nebraska Press, 1995), 68.

35. Pauline Marks Frumerman, interview by Stephanie Benson and Nancy Holmes, March 18, 1976, National Council of Jewish Women (NCJW), Pittsburgh Section Papers, University of Pittsburgh.

36. Caley, "Historical, Social and Economic," 12.

37. Ibid., 16–17; and Bigham, *Class Book*, 108–9.

38. Bigham, *Class Book*, 108–9; and Chris Adamski, "Schenley Teams Go Out as Winners," *P-G*, May 15, 2011, C-12.

39. Caley, "Historical, Social and Economic," 11.

40. Alumni Association, *Alumni Register*, 80–83.

41. *Fourteenth Annual Report of the Condition of the Public Schools of Pittsburgh, for the School Year Ending August 31, 1882* (Pittsburgh: Board of Public Education, 1883), 9; *High School Journal*, September 1897, 17; Caley, "Historical, Social and Economic," 23n4; and ibid., 23.

42. Thorpe, interview; "Central Boarders Meet," *Daily Post*, September 15, 1886. "It is alleged that some parents have even gone so far as to purchase lots and build small houses in the rural districts of the city, so as to be able to set up the claim of being taxpayers and have a place for their children to reside while attending the high school"; see "Prepared to Fight," *Press*, January 27, 1895, 2.

43. Fleming, *My High School Days*, 59, 72, 87; "Obituary News: Miss Frances C. Parry," *Post*, October 19, 1920, 7; and "German Teacher Elected," *Pittsburgh Commercial*, October 27, 1869.

44. Hadley, "Central High School," 74–75; "Pulitzer Prizes in Journalism Announced," *Altoona (PA) Tribune*, May 16, 1923, 11; "Success with Roentgen Rays," *Daily Democrat* (Huntington, IN), April 11, 1896; and Fleming, *My High School Days*, 151.

45. The principal was paid $2,000 in 1855, $1,200 in 1864, $2,500 in 1888, and $3,000 in 1912; see "The Pittsburgh High School," *Daily Pittsburgh Gazette*, July 14, 1855; "Central Board of Education," *Daily Pittsburgh Gazette*, July 13, 1864; "A New Salary Schedule," *Post*, December 19, 1888, 3; and "Education Board Assigns Teachers and Compensation," *Post*, May 29, 1912, 4.

46. "More Room Needed," *Pittsburgh Commercial Gazette*, September 11, 1895, 2. In 1907, Central was so crowded that fifty students were sent to nearby Letsche Elementary, and every room in Central "had at least one-third more pupils than normal capacity"; see William D. McCoy, *History of Pittsburgh Public Schools to 1942* (Pittsburgh, 1959), 5–6:21.

47. Lila Ver Planck North, "Pittsburgh Schools," in *The Pittsburgh District: Civic Frontage*, ed. Paul Underwood Kellogg (New York: Russell Sage Foundation Publications, 1914), 302.

48. W. P. Botsford, "Schools Grows Amazingly in Past 50 Years," *Press*, June 23, 1934, 32; and Caley, "Historical, Social and Economic," 16.

49. "More Room Needed," *Pittsburgh Commercial Gazette*, September 11, 1895, 2.

50. The property was on South Negley Avenue in Squirrel Hill, 330 yards south of Fifth Avenue; see "Protests in Plenty for School Solons," *Post*, December 13, 1898, 2.

51. "Shady Avenue Site Selected," *Post*, November 3, 1899, 3; and "Title to Site All Right," *Post*, January 14, 1900, 14.

52. "Board Wishes a Better Site," *Pittsburgh Gazette*, October 14, 1903, 7.

53. "Talking of School Site," *Post*, November 10, 1903, 9; and Steven Bernstein, "Pittsburgh's Benevolent Tyrant: Christopher Lyman Magee," *Western Pennsylvania History* 86, no. 2 (Summer 2003): 37.

54. "School Site Is Adopted Amid Storm," *Post*, November 11, 1903, 1; and "Advertises for Bids for High School," *Press*, February 1, 1911, 14.

55. "Realty Deal Is Criticized," *Press*, June 21, 1905, 2.

56. "Proposed Academic and Schenley District High School Building," *The Builder* 28, no. 11 (March 1911): 16, 38; Pittsburgh Central Board of Education, "Catalogue of Pittsburgh High School 1911–1912."

57. McCoy, *History of Pittsburgh Public Schools*, 5–6: 25–29.

58. "Board to See Public Gets Money's Worth," *GT*, December 17, 1912, 9; "Trade of Sites Now Proposed," *Post*, December 31, 1912, 4; Robert M. Ginter, "Stimson Agrees to Trade of Properties," *GT*, January 5, 1913, sec. 1, 1; "Two Offers Made for Magee High School Site," *GT*, January 7, 1913, 2; and "Magee Site Will Be Sold to the City," *GT*, January 15, 1913, 2.

59. "Official—Pittsburgh," *Post*, June 30, 1913, Sporting 2; and "Check for Magee

Site Is Received by Board," *Post*, October 11, 1913, 7.

60. "School Board Clashes Over Public's Right," *Post*, October 23, 1912, 9; and "Board to See Public Gets Money's Worth," *GT*, December 17, 1912, 9.

61. National Register of Historic Places, Schenley High School, Pittsburgh, Allegheny County, Pennsylvania, National Register #86002706; National Register of Historic Places, Schenley Farms Historic District, Pittsburgh, Allegheny County, Pennsylvania, National Register #83002213; and John F. Bauman and Edward K. Muller, *Before Renaissance: Planning in Pittsburgh, 1889–1943* (Pittsburgh: University of Pittsburgh Press, 2006), 60–62.

62. "Magee Site Will Be Sold to the City," *GT*, January 15, 1913, 2; "Two Land Deals Closed by Board," *GT*, October 15, 1913, 6; and Robert M. Ginter, "Stimson Agrees to Trade of Properties," *GT*, January 5, 1913, sec. 1, 1.

Chapter 2

1. Altenbaugh, *American People*, 231.

2. US National Education Association, Commission on the Reorganization of Secondary Education, "Cardinal Principles of Secondary Education," *US Bureau of Education Bulletin*, no. 35 (1918): 25.

3. Altenbaugh, *American People*, 231.

4. US National Education Association, Commission on the Reorganization of Secondary Education, "Cardinal Principles," 25.

5. "Cosmopolitan Schools Wanted," *GT*, May 12, 1912, sec. 1, 4.

6. "New Officials for Schools Provided," *GT*, May 29, 1912, 3.

7. "Fifth Avenue High School Pupils Open Campaign to Have an Annex Built," *GT*, March 6, 1924, 16.

8. Caley, "Historical, Social and Economic," 25.

9. "Late Dr. M'Kelvy Honored By Board," *Post*, January 6, 1914, 10; George Thornton Fleming, *History of Pittsburgh and Environs* (New York and Chicago: American Historical Society, 1922), 2: 215–16; Bauman and Muller, *Before Renaissance*, 60–62; and Oresick, "What's in a Namesake?," 22–33.

10. "New High School Plans Disclosed," *GT*, February 17, 1914, 2; and "Board Members See High School Plans," *Press*, February 17, 1914, 18.

11. "Another Affront to Pittsburg Taxpayers," *Press*, June 15, 1916, 12; "Sharp Debate Over New High School at Meeting of Board," *Press*, April 22, 1914, 5. The total cost included $249,765.23 for the land, $1,000,249.49 for construction, and $180,000.00 for equipment; see "Splendid Schenley High, Erected at a Cost of Nearly $1,500,000, Ready for Occupancy," *Press*, September 17, 1916, Theatrical 6. Present-day construction cost was determined by the US Bureau of Labor Statistics inflation calculator; see "CPI Inflation Calculator," *US Bureau of Labor Statistics*, accessed June 5, 2016, http://data.bls.gov/cgi-bin/cpicalc.pl.

12. Franklin Spencer Edmonds, *Proceedings of the Dedication of the New Buildings of the Central High School, Philadelphia* (Philadelphia: Philadelphia Board of Education, 1910), 15; and "Schenley High Equipment Is to Cost More," *GT*, February 23, 1915, 2.

13. George W. Gerwig, "Fifty Years in Pittsburgh Schools," *Western Pennsylvania Historical Magazine* 25, nos. 3–4 (September–December 1942): 153.

14. Pittsburgh Board of Education, *Meeting Minutes, September 22, 1914* (Pittsburgh, [1915]); and "Davidson Plans Many Changes," *GT*, September 23, 1914, 9.

15. "Another Affront to Pittsburg Taxpayers," *Press*, June 15, 1916, 12.

16. "School Case to Be Pushed," *GT*, November 17, 1914, 9; "School Board Will Reconsider Stuart Schenley High Pay," *Press*, May 18, 1915, 4; and "Labor Row May Halt New Schenley High," *GT*, June 21, 1916, 1.

17. "Economy in Stone Construction," *Stone* 42 (January–December 1921): 252; and D. H. Colcord, "Electric Motor Drive in the Schenley High School in Pittsburgh," *Electrical Review* 74 (January 4, 1919–June 28, 1919): 331.

18. "Splendid Schenley High, Erected at a Cost of Nearly $1,500,000, Ready for Occupancy," *Press*, September 17, 1916, Theatrical 6.

19. Pennsylvania Historical and Museum Commission, "Historic Resource Survey Form for Schenley High School," May 1985.

20. Patricia Lowry, "Historic, Asbestos-Plagued Schenley Deserves Reprieve and Makeover," *P-G*, February 22, 2006, C-2; Larkin Page-Jacobs, "Asbestos and the End of Schenley High," *WESA.FM*, June 13, 2012, accessed May 18, 2016, http://wesa.fm/post/asbestos-and-end-schenley-high; and "Fine Art Works Hung in New High School," *Pittsburgh Sun*, September 17, 1916.

21. Colcord, "Electric Motor," 331–32; and Nick Bisceglia, e-mail to author, August 20, 2014.

22. "Splendid Schenley High, Erected at a Cost of Nearly $1,500,000, Ready for Occupancy," *Press*, September 17, 1916, Theatrical 6.

23. Ibid.; Clara E. Howard, "Organizing a New High School Library," *Bulletin of the American Library Association* 11 (January–November

1917): 176–79; and Caley, "Historical, Social and Economic," 27–28.

24. "Recent School Buildings in Pittsburgh, Pa.," *American School Board Journal* 53, no. 6 (December 1916): 32; John J. Donovan, *School Architecture: Principles and Practices* (New York: Macmillan, 1921), 663–66; *The American Architect* 111, no. 2146 (February 7, 1917); and "Helpful Economy News to All Mothers of School Boys and Girls," *GT*, September 29, 1916, 6.

25. "Symbol of City's Progress," *Pittsburgh Sunday Post*, August 13, 1916, sec. 2, 2; "Western Pennsylvania Schools and Colleges Increase Attendance," *GT*, August 5, 1916, 9; and "Splendid Schenley High, Erected at a Cost of Nearly $1,500,000, Ready for Occupancy," *Press*, September 17, 1916, Theatrical 6.

26. "Splendid Schenley High, Erected at a Cost of Nearly $1,500,000, Ready for Occupancy," *Press*, September 17, 1916, Theatrical 6; "Board May Amend Marriage Ruling," *Post*, September 22, 1916, 9; and "Public to Inspect New School This Week," *Post*, October 9, 1916, 12.

Chapter 3

The epigraph to this chapter is drawn from James N. Rule, "Greetings from Principal Rule," *Journal*, December 1916, 13.

1. James N. Rule, "The Place of the Modern Secondary School in a Democracy," *Third Yearbook of the National Association of Secondary Principals*, 1920, 18–20.

2. Beginning in 1915, it appears the exam was no longer given to the District's elementary school graduates, but it was still required for applicants from parochial or suburban elementary schools; see "1,983 Graduated by Grade Schools," *Post*, June 25, 1915, 8; and "101 Pass 'Exams' for High School," *Press*, June 24, 1916, 8. Carrick High School is counted among these seven but was constructed in 1924 by Carrick Borough, before the borough was annexed by the City of Pittsburgh in 1927; see "Meeting Backs Carrick Bonds," *GT*, April 1, 1924, 3; and "Carrick's Annexation to Pittsburgh Approved," *GT*, March 6, 1926, 1. For a comprehensive list of District high schools, see appendix E.

3. "700,000 Pupils at Schools on Opening Day," *GT*, October 3, 1916, 1, 3.

4. Milton Susman, interview by Judy Rubenstein and Nancy Holmes, November 10, 1976, National Council of Jewish Women (NCJW), Pittsburgh Section Papers, University of Pittsburgh.

5. Ibid.

6. Ibid.; and Caley, "Historical, Social and Economic," 20, 24.

7. *Journal*, March 1917, 22.

8. Hugh Patton, "Enrollment of Schenley 300 More Than That of Any Other High School in the City," *Triangle*, September 19, 1924; and Edward Sauvain, *Report on a Questionnaire Submitted to the Principal of the Pittsburgh Public School by the Survey Commission, Schenley High School* (Pittsburgh: Schenley High School, 1927), 19, 29. Enrollment was 2,562 in 1927–28; see Pittsburgh Board of Public Education, *Sixteenth Annual Report for the Year Ending December 31, 1927* (Pittsburgh, 1928), 53. For information on enrollment in 1922, see Caley, "Historical, Social and Economic," 52.

9. Sauvain, *Report on a Questionnaire*, 24.

10. *Journal*, February 1929, 11–45; and *Journal*, June 1929, 11–67.

11. "Board of Education Fixes Basic Salaries," *Press*, June 23, 1920, 14; Stanley W. Rosenbaum, interview by Pat Meltzer and Betty Alpern, December 27, 1987, National Council of Jewish Women (NCJW), Pittsburgh Section Papers, University of Pittsburgh; and W. Stewart Townsend, Mary Townsend Summers, E. Dudley Townsend, Anne E. Townsend, Jane W. Townsend, and Rebecca P. Townsend, "Letter to Edward Sauvain," *Triangle*, October 8, 1940.

12. Susman, interview; "Elmer Kenyon, Teacher of Theater, Dies," *Press*, May 13, 1949, 2.

13. Nancy Newman Frank, interview by Jane Berkey and Natalie Mandelblatt, November 12, 1975, National Council of Jewish Women (NCJW), Pittsburgh Section Papers, University of Pittsburgh.

14. "Elmer Kenyon, Teacher of Theater, Dies," *Press*, May 13, 1949, 2.

15. Clifford G. Shull, "Biography of Clifford G. Shull," in *Nobel Lectures in Physics, 1991–1995*, ed. Gosta Ekspong (Singapore: World Scientific, 1997), 141; and Alexander Jackson, interview by Marion Kabet and Stephanie Benson, January 21, 1976, National Council of Jewish Women (NCJW), Pittsburgh Section Papers, University of Pittsburgh.

16. Jackson, interview.

17. "Sara Soffel, 89, County Ex-Judge," *P-G*, October 7, 1976, 24.

18. M. G. Thomas, "The Fine Life," *Triangle*, October 4, 1930.

19. Jackson, interview; "Deaths of the Day: Emma M. Campbell," *New Castle (PA) News*, April 22, 1969, 3; and Sylvia Bernstein, "Mr. Rupert Publishes Book of Poetry," *Triangle*, September 12, 1930.

20. Myrtle M. Fisher, interview by Selma Berkman and Estelle Kruman, December 11, 1975, National Council of Jewish

Women (NCJW), Pittsburgh Section Papers, University of Pittsburgh.

21. Frank, interview.

22. "Opening Day," *Journal*, December 1916, 58; and Pittsburgh Architectural Club, Inc., *Yearbook of the Pittsburgh Architectural Club, Inc.* (Pittsburgh, 1917).

23. Rule, "Greetings from Principal Rule," 13.

24. Rule, "Modern Secondary School," 16–20.

25. Caley, "Historical, Social and Economic," 20, 24; and D. H. Colcord, "Electrical Equipment in a Pittsburgh High School," *The American City* 20 (January–June 1919): 585.

26. Sauvain, *Report on a Questionnaire*, 21; and Colcord, "Electrical Equipment," 583.

27. David Anderson et al., "The Hill District Community Collaborative: An Oral History" (course project, Carnegie Mellon University, 2001); and M. R. Goldman, "Hill District of Pittsburgh, as I Knew It," *Western Pennsylvania Historical Magazine* 51, no. 3 (July 1968): 279, 290. Between 1910 and 1930, the neighborhood had approximately 45,000 residents over 1.4 square miles, while present-day New York City has a population density of less than 28,000 people per square mile; see Alonzo G. Moron, "Distribution of the Negro Population in Pittsburgh, 1910–1930" (MA thesis, University of Pittsburgh, 1933), 29; Lynette Clemetson, "Revival for a Black Enclave in Pittsburgh," *New York Times*, August 9, 2002, A1; and Jim Gorzelany, "Putting on the Breaks," *Akron Beacon Journal*, May 9, 2013, D2. Kate Benz, "Standing at the Crossroads," *Pittsburgh Tribune-Review*, February 21, 2015, D4; Bob Bauder, "Can New Equal the Old?" *Pittsburgh Tribune-Review*, February 24, 2014, B1; Colter Harper, "'The Crossroads of the World': A Social and Cultural History of Jazz in Pittsburgh's Hill District, 1920–1970" (PhD diss., University of Pittsburgh, 2011), 58–59, 125, 49–50, 12–14; Kevin Kirtland, "Greenlee Field Site Earns Place in History," *P-G*, July 17, 2009, D-5; Laurence Glasco, "Double Burden: The Black Experience in Pittsburgh," in *African Americans in Pennsylvania: Shifting Historical Perspectives*, ed. Joe William Trotter Jr. and Eric Ledell Smith (University Park: Pennsylvania State University Press; Harrisburg: Pennsylvania Historical Museum Commission, 1997), 416–17; Jacob Feldman, *The Jewish Experience in Western Pennsylvania: A History, 1755–1945* (Pittsburgh: Historical Society of Western Pennsylvania, 1986), 183; Perry Bush, "A Neighborhood, a Hollow, and the Bloomfield Bridge: The Relationship Between Community and Infrastructure," *Pittsburgh History* 74, no. 4 (Winter 1991): 163; Scott Smith and Steven Manaker, "Pittsburgh's African-American Neighborhoods, 1900–1920," *Pittsburgh History* 78, no. 4 (Winter 1995–96): 160–61; and Ervin Dyer, "The Sweet Life," *P-G*, July 17, 2005, E-1, E-8.

28. Walter Dassdorf, interview by author, July 13, 2014; Goldman, "Hill District," 279; Charles F. Danver, "Christmas Customs of Old World Recalled in Hill District Colonies," *P-G*, December 23, 1932, 13; and Sauvain, *Report on a Questionnaire*, 16(a).

29. Official demographic data are unavailable, but an estimate of 25 percent by Stanley W. Rosenbaum '24 is supported by a yearbook audit of graduating seniors in which Jews ranged from 17 percent (1919–20) to 27.4 percent (1928–29); see Rosenbaum, interview; *Journal*, January 1920, 18–39; *Journal*, June 1920, 16–57; *Journal*, February 1929, 11–45; and *Journal*, June 1929, 11–67. For more information on Pittsburgh's Jewish population, see H. S. Linfield, "Statistics of Jews," *American Jewish Yearbook* 29 (1927–28): 245.

30. Blacks constituted 2 percent (1918–19) to 7.4 percent (1927–28) of the era's graduating classes; see *Journal*, January 1919, 20–39; *Journal*, June 1919, 29–48; *Journal*, January 1928, 11–51; *Journal*, June 1928, 21–77; and Michael Srulevich, "A Positive Look Back," *Jewish Chronicle* (Pittsburgh), August 18, 1994, 32.

31. "Miss Anderson Sings to Large Audience at Schenley High," *Courier*, December 11, 1926, sec. 1, 6; "Varied Activities," *Jewish Criterion* (Pittsburgh), January 2, 1925, 24; and "Clubs," *Jewish Criterion* (Pittsburgh), February 18, 1927, 41.

32. "Blind Students at Schenley High," *Journal*, October 1917, 25.

33. Caley, "Historical, Social and Economic," 67.

34. Richard J. Herrnstein and Charles Murray, *The Bell Curve: Intelligence and Class Structure in American Life* (New York: Free Press, 1994), 29–36; "Schenley's Alumni at College," *Journal*, June 1920, 81; and Claudia Goldin, "America's Graduation from High School: The Evolution and Spread of Secondary Schooling in the Twentieth Century," *Journal of Economic History* 58, no. 2 (June 1998): 351.

35. Glasco, "Double Burden," 416–17; and Feldman, *The Jewish Experience*, 183.

36. Milton Susman '24 recalled his own difficulty in becoming the first Jewish student body president; see Susman, interview.

37. This inference is partly based on evidence that ethnic differences in the early 1900s Hill District "frequently caused serious contentions"; see Goldman, "Hill District," 289–90. Harry Barnhardt, "Nicknames," *Triangle*, January 16, 1920.

38. For more information on class presidents, see *Journal,* February 1917 through *Journal,* June 1929. Confirmed Jewish leaders include student body presidents Milton Susman '24 (1923–24) and Arthur Goldberg '29 (1929), and class president Jack Levy '27 (June 1927); see Susman, interview; Sarah Patterson and Anna Kaufman, "Clubs," *Journal,* June 1929, 106; and *Journal,* June 1927, 13. For more information on female leaders, see *Journal,* January 1922, 67; *Journal,* June 1922, 83; and "Alice Dykema Elected President of Schenley," *Triangle,* October 3, 1947.

39. Sauvain, *Report on a Questionnaire,* 16. The Pittsburgh Public Schools had not hired a full-time black teacher since the end of de jure segregation. The valedictorian of its Teachers' Training School was passed over for her white classmates; see Proctor, "Racial Discrimination," 39, 58–59.

40. "Wm. Randolph First in City-Wide Contest," *Courier,* May 3, 1924, 1; and "Randolph Is Again Winner in Big Contest," *Courier,* May 10, 1924, 1.

41. "Afro-American Notes," *Press,* June 10, 1917, Theatrical 4.

42. Jerry Vondas, "Alderman's a Winner in Life," *Press,* October 29, 1973, 12; and *Journal,* May 1917, 29–31.

43. "Schenley—A School of Schools," *Journal,* December 1916, 56; and "M. M. F.," *Journal,* December 1916, 57.

44. Sauvain, *Report on a Questionnaire,* 37; and James Reed, "Schenley Spirit," *Journal,* January 1925, 53–54.

45. "What Do You Think?" *Journal,* February 1917, 47.

46. "Schenley's Alumni at College," 81; and Goldin, "America's Graduation," 351. For more information on Schenley's athletic history, see appendix C.

47. *Journal,* June 1918, 75–76; "Russian Soviet Rule Is Upheld," *Press,* April 21, 1929, Society 12; Schenley High Library Staff, *Journal of Schenley High School,* November 3, 1916–January 2, 1924, 15, William R. Oliver Special Collections Room, Carnegie Library of Pittsburgh; and *Journal,* June 1922, 4–5.

48. Other speakers included actors Walter Hampden, Julia Marlowe, and E. H. Sothern; see Caley, "Historical, Social and Economic," 45; and *Journal,* June 1917, 83. Hanly, the Prohibition Party's 1916 presidential candidate, held a campaign rally at Schenley; see "Prohibition Candidates Assail Other Parties," *GT,* October 21, 1916, 2.

49. Sauvain, *Report on a Questionnaire,* 30; P. L. Windsor, "University of Illinois Library School," *Library Journal* 44 (January–December 1919): 410; and Howard, "Organizing a New High School Library," 176–79.

50. "Smoky City Has Redeeming Features," *Washington (DC) Herald,* March 24, 1922, 8; and "Daily Radio Programs," *Altoona (PA) Tribune,* August 9, 1922, 7.

51. For more information on Kerr's coaching career, see appendix B.

52. "American Tennis Players and Swimmers Capture All Events," *Cincinnati Enquirer,* July 21, 1924, 10; and "New Records for Mercersburg," *Harrisburg (PA) Telegraph,* January 29, 1923, 17.

53. AP, "Mr. Sauvain Assists at the Inaugural," *Triangle,* March 4, 1921; and Donald Kirby, "Mr. Sauvain's Visit to Washington," *Triangle,* March 11, 1921.

54. "Mrs. Roosevelt Thanks Schenley," *Triangle,* October 17, 1919.

55. "US Now at War with Kaiser," *Press,* April 6, 1917, 1; and "Central-Schenley High Will Honor Veterans of War," *GT,* August 15, 1920, sec. 6, 2.

56. "Schenley Wins Title," *Press,* March 28, 1917, 28; and Merle C. Knapp, "On Active Duty with the American Expeditionary Force," *Journal,* February 1918, 22.

57. Cecil H. Dean, "The Work of the Schenley High School Auxiliary of the Red Cross," *Journal,* January 1918, 61; *Journal,* June 1919, 63; Caley, "Historical, Social and Economic," 32; *Journal,* May 1917, 3–7, 13; and "Letters from the Front," *Journal,* June 1918, 87–93.

58. "Rule Named by Dr. Finegan to Succeed Lewis," *Evening News (Harrisburg, PA),* January 20, 1923, 1. Rule became principal of Washington & Jefferson College's preparatory academy in 1900, thirty-eight years before his obituary indicated that he passed away at age sixty-one; see "Alumni of W. & J. Hold Reunions," *Post,* June 20, 1900, 9; and "Dr. Rule Is Dead; Guided Schools in Financial Crisis," *Harrisburg (PA) Telegraph,* April 11, 1938, 7.

59. Maude W. Miller, "Mr. Rule Leaves for Washington!," *Triangle,* September 26, 1919.

60. "Dr. Rule Is Dead; Guided Schools in Financial Crisis," *Harrisburg (PA) Telegraph,* April 11, 1938, 7.

61. "Special Study Directors Get Pay Increase," *GT,* June 23, 1920, 4; and "All Schools to Open Soon," *Press,* August 19, 1903, 1.

Chapter 4

1. Cecil F. Poole, "Civil Rights, Law, and the Federal Courts: The Life of Cecil Poole, 1914–1997," oral history by Carole Hicke, 1993, Regional Oral History Office, The Bancroft Library, University of California, Berkeley, 13–14; and Kurt Pine, "The Jews in the Hill

District of Pittsburgh, 1910–1940: A Study of Trends" (MS thesis, University of Pittsburgh, 1943), 46.

2. Monica L. Haynes, "Schenley's Class of '33 Gathers to Celebrate 70th Reunion," P-G, June 23, 2003, C-2.

3. "[S]tringent financial conditions" drastically scaled back some activities, like girls' interscholastic athletics, which was eventually eliminated until 1972–73; see Journal, June 1933, 86–91; James Bullock, "Sports," Triangle, January 12, 1973.

4. Dassdorf, interview.

5. Pittsburgh Board of Public Education, Twentieth Annual Report for the Year Ending December 31, 1931 (Pittsburgh, 1932), 89; Pittsburgh Board of Public Education, Twenty-Fifth Annual Report for the Year Ending December 31, 1936 (Pittsburgh, 1937), 31; and Journal, June 1930, 18–70.

6. Lilian McKibbin Steiner, "'Sugar Top' and the 'Cobblestone Jungle': Urban Redevelopment in Pittsburgh's Hill District, 1955–1959" (thesis, Haverford College, 2010), 32; and McCoy, History of Pittsburgh Public Schools, 1:230.

7. Leonard Weitzman, interview by Jean Simon and James Balter, November 29, 1990, National Council of Jewish Women (NCJW), Pittsburgh Section Papers, University of Pittsburgh; and Paul S. Caplan, interview by Ruth Winer and Bess Karelitz, May 3, 1998, National Council of Jewish Women (NCJW), Pittsburgh Section Papers, University of Pittsburgh.

8. Journal, June 1930, 18–70.

9. W. Stewart Townsend et al., "Letter to Edward Sauvain," Triangle, October 8, 1940.

10. Shull, "Biography of Clifford G. Shull," 141.

11. Herbert S. Parnes, A Prof's Life: It's More than Teaching (Lincoln, NE: iUniverse, 2001), 7; William Grace, survey, January 29, 2015; and Samuel E. Tisherman, interview by Ruth Saul and Gene Dickman, May 5, 1998, National Council of Jewish Women (NCJW), Pittsburgh Section Papers, University of Pittsburgh. Byrne was at Schenley as early as November 1918 and retired after the 1954–55 school year; see Leila H. Rupp, Graduation Memory Book (1919), 173, Detre Library & Archives, Heinz History Center; and "Two Faculty Members Bid Adieu to S.H.S.," Triangle, June 14, 1955.

12. "Two Faculty Members Bid Adieu to S.H.S.," Triangle, June 14, 1955.

13. Albert W. Bloom, interview by Elinor Cohen and Harold Kimball, May 3, 1984, National Council of Jewish Women (NCJW), Pittsburgh Section Papers, University of Pittsburgh.

14. During Bloom's distinguished journalism career, he covered the White House during World War II, wrote for the Post-Gazette, and founded the Pittsburgh Jewish Chronicle; see "Albert Bloom, Editor Emeritus of Jewish Paper," P-G, January 29, 1990, 8; and A. Bloom, interview.

15. "Two Faculty Members Bid Adieu to S.H.S.," Triangle, June 14, 1955; and "Duquesne Names Dean of Women," Press, August 13, 1955, 4.

16. "Meet the Faculty," Triangle, March 17, 1941; and Tisherman, interview.

17. "Squirrel Hill Youth Wins Chemistry Scholarship," Press, September 18, 1932, 5; "Schenley Players Retain City Chess Championship," Triangle, December 16, 1938; and Clay Lynch, "Chess Blindfolded Is Easy for Schenley High Senior," P-G, February 7, 1939, 2.

18. Harry Schwalb, "Blast Furnace in Miniature," P-G, February 21, 1939, 22.

19. "Six Take Over Faculty Positions Left Vacant," Triangle, September 13, 1940; "Mr. Harvey P. Roberts Begins Work as Principal," Triangle, September 13, 1940; and "Mr. Bernard McCormick Schenley's New Principal," Triangle, September 23, 1946.

20. Elizabeth Malick, "Dedication," Triangle, October 8, 1940.

21. Dassdorf, interview.

22. "Veteran Head of Schenley High Retires," P-G, June 19, 1940, 9.

23. "Mr. Harvey P. Roberts Begins Work as Principal," Triangle, September 13, 1940.

24. "Reader Forum: Share Your Memories of Pittsburgh's Schenley High School," P-G, June 11, 2008, accessed May 20, 2016, http://www.post-gazette.com/news/educa tion/2008/06/11/Reader-Forum-Share-your -memories-of-Pittsburgh-s-Schenley-High -School/stories/200806110225.

25. "Letters from Our Readers: Schenley High Students also Oppose War," Press, June 14, 1935, 21.

26. Samuel Foner, "Mussolini Communicates with Schenley Students," Triangle, December 6, 1935.

27. Joseph J. Bruno, interview by Nicholas Ciotola, May 17, 2004, 8, Italian American World War II Veterans Oral History Collection, Detre Library & Archives, Heinz History Center.

28. "Nine Schenley Pupils Join Armed Forces to Fight Axis," Triangle, December 22, 1941.

29. Journal, 1943.

30. Joyce Gannon, "Obituary: Milton Field / Code Breaker in WWII Who Helped Develop Bar Codes," P-G, January 7, 2009, 9; and "Former Schenley Student Torpedoed in Mid-Ocean When Manning Tanker," Triangle, September 29, 1942.

31. "Former Pupil Dies in Crash," *Triangle*, January 26, 1942; "Former Student Killed in Action," *Triangle*, November 2, 1942; and UP, "Seaman, Reported Dead, Telephones to Mother," *Evening News* (Harrisburg, PA), April 28, 1942, 14.

32. "Pupils Inducted into Victory Corps," *Triangle*, March 16, 1943; Doris Kalet and Marilyn Sparks, "Schenley in Wartime I," *Journal*, 1943; and Ruth Tisherman, "Messenger Course Is Opened," *P-G*, March 17, 1942, 6.

33. Kalet and Sparks, "Schenley in Wartime I"; and Ruth Tisherman, "Schoolgirls Sewing to Help the Army," *P-G*, May 12, 1942, 7.

34. Victor Bockris, *Warhol: The Biography* (New York: Da Capo Press, 2003), 51–52.

35. Lisa L. Ossian, *The Forgotten Generation: American Children and World War II* (Columbia: University of Missouri Press, 2011), 35–37, 72–77; and Edith Flom Schneider, interview by author, December 30, 2014.

36. Pittsburgh Board of Public Education, *Annual Report of the Superintendent, 1947–1948* (Pittsburgh, 1948), 53; and Pittsburgh Board of Public Education, *Annual Report of the Superintendent, 1948–1949* (Pittsburgh, 1949), 79.

37. "Pupils Voice Various Opinions About Girls on Safety Patrol," *Triangle*, April 16, 1945.

38. "Schenley High 2,159 Strong," *Triangle*, October 14, 1946; "Alice Dykema Elected President of Schenley," *Triangle*, October 3, 1947; and *Journal* June 1922, 83.

39. "Elect Ex-Press Girl Reporter," *Press*, February 9, 1930, Radio 6; and "Girl Crashes Chess Club," *Press*, November 9, 1930, World of Today 5.

40. "Girl Crashes Chess Club," *Press*, November 9, 1930, World of Today 5.

41. AP, "Co-eds Won't End Privacy at Lunch," *Reading (PA) Times*, January 11, 1938, 10.

42. Pittsburgh Board of Public Education, *Twenty-Ninth Annual Report for the Year Ending December 31, 1940* (Pittsburgh, 1941), 27; and "Enrollment at Low Ebb," *Triangle*, March 1, 1955.

43. "Miss Baker, Mr. Cheesebrough, Mr. Hildebrand Retire," *Triangle*, June 13, 1940; "Mr. Chester Story Retires from Schenley Faculty," *Triangle*, June 6, 1947; and Bockris, *Warhol*, 53.

44. "Enrollment at Low Ebb," *Triangle*, March 1, 1955; Ossian, *Forgotten Generation*, 35–37. Population data do not include Shadyside, which was split between Schenley and Peabody; see Department of City Planning, *1990 Census of Population and Housing Reports, Report No. 1: Pittsburgh Population by Neighborhood, 1940 to 1990* (Pittsburgh, 1991).

45. Department of City Planning, *1990: Pittsburgh*; and Joe W. Trotter and Jared N. Day, *Race and Renaissance: African Americans in Pittsburgh Since World War II* (Pittsburgh: University of Pittsburgh Press, 2010), 38.

46. Arnold Sowell, interview by author, July 23, 2014.

47. Caley, "Historical, Social and Economic," 56.

48. From 1930 to 1950, black population in the Upper Hill District alone increased from 64.2 percent to 96.6 percent. From 1924 to 1940, the number of Jews in the entire Hill District decreased by 80.8 percent; see John Bodnar, Roger Simon, and Michael P. Weber, *Lives of Their Own: Blacks, Italians, and Poles in Pittsburgh, 1900–1960* (Urbana: University of Illinois Press, 1982), 211, 225–26; and Pine, "Jews in the Hill District," 28. Edith Flom Schneider, interview by author, October 19, 2015; and Trotter and Day, *Race and Renaissance*, 46–48.

49. The figures for Jews in 1931 represent only graduates, while the other figures represent all Schenley students; see *Journal*, January 1931, 12–43; *Journal*, June 1931, 14–56; Katherine Waters and Herman McClain, "Schenley High School," *Courier*, November 14, 1931, sec. 2, 6; Pittsburgh Board of Education, *Twentieth Annual Report*, 1931, 89; and Caley, "Historical, Social and Economic," 58, 65.

50. Caley, "Historical, Social and Economic," 61.

51. Julia Jones, "Talk o' Town," *Courier*, April 12, 1941, 9; Julia Jones, "Talk o' Town," *Courier*, April 10, 1943, 9; and "Four Prominent Churches Will Present 'Passion and Triumph,'" *Courier*, March 23, 1935, sec. 1, 6.

52. "Scully Okays Carver Week," *Courier*, January 1, 1944, 1; and "Honor Noted Scientist During 'Carver Week,'" *Courier*, January 15, 1944, 10.

53. Caley, "Historical, Social and Economic," 58.

54. Only five Asian students are believed to have graduated in the era; see *Journal*, 1938, 20–36; *Journal*, 1943; *Journal*, 1945; and *Journal*, 1947.

55. Ralph Proctor Jr., *Voices from the Firing Line: A Personal Account of the Pittsburgh Civil Rights Movement* (Pittsburgh: Introspec Press, 2013), 355.

56. Ibid., 24, 47, 31; and Albert W. Bloom, "Hospitals End Segregation," *P-G*, December 26, 1958, 11.

57. Proctor, *Voices from the Firing Line*, 59.

58. Ibid., 23; and Proctor, "Racial Discrimination," 22–23.

59. Proctor, "Racial Discrimination," 56.

60. Ibid., 48, 46.

61. Ibid., 75–76.

62. Ibid., 91, 76.

63. *Journal*, June 1931, 14–56; and Katherine Waters and Herman McClain, "Schenley High School," *Courier*, November 14, 1931, sec. 2, 6.

64. Katherine Waters and Herman McClain, "Schenley High School," *Courier*, November 14, 1931, sec. 2, 6; and Katherine Waters and Herman McClain, "Schenley High School," *Courier*, December 5, 1931, sec. 2, 6.

65. School-wide demographic data are not available for 1946–47, but the senior class was 66.7 percent white; see *Journal*, 1947. In June 1949, the first school-wide demographic survey indicated 35 percent black enrollment; see Caley, "Historical, Social and Economic," 58. "Henry Burwell Captures Election for President," *Triangle*, October 14, 1946; and Mary Niederberger, "William E. Green: A Leader at City Schools for Decades," *P-G*, March 21, 2013, C-3.

66. Betty Kieffer, interview by author, December 15, 2012.

67. Thelma Lovette Morris, e-mail to author, February 1, 2015.

68. Bockris, *Warhol*, 52.

69. June 1944 marked the first time Jews constituted less than 10 percent of Schenley's graduating class; see *Journal*, 1944. For more information on anti-Semitism in Pittsburgh, see Jacob L. "Jake" Weinberg, interview by Frisch and Weinberg, 1993, National Council of Jewish Women (NCJW), Pittsburgh Section Papers, University of Pittsburgh; and Jack Buncher, interview by Shirley Stolzer and Judy Rubinstein, May 26, 1994, National Council of Jewish Women (NCJW), Pittsburgh Section Papers, University of Pittsburgh. Evelyn Glick Bloom, interview by Bernice Herzog and Marvin Herzog, February 19, 1998, National Council of Jewish Women (NCJW), Pittsburgh Section Papers, University of Pittsburgh; and Milton Hirsch, interview by author, July 16, 2014.

70. Mina (Serbin) Kavaler, interview by Angela Leibowicz, October 5, 1999, National Council of Jewish Women (NCJW), Pittsburgh Section Papers, University of Pittsburgh.

71. "Mina Kavaler: A Calling of Calling—and Much More," *The Insider* (Jewish Federation of Greater Pittsburgh), April 2014, accessed June 6, 2016, http://www.jfedpgh .org/mina; Kavaler only left the NAACP board because "Tim Stevens ['63] came in and threw off all the whites"; see Kavaler, interview.

72. Bockris, *Warhol*, 55; and Matthew Shaffer, interview by author, July 15, 2014.

73. Shaffer, interview, 2014.

74. "Reader Forum: Share Your Memories of Pittsburgh's Schenley High School," *P-G*, June 11, 2008.

75. Dassdorf, interview.

76. Monica L. Haynes, "Schenley's class of '33 gathers to celebrate 70th reunion," *P-G*, June 23, 2003, C-2.

77. "Reader Forum: Share Your Memories of Pittsburgh's Schenley High School," *P-G*, June 11, 2008.

78. Kieffer, interview.

79. Monica L. Haynes, "Schenley's Class of '33 Gathers to Celebrate 70th Reunion," *P-G*, June 23, 2003, C-2.

80. "Schenley High May Be Called Great School of Autographing," *Press*, April 27, 1932, 18.

81. "Schenley Baseball Chances Hinge on Susce's Success," *Triangle*, April 9, 1948; and Tom Shorall, "Josh Gibson Supplies Lusty Batting Punch," *Triangle*, May 21, 1948.

82. "Schenley Baseball Chances Hinge on Susce's Success," *Triangle*, April 9, 1948; and Mark Ribowsky, *The Power and the Darkness: The Life of Josh Gibson in the Shadows of the Game* (New York: Simon & Schuster, 1996), 3–4.

83. Ribowsky, *The Power and the Darkness*, 211–12.

84. Ibid., 302–3; "2 Baseball Families to Team Up at Altar," *Press*, March 30, 1956, 20; Isabel Lubovsky, "Pie Traynor, Greatest Third Baseman of Them All, Grants *Triangle* Interview," *Triangle*, May 28, 1948; and Al Abrams, "Traynor Third Pirate to Enter Hall of Fame," *P-G*, February 28, 1948, 14.

85. Albert W. Bloom, "Coach Warner Praises High School Coaching," *Triangle*, October 25, 1935; A. Wranitzky, "Knute Rockne Gives Views on Football," *Triangle*, October 31, 1930; Irving Kaufman, "Private Interview with Otis Skinner Delights Reporters," *Triangle*, October 25, 1935; Beatrice Cohen, "Ida Tarbell, Famous Author, Grants '*Triangle*' Interview," *Triangle*, September 30, 1932; and Parnes, *A Prof's Life*, 7–8.

86. Parnes, *A Prof's Life*, 7–8.

87. *Schenleyan*, 1938, 10–13; and "Offer Full Hi School Course," *P-G*, September 16, 1928, Theatrical and Photoplay 6.

88. "Free Night School Planned in North Hills," *North Hills (PA) News Record*, September 16, 1964, 1.

89. "Father Rice, Hacker Debate Communism," *Press*, February 1, 1938, 10; and "Priest and Editor Talk Communism," *Press*, October 11, 1938, 16.

90. "Board Forbids Use of School to Honor Lenin," *P-G*, January 21, 1936, 28; and "Board Bans Use of School Hall by Communists," *Press*, September 19, 1939, 3.

91. Kermit McFarland, "Lawrence Puts Smoke Control at Top of List," *Press*, November 9, 1945, 1; and Michael P. Weber, *Don't Call Me Boss: David L. Lawrence, Pittsburgh's Renaissance Mayor* (Pittsburgh: University of Pittsburgh Press, 1988), 228.

92. Weber, *Don't Call Me Boss*, 235–37; "PRR Sells 13 Acres for Point Park," *Press*, February 13, 1948, 1; W. L. Russell, "$50 Million Point Project Most Modern in World," *Press*, September 21, 1949, 1; and "30 Blocks to Be Cleared for Plant in Southside Area," *P-G*, August 14, 1949, 1.

93. "Huge Civic Center Studied for Lower Hill," *Press*, October 30, 1947, 1.

Chapter 5

1. "Begin Land-Buying in Lower Hill Area," *Courier*, March 24, 1956, 3; and Dan Fitzpatrick, "A Story of Renewal," *P-G*, May 21, 2000, C-3.

2. Harper, "'Crossroads of the World,'" 4; and Weber, *Don't Call Me Boss*, 270–75.

3. Dan Fitzpatrick, "The Story of Renewal," *P-G*, May 21, 2000, C-3.

4. Michael A. Fuoco, "Return to Glory," *P-G*, April 11, 1999, A-11. For more information on Lower Hill residents' anger, see Proctor, *Voices*, 33; and "Hill Office Open to Give Answers," *Courier*, April 14, 1956, 10.

5. Weber, *Don't Call Me Boss*, 271–73.

6. Ann (Sharpe) Haley, e-mail to author, February 9, 2015.

7. Pittsburgh Board of Public Education, *The Quest for Racial Equality in the Pittsburgh Public Schools* (Pittsburgh, 1965), 12.

8. Ibid.

9. Ibid., 7.

10. Robert C. Alberts, *Pitt: The Story of the University of Pittsburgh, 1787–1987* (Pittsburgh: University of Pittsburgh Press, 1986), 198–209, 262–70.

11. Official demographic data are unavailable, and these percentages represent yearbook audits of only graduating seniors; see *Journal*, 1950, 35–68; and *Journal*, 1964, 34–62.

12. "Enrollment at Low Ebb," *Triangle*, March 1, 1955; Schenley High School, *The History of Schenley High School* (Pittsburgh, [1963]), 1, William R. Oliver Special Collections Room, Carnegie Library of Pittsburgh; Stephanie Flom, interview by author, February 15, 2015; and "Enrollment Same in City Schools," *Press*, November 6, 1964, 12.

13. "Requests for School Transfers in Decline," *P-G*, April 3, 1964, 17.

14. "Youngster, Crippled Since Birth, Will Be 16; Takes First Steps," *News-Herald* (Franklin, PA), October 8, 1958, 8; and "Schenley Welcomes New Student," *Triangle*, November 28, 1956. The Upper Hill's Jean Green '53 was rarely able to leave her bed and thus never physically attended Schenley, but she "talked excitedly" about attending her commencement. Green passed away in April 1953, "a few days" after confirmation that she would graduate with Schenley's June class, and just hours before her father died of illness. Eight weeks later, Green's mother received her daughter's Schenley diploma in an emotional ceremony at Soldiers & Sailors Memorial Hall; see "Dead Girl's Diploma Presented to Mother," *P-G*, June 16, 1953, 17; and "Her Posthumous Diploma," *P-G*, April 24, 1953, 1.

15. "Helga Barcs, 'Fighter for Freedom,'" *Triangle*, February 1961.

16. "Israeli Student Enrolled in Schenley," *Triangle*, October 10, [1956]; "Native of Vienna Attends Schenley," *Triangle*, November 27, 1957; "Students from British Guiana," *Triangle*, February 1962; "Anthony Joins USA," *Triangle*, [November 1959]; "Puerto Rican, Student Learning Teaching Methods in 324," *Triangle*, September 30, 1957; and "Two Boys from Blind School Attend Schenley," *Triangle*, October 12, 1954.

17. Pittsburgh Board of Public Education, *Quest for Racial Equality*, 7.

18. Ralph Falbo, interview by author, April 28, 2014.

19. Sowell, interview.

20. AP, "Soldiers Integrate School," *P-G*, September 26, 1957, 1; *Journal*, 1958, 16.

21. *Journal*, 1951, 11; and *Journal*, 1952, 24; and *Journal*, 1958, 30.

22. Meg Sandridge, e-mail to author, January 31, 2015; and Meg Sandridge, e-mail to author, February 1, 2015.

23. Ibid.

24. Falbo, interview.

25. Leslie (Hill) Horne, survey, September 2, 2014; Richard Nicklos, interview by author, November 27, 2012.

26. "Reader Forum," *P-G*, June 11, 2008, accessed May 20, 2016.

27. Simon Noel, interview by author, July 14, 2014.

28. Proctor, *Voices from the Firing Line*, 123; and Ralph Proctor Jr., interview by author, December 15, 2015.

29. Ann (Sharpe) Haley, interview by author, February 3, 2015; and Meg Sandridge, e-mail to author, February 1, 2015.

30. Proctor, interview.

31. Proctor, "Racial Discrimination," 113.

32. Proctor, interview.

33. Proctor, "Racial Discrimination," 112–13.

34. Ibid., 113–15.

35. J. Gordon Hylton, "Before the Redskins Were the Redskins: The Use of Native

American Team Names in the Formative Era of American Sports, 1857–1933," *North Dakota Law Review* 86, no. 4 (2010): 890; "Schenley Is Easy Winner Over Peabody," *GT*, March 10, 1917, 8; "Peabody Girls Pass Schenley High in Race," *Post*, March 9, 1918, 8; Fred Landucci, "Powell Stars in City Title Grid Contest," *Press*, November 22, 1929, 1; James D. Van Trump, "The Church of the Ascension, Pittsburgh: A Brief Chronicle of Its Seventy-Five Years," *Western Pennsylvania Historical Magazine* 48, no. 1 (January 1965): 2; Fleming, *History of Pittsburgh*, 2:215–16; and Cliff J. Ryan, "High Schools Open Grid Season Today," *GT*, September 29, 1922, 13. Westinghouse abandoned their informal geographic moniker, Silver Lakers, for their current Bulldog mascot; see Paul Kurtz, "Playoff Benefit Game at Stadium Saturday—Westinghouse Favored to Beat Perry for City League Title," *Press*, November 8, 1944, 22. Leland D. Baldwin, *Pittsburgh: The Story of a City, 1950–1865* (Pittsburgh: University of Pittsburgh Press, 1995), 235; Edith Flom Schneider, interview by author, July 29, 2015; "*Triangle* to Poll Students for New Team Nickname," *Triangle*, May 7, 1945; "Here's Your Chance! Name the New Mascot," *Triangle*, October 27, 1953; Ralph Falbo, interview by author, April 28, 2014; and Proctor, interview.

36. Proctor, interview.

37. Glasco, "Double Burden," 416–17; Ralph Lemuel Hill, "A View of the Hill: A Study of Experiences and Attitudes in the Hill District of Pittsburgh, Pennsylvania from 1900 to 1973" (PhD diss., University of Pittsburgh, 1973), 27–28; and Andrew Buni, *Robert L. Vann of the 'Pittsburgh Courier': Politics and Black Journalism* (Pittsburgh: University of Pittsburgh Press, 1974), 32.

38. Hill, "A View of the Hill," 129–30.

39. Mary Thomas, "Photos at Exhibition," *P-G*, March 18, 2001, G-10.

40. Buni, *Robert L. Vann*, 32; Glasco, "Double Burden," 418; and Ervin Dyer, "The Sweet Life," *P-G*, July 17, 2005, E-8.

41. Proctor, interview.

42. Ann (Sharpe) Haley, e-mail to author, February 9, 2015; and Marvin Snowden, interview by author, July 24, 2015.

43. Proctor, interview.

44. Jeff Sewald, "What Do I Know?: Sala Udin," *Pittsburgh Quarterly*, Fall 2013, 18.

45. Sowell, interview.

46. 1958 Schenley graduate (name withheld by request), interview by author, August 29, 2015. The border between feeder districts was historically the Middle Hill's Kirkpatrick Street but was moved east in the 1980s for better racial balance at both Schenley and Brashear High, Fifth Avenue's successor; see Proctor, interview; and *Enter to Learn, Go Forth to Serve: The Story of Schenley High School (1916–2011)* (Pittsburgh: City of Pittsburgh Housing Authority, Creative Arts Corner), 2013, film.

47. Sowell, interview.

48. Sheldon Monsein, interview by author, January 3, 2015.

49. Bruno Sammartino, Bob Michelucci, and Paul McCollough, *Bruno Sammartino: An Autobiography of Wrestling's Living Legend* (Pittsburgh: Imagine, Inc., 1990), 17–19, 70.

50. Carol Dianne (Williams) Colbert, e-mail to author, August 15, 2014; Horne, survey; and Meg Sandridge, e-mail to author, January 31, 2015; and Janet I. Foster, e-mail to author, June 25, 2008. Enrollment fell 16.1 percent between 1950 and 1959; see Proctor, "Racial Discrimination," 113.

51. Arthur Hoppe, "Curriculum Developments," *Education Leadership* 18, no. 6 (March 1961): 391; Herbert Stein, "Advanced Courses at Schenley," *Pittsburgh Post-Gazette and Sun-Telegraph*, August 12, 1960, 19; and "Freshmen Again," *Triangle*, January 1960.

52. Carol Dianne (Williams) Colbert, e-mail to author, August 15, 2014; Horne, survey; Meg Sandridge, e-mail to author, January 31, 2015. Continuum was originally to be piloted at Allderdice High, but its directors ultimately chose Schenley for its heterogeneous student body and central location; see J. Steele Gow Jr., *Curriculum Development Through School and University Collaboration: The Pittsburgh Curriculum Continuity Demonstration* (Pittsburgh: Regional Commission on Educational Coordination and the Learning Research and Development Center, University of Pittsburgh, 1965), 14.

53. Charles Alan Roth, *The Changing Facilities of Pittsburgh High Schools from 1860 to 1960* (Research paper for Education 61, University of Pittsburgh, 1960), 5; Pittsburgh Board of Public Education, *Annual Report of the Superintendent, 1959–1960* (Pittsburgh, 1960).

54. "Social Living Class," *Triangle*, April 4, 1956; and "Social Living Class," *Triangle*, November 28, 1956.

55. "Mr. McCormick Observes Tenth Anniversary," *Triangle*, May 23, 1956; "Schenley's Loss Is Allderdice's Gain," *Triangle*, June 11, 1958; and "Dr. McMarland Resigns, Top Aide Gets Post," *P-G*, June 7, 1968, 1.

56. Gary Rotstein, "Virgil D. Cantini: Acclaimed Artist, Longtime Pitt Professor," *P-G*, May 5, 2009, A-9.

57. Falbo, interview; and UP, "Football Career Ends for Injured Cantini," *Daily Notes* (Canonsburg, PA), November 3, 1941, 8.

58. "Eureka Graduate Has Book on
School Problems, Critics," *The Pantagraph*
(Bloomington, IL), December 18, 1955, 14; and
PNS, "Percy B. Caley, 75, Dies at Mackinaw,"
The Pantagraph (Bloomington-Normal, IL),
January 26, 1972, A-5.

59. "Schenley's Loss, County's Gain,"
Triangle, February 1960; "Health Probe Urges
City to Change Setup," *P-G*, September 9,
1941, 8; "Speaker Traces Nation's Growth,"
Record-Argus (Greenville, PA), August 25, 1954,
3; and Anne Arden, "In Hosack School," *North
Hills (PA) News Record*, August 23, 1972, 8.

60. "The Faculty and Students Welcome New Teachers," *Triangle*, September 30,
1957; "Three Depart from Faculty," *Triangle*,
September 28, 1955; and "Former Teacher
Edits New Book," *Triangle*, [September 1958].

61. John Young, interview by author,
June 24, 2014; and Rebecca Lewis Smith,
survey, August 1, 2014.

62. Meg Sandridge, e-mail to author,
January 31, 2015.

63. "On Her Toes," *Triangle*, October
31, 1958; "Schenley Student to Tour Mexico,"
Triangle, May 3, 1955; and "Oakland Girl at
Case 1 of 10 with 1500 Men," *Press*, November
12, 1961, sec. 3, 12.

64. Meg Sandridge, survey, January 27,
2015.

65. "Batter-Up," *Triangle*, January 1964.

66. "Schenley Choir Performs on
WQED," *Triangle*, January 18, 1956; "Schenley
Students Participate in T.V.," *Triangle*, April 4,
[1956]; and "Schenley Saluted In WQED Program," *Triangle*, October 31, 1956.

67. Pat O'Neill, "Mrs. FDR Backs Bomb
Test Ban," *P-G*, October 19, 1956, 1.

68. "War on Polio Is Gaining," *P-G*,
June 7, 1950, 21. In 1954, Salk field tested a
polio vaccine at nearby Arsenal Elementary in
Lawrenceville; see "Polio Tests Are Started on
Our School Children Here," *P-G*, February 24,
1954, 1; and "Schenley Students Get Shot,"
Triangle, March 20, 1957.

69. Jack Hernon, "Robinson Not
Interested in Managers Job," *P-G*, December
11, 1954, 13; and Teenie Harris, "Bernard
McCormick, Brooklyn Dodgers baseball player
Jackie Robinson, and C. F. Kortner standing in
front of landscape painting in Schenley High
School," 1954, The Teenie Harris Archive, Carn-
egie Museum of Art, Pittsburgh, 2001.35.6581.

70. "'Big Break of 1953' Show in Pittsburgh Sept. 26," *Courier*, September 20, 1952,
19; and Rhonda Kubrick, "Eddie Fisher Visits
Schenley," *Triangle*, February 8, [1956].

71. Monte Buchsbaum, "Interview with
James Stewart," *Triangle*, April [1957]; "Bill
Haley Interviewed," *Triangle*, May 21, 1958;
"Reporters Interview Jimmy Dean," *Triangle*,

September 30, 1957; "Two Schenley Girls
Interview Richard Egan," *Triangle*, October 31,
1956; "*Triangle* Editor Interviews Dinah Shore,"
Triangle, February 1957; Joan Dickerson,
"Patty McCormick Interviewed," *Triangle*, April
1960; Jay Adlersberg and Bob Lavelle, "Eddie
Hodges Interviewed," *Triangle*, May 1960; and
"Miiko Taka Interviewed," *Triangle*, November
27, 1957.

72. Young, interview.

73. Joni Perri, e-mail to author, March 27,
2014; Joni Perri, interview by author, December 17, 2014, and Joni Perri, e-mail to author,
December 18, 2014.

74. Horne, survey.

Chapter 6

1. Thomas Sumpter, interview by author,
February 12, 2015.

2. Sumpter and Picciafoco were well
acquainted from their scholars courses, the
Triangle staff, and the baseball and volleyball
teams. See Sumpter, interview; and Gene
Picciafoco, interview by author, July 31, 2014.

3. Picciafoco, interview.

4. Jain Williams, survey, January 31,
2015; and AP, "Vandalism Erupts in Pittsburgh," *The Derrick* (Oil City, PA), April 6,
1968, 14.

5. Sylvia Jelks, e-mail to author, January 27,
2015.

6. "City Is Calm After 4 Nights of
Disorders," *P-G*, April 10, 1968, 1.

7. "Pittsburgh Hit by Gangs in Hill District," *P-G*, April 6, 1968, 1.

8. Denise (Fulton) Lamar, survey, January
28, 2015.

9. "City Is Calm After 4 Nights Of
Disorders," *P-G*, April 10, 1968, 1, 4; and
"Guard, State Troopers Sent in to Quell Hill
District Disorder," *P-G*, April 8, 1968, 1.

10. Joseph B. Browne, "Mayor's Task
Force Assigns Top Priority to Maintaining
Law," *P-G*, June 29, 1968, 5.

11. Wrenna Watson, interview by author,
March 23, 2015.

12. Sumpter, interview; Picciafoco, interview; and Denise (Fulton) Lamar, e-mail to
author, February 1, 2015.

13. The two-thirds approximation is based
on enrollment data from 1965 (65.8 percent
black) and 1969 (72.5 percent black), as this
investigation was unable to procure 1967–68
figures; see Pittsburgh Board of Public Education, *Quest for Racial Equality*, 12; Susan
Mannella, "Racial Mix of City Students Has
Changed Little," *P-G*, February 20, 1980, 2; and
Picciafoco, interview.

14. Saul Berliner, "Invading Gangs Force
Closing of 3 Schools," *P-G*, June 7, 1968, 1, 8;

and "Gang Attacks PAT Driver in Hill District," *P-G*, June 7, 1968, 1.

15. Between 1955 and 1965, Schenley lost approximately 357 white students, while its overall enrollment fell by only 22; see Pittsburgh Board of Public Education, *Quest for Racial Equality*, 12; "Enrollment at Low Ebb," *Triangle*, March 1, 1955; and "The 'Student' Explosion," *Triangle*, October 1965.

16. "Catholics Rap Diocese Delay on Integration," *P-G*, June 9, 1967, 19; and Bob Voelker (AP), "Two Priests Protest School Aid Campaign," *Indiana (PA) Gazette*, November 30, 1967, 4. John B. McDowell, an auxiliary bishop and superintendent of Catholic schools, stated a desire to retain whites but denied wanting to "sap white students" from Schenley; see "Bishop Denies Integration 'Lax,'" *Press*, June 13, 1967, 14.

17. R. F. Karlovitz, "Lawrenceville Is His 'Parish,'" *Press Roto*, April 23, 1972, 40.

18. Barbara Gubanic, "School Transfer Control Sought," *P-G*, October 7, 1982, 4; Carole Patton Smith, "It's 'Cool to Be Smart' Now at Schenley High School," *P-G*, February 15, 1988, 1; and Vincent Carr, e-mail to David Singer, June 17, 2016. The Hill District's Mary Myers, a future *Parade* basketball All-American, was one of many who transferred under the District's open enrollment policy, taking two buses each way to attend Allderdice; see "*P-G*'s Athlete of the Week," *P-G*, February 23, 1979, 10; Mike White, "Myers Makes Loud Noises," *P-G*, June 26, 1980, East 9; and Susan Mannella, "Racial Mix of City Students Has Changed Little," *P-G*, February 20, 1980, 2. Stephanie Flom, e-mail to author, June 17, 2016.

19. George Lies, "3 Black Principals Making Strides," *Press*, January 25, 1970, sec. 1, 2; and Pittsburgh Public Schools, *Membership Report as of October 1, 1979* (Pittsburgh, 1979), 10.

20. Hill, "A View of the Hill," 224–25; Watson, interview; and Douglas Smock, "Many Ask Busing to Transfer Schools," *P-G*, January 27, 1972, 7.

21. "The 'Student' Explosion," *Triangle*, October 1965; *Membership Report*, 1979, 10.

22. "Editorial: Manslaughter in the 'Jon,'" *Triangle*, December 1969; "Truth Column: A Need to Go," *Triangle*, [October 12, 1973]; Gabriel Mejail, interview by author, January 21, 2015; "Schenley High Fracas Holds 3," *Press*, October 3, 1969, 1; "Schenley High 'Alcohol' Hunted," *Press*, April 18, 1973, 13; "Give Up Graffiti," *Triangle*, [October 12, 1973]; and "Editorial: Stay in School," *Triangle*, March 1974.

23. "Fans in Fight, Halt Allderdice, Schenley Game," *P-G*, October 28, 1972, 1.

24. "Officials Blamed for Free-for-All Fight at Schenley Homecoming," *New Pittsburgh Courier*, November 4, 1972, 25.

25. Bob Wolfley, "Leaving MU was a Drama for Lucas," *Milwaukee Journal Sentinel*, November 3, 2010, accessed May 23, 2016, http://www.jsonline.com/blogs/sports/106646423.html; Trudy Tynan (AP), "Hawkins, Lanier, 7 Others Make Hall of Fame," *Advocate-Messenger* (Danville, KY), January 31, 1992, B6; and Carol (Gift) Sperandeo, interview by author, January 5, 2013.

26. Sperandeo, interview.

27. "Fire," *Triangle*, February 1967; and "Fire Damages Schenley High," *New Pittsburgh Courier*, April 22, 1967, 1.

28. "Third School Fire in 3 Weeks Hits Schenley," *New Pittsburgh Courier*, February 26, 1972, 33.

29. "College Acceptances," *Triangle*, [June 1972].

30. Carole Patton Smith, "City Test Scores Show Schenley Turnaround," *P-G*, August 28, 1987, 4.

31. Haley, interview.

32. In a feature in the *Triangle* on the 1975 basketball team, Carry Yates '75 and Jerry Hughes '77 criticized Schenley's quality of instruction; see "Team Viewpoints," *Triangle*, April 1975.

33. Pohla Smith (UPI), "Panther Wayne Williams's World Poetry in Motion," *Press*, January 27, 1978, B-7.

34. Michelle Terry, "Tighten Loose Ends," *Triangle*, May 1978.

35. Haley, interview.

36. Watson, interview.

37. "Editorial: Hear Our Plea," *Triangle*, October 1978; Marlene Gary Hogan, e-mail to author, February 6, 2015; and Jim Burwell, e-mail to author, October 30, 2014.

38. "Make Every Day Count," *Triangle*, October 1978; "Editorial: Hear Our Plea," *Triangle*, October 1978; and Jackie Collier, "Schenley and Peabody, Best of Two Worlds," *Triangle*, October 1979.

39. Sperandeo, interview; Mejail, interview; and Watson, interview.

40. Watson, interview.

41. Mallorie Michael, "Why Black Students Face Tough Road," *Triangle*, May 1978.

42. Young credited Schenley's Doris Douglas for his testing out of freshman English at Case Western Reserve University; see Greg C. Young, e-mail to author, August 14, 2014.

43. Mejail, interview.

44. Stanley Page, interview by author, August 18, 2014.

45. Michelle Terry, "Tighten Loose Ends," *Triangle*, May 1978.

46. Greg C. Young, e-mail to author, August 13, 2014; Watson, interview; Page, interview; and Sylvia Jelks, survey, January 24, 2015.

47. Mejail, interview.

48. "Obituaries: Virginia Musmanno Berardino," *P-G*, April 28, 2003, B-6; Thelma Lovette Morris, e-mail to author, January 31, 2015; Horne, survey; Nancy Primus Greene, survey, September 26, 2014; Williams, survey; and Jelks, survey.

49. For more information on Trumbull, see Jim Burwell, survey, October 4, 2014; Nancy Jarzynka Wood, survey, January 27, 2015; and Sharon Goode Ryan, survey, January 27, 2015. For more information on Berkebile, see Jeffrey Burton, e-mail to author, February 2, 2015; Judy Tornoff Duffy, survey, August 13, 2014; Greene, survey; Williams, survey; Meg Sandridge, e-mail to author, January 31, 2015; and Sharrieff Mustakeem (Howard Wood), survey, February 2, 2015. For more information on Waldman, see Watson, interview; Mejail, interview; Page, interview; "Asking for Criticism," *Press*, April 30, 1979, B-2; and Ginny Thornburgh, "Letter to the Editor: State Jobs Defended for Waldman, Wife," *Press*, May 20, 1979, B-6.

50. Susan Mannella, "City Schools Shuffling Principals," *P-G*, July 22, 1981, 2; and Patricia Curry Howard, survey, January 28, 2015.

51. Toki Schalk Johnson, "Mother, Daughter Say: Teaching Those Who Want to Learn Is Labor of Love . . . ," *Courier*, October 3, 1970, 12; "'Second Chance' School Headed by Lois Golden," *Courier*, October 30, 1965, 6; and "School Official Aids in Birth," *Press*, June 13, 1977, A-8.

52. Marylynne Pitz, "Ernestine Gloster Parks: Respected Civic Leader," *P-G*, January 5, 2004, B-6; Rochelle (Jackson) Landingham, e-mail to author, January 31, 2015; Marlene Gary Hogan, survey, January 28, 2015; and Gail Biggs Jackson, survey, January 29, 2015.

53. Linda Tardy Wilson, survey, January 28, 2015; Thelma Lovette Morris, survey, January 27, 2015; Marlene Gary Hogan, e-mail to author, February 6, 2015; Greg C. Young, survey, July 30, 2014; and Greg C. Young, e-mail to author, August 13, 2014.

54. Fred Lucas, interview by author, December 5, 2012. The block run was a 1,015-yard, mostly uphill, counterclockwise dash around the building's perimeter that all students were required to complete in under four minutes; see Fred Lucas, e-mail to author, April 27, 2015.

55. *Enter to Learn, Go Forth to Serve: The Story of Schenley High School (1916–2011)* (Pittsburgh: City of Pittsburgh Housing Authority, Creative Arts Corner, 2013), film.

56. Darrick Suber, interview by author, January 15, 2015.

57. Mike White, "Schenley Shines for City," *P-G*, May 8, 1993, D-3; *Journal*, 1977, 98–99; and Fred Lucas, e-mail to author, April 27, 2015.

58. Watson, interview; Jojo Dixon, "Pledge of Blackness," *Triangle*, May 1976; J. Collier, "Poetry Corner: To My Black Man," *Triangle*, April 1978; Michelle Williams, "Black Features: Naturally Be Natural," *Triangle*, December 1969; and C. Barkley, "Roots," *Triangle*, March 1977.

59. *Journal*, 1969, 10–40; *Journal*, 1978, 31–58; Mejail interview; Watson, interview; and Young, interview.

60. Mejail, interview.

61. The seven schools included Oliver, Allegheny, Perry, Langley, Allderdice, South Hills, and Carrick; see Jack Ryan, "City Police Sent to Keep Order at Oliver High," *P-G*, November 3, 1967, 1; "Students Warned on Disorders," *P-G*, September 24, 1969, 1; Vince Gagetta, "City Police Patrol Perry High Halls, Students Peaceful," *P-G*, September 17, 1970, 29; Vince Gagetta, "Students at Langley 'Talk It Out,'" *P-G*, January 28, 1971, 25; and Vince Gagetta, "Police Ordered to Carrick High in Race Clashes," *P-G*, April 3, 1971, 13.

62. Mejail, interview; and Richard Goldstein, "Maurice Lucas, 58, N.B.A. Star, Dies," *New York Times*, November 2, 2010, A29.

63. Page, interview.

64. Greg C. Young, e-mail to author, August 13, 2014.

65. Snowden, interview.

66. Linda Leffakis, interview by author, March 5, 2016.

67. Jim Burwell, e-mail to author, October 30, 2014; Mejail, interview; and Roberta (Thompson) Woods, survey, January 27, 2015.

68. Greene, survey; Wilson, survey; and Hogan, survey.

69. Picciafoco, interview.

70. Page, interview.

71. Fred Lucas referenced a widely held belief that Mrs. Parks preferred light-skinned girls to be cheerleaders (interview). Wrenna Watson '72 dismissed this, and cited two specific "brown-skinned" cheerleaders from the mid-1960s. However, "[the brown-skinned cheerleaders] still all lived up in the Schenley Heights area. None of them lived past Herron Avenue. That I knew of" (interview).

72. Watson, interview.

73. "Reader Forum," *P-G*, June 11, 2008, accessed May 20, 2016.

74. For a comprehensive list of championships and season-by-season results, see appendix C. Schenley lost to Westinghouse on February 5, 1965, but did not lose another regular season league game until February 11, 1969; see Marino Parascenzo, "Bulldogs Stun Unbeaten Schenley, 78–71," *P-G*, February 6, 1965, 11; and UPI, "Schenley's Win Streak Ends at 61 Straight," *Daily Republican* (Monongahela, PA), February 12, 1969, 10.

75. Peter Oresick, interview by author, February 16, 2015; C. V. Burns, "Sports Slants," *Cumberland (MD) News*, December 7, 1966, 34; and Mario Parascenzo, "Schenley Tops Fifth Ave. in City Thriller," *P-G*, January 31, 1965, 11.

76. For more information on Schenley's collegiate and professional basketball alumni, see appendix C.

77. Snowden, interview.

78. Lamar, survey; Wood, survey.

79. "Reader Forum," *P-G*, June 11, 2008, accessed May 20, 2016.

80. Noel, interview.

81. "A Star is Born," *Triangle*, February 1977; and A. Bradberry, "A Star is Born," *Triangle*, November 1976.

82. "Schenleyesque," *Triangle*, April 1975; and Joe Bennett, "Pittsburgh's Champs Go for All the Marbles," *Press* Roto, March 9, 1975, 12–13.

83. Roy McHugh, "Press Box: High Noon at Schenley High," *Press*, May 17, 1970, sec. 4, 2.

84. Picciafoco, interview; Meg Sandridge, e-mail to author, May 12, 2016; Ilene (Flom) Singer, e-mail to author, May 13, 2016; and Jim Burwell, e-mail to author, October 30, 2014.

85. Jim Burwell, e-mail to author, October 30, 2014; and Andra Powell, survey, July 30, 2014.

86. Jackie Collier, "Schenley and Peabody, Best of Two Worlds," *Triangle*, October 1979.

87. Peabody was 43.8 percent black in 1976–77; see Pittsburgh Public Schools, *Membership Report as of October 4, 1976* (Pittsburgh, 1976), 9. For more information on the East End's 1970s demographic shift, see Department of City Planning, *1990 Census of Population*; David Guo, "City's Urban Renewal Areas Lose Most in Population," *P-G*, July 10, 1980, 3; Mike Bucsko, "Crime Trial's Roots Started in East Liberty," *P-G*, November 5, 1990, 1; and R. LaMont Jones Jr., "Kingsley House at 100 a Survivor of Struggle and Change," *P-G*, September 7, 1993, D-1. For more information on the East End's middle-class neighborhoods, see "City Social, Economic Character Detailed," *Press*,

February 14, 1975, 2; and James N. Crutchfield, "Tokenism Is Trademark of Blacks in Quest for Greener Real Estate," *P-G*, August 6, 1973, 19.

Chapter 7

1. Jack Dougherty, "Northern Desegregation and the Racial Politics of Magnet Schools in Milwaukee, Wisconsin," in *With All Deliberate Speed: Implementing* Brown v. Board of Education, ed. Brian J. Daugherity and Charles C. Bolton (Fayetteville: University of Arkansas Press, 2008), 219.

2. Pittsburgh Board of Public Education, *Quest for Racial Equality*, 36.

3. Isadore Shrensky, "'Speedy' Is Slow in School Mixing," *Press*, July 28, 1968, sec. 1, 20; and Marcella DeMarco, "Magnet Programs in the Pittsburgh Schools: Development to Implementation, 1977 through 1982" (PhD diss., University of Pittsburgh, 1983), 75.

4. William Dodge Rutherford, "The 'Unraveling': Resistance to Desegregation in the Pittsburgh Public Schools, 1971–1998" (BA thesis, Tufts University, 2014), 13; and Gerald Grant, "Pittsburgh Plan Boldly Attacks Massive School Problems," *The Blade* (Toledo, OH), May 14, 1967, B-2.

5. Jack Hillwig, "City Drops 'Impractical' Great High Schools," *Press*, June 24, 1970, 2; and Isadore Shrensky, "'Speedy' Is Slow In School Mixing," *Press*, July 28, 1968, sec. 1, 20.

6. Trotter and Day, *Race and Renaissance*, 100.

7. Rutherford, "The 'Unraveling,'" 6n4.

8. Joyce Gemperlein, "City Plans to Renovate, Integrate Schools," *P-G*, September 9, 1975, 1.

9. Rutherford, "The 'Unraveling,'" 16–19, 39–40; and *Pennsylvania Human Relations Commission v. School District of Philadelphia*, et al., 390 A.d 1238 (Pa. 1978).

10. Rutherford, "The 'Unraveling,'" 67–78.

11. Douglas Smock, "Plan Punishes Blacks, Says Mrs. McNairy," *P-G*, February 21, 1973, 1; Ron Suber, "E. End and Hill Schools Remain Black Under Citywide Plan," *New Pittsburgh Courier*, September 27, 1975, 8; and Rutherford, "The 'Unraveling,'" 23–24, 45–46.

12. Rutherford, "The 'Unraveling,'" 17–18, 24–30, 32–33, 36–38, 41, 77, 81. East End elementary schools "appeared to be unaffected" by a 1980 boycott; see Susan Mannella, "Busing Boycott Skyrockets Absenteeism," *P-G*, February 7, 1980, 1–2; and Pittsburgh Public Schools, *Membership Report, 1979*, 10.

13. Beth Dunlop, "City Relations Panel Calls Pete's Busing Stand Divisive," *Press*, December 8, 1972, 2; and Sherley Uhl, "Clean Sweep for Re-Pete," *Press*, May 16, 1973, 1.

14. David Nilsson, "Boards Oks Brashear Plan, Fifth, Gladstone Closings," *Press*, December 24, 1975, 1; Thomas P. Benic, "Touring Student Leaders Take to Brashear High," *P-G*, June 4, 1976, 11; Pittsburgh Public Schools, *Membership Report, 1976*, 9; and Richard Arnold, "Guns, Knives Found at Brashear," *Press*, March 17, 1978, A-1, A-4.

15. Young, interview; Rutherford, "The 'Unraveling,'" 24; Robert A. Oberlin letter to Brookline Elementary School parents, February 28, 1967, Detre Library & Archives, Heinz History Center; and Jack Tager, *Boston Riots: Three Centuries of Violence* (Boston: Northeastern University Press, 2001), 209–27.

16. Jerry Byrd, "Carrick Parents' Warning: Don't Bus Our Kids," *Press*, March 15, 1979, A-2. The nine schools were Oliver, Gladstone, Allegheny, Perry, Langley, South Hills, Alldderdice, Carrick, and Brashear; see Jack Ryan, "City Police Sent to Keep Order at Oliver High," *P-G*, November 3, 1967, 1; "Police Curb Flareups at 2 High Schools," *P-G*, October 10, 1968, 1; "Students Warned on Disorders," *P-G*, September 24, 1969, 1; Vince Gagetta, "City Police Patrol Perry High Halls, Students Peaceful," *P-G*, September 17, 1970, 29; Vince Gagetta, "Students at Langley 'Talk It Out,'" *P-G*, January 28, 1971, 25; Vince Gagetta, "Police Ordered to Carrick High in Race Clashes," *P-G*, April 3, 1971, 13; and Richard Arnold, "Guns, Knives Found at Brashear," *Press*, March 17, 1978, A-1.

17. Vince Gagetta, "Police Ordered to Carrick High in Race Clashes," *P-G*, April 3, 1971, 13; and Rutherford, "The 'Unraveling,'" 24.

18. David Nilsson, "Black Close-Carrick Plea Fails," *Press*, April 6, 1971, 4.

19. Rutherford, "The 'Unraveling,'" 16.

20. Ibid., 64–67.

21. Thomas P. Benic, "Olson Desegregation Proposal: Schools' Voluntary Enrollment," *P-G*, May 11, 1977, 1; and DeMarco, "Magnet Programs in the Pittsburgh Schools," 22–24.

22. DeMarco, "Magnet Programs in the Pittsburgh Schools," 120.

23. Thomas P. Benic, "Olson Desegregation Proposal: Schools' Voluntary Enrollment," *P-G*, May 11, 1977, 2; and Rutherford, "The 'Unraveling,'" 71.

24. A Lawrenceville resident and retired truck driver, Widina once declared "the Supreme Court is wrong" on desegregation, derisively likened the Catholic diocese to Communists, and said that a proposed sex education curriculum—which he admittedly had not read—would "turn our classrooms into sex schools"; see Susan Mannella, "Widina Predicts Landslide Win in School Board Primary," *P-G*, April 19, 1979, 2; David Nilsson, "Board Member Blasts Sale of City School to Diocese," *Press*, April 28, 1977, A-16; and Caren Marcus, "City Parents Fume Over Sex Education," *Press*, February 16, 1982, A-2. John Golightly, "City Board Sets Poll on Magnet Schools," *P-G*, November 23, 1977, 2.

25. Susan Mannella, "Widina Predicts Landslide Win in School Board Primary," *P-G*, April 19, 1979, 2; and Rutherford, "The 'Unraveling,'" 64.

26. Rutherford, "The 'Unraveling,'" 73–77; and Susan Mannella, "School Board Trims Desegregation Plan," *P-G*, March 22, 1979, 1–2.

27. Caren Marcus, "Stunned Olson Proud of Accomplishments," *Press*, March 27, 1980, A-1, A-4; *Membership Report, 1979*, 3–4.

28. Richard C. Wallace Jr., interview by author, June 7, 2014.

29. David Guo, "City Selects Mass. Educator as School Chief," *P-G*, August 7, 1980, 1, 5.

30. Wallace, interview.

31. Susan Mannella, "City's New School Chief Wins Board Approval, 8–1," *P-G*, August 28, 1980, 3; Wallace, interview; and Caren Marcus, "Al Fondy: His Teachers Are Pioneers," *Press*, September 6, 1981, Roto 9.

32. Wallace, interview.

33. DeMarco, "Magnet Programs in the Pittsburgh Schools," 146, 247–48; and Susan Manella, "5,100 Students Apply for 'Magnet' Programs," *P-G*, May 3, 1980, 2.

34. DeMarco, "Magnet Programs in the Pittsburgh Schools," 138–39, 145; and Michelle Broadus, e-mail to author, March 18, 2016.

35. Michelle Broadus, e-mail to author, March 18, 2016; Eleanor Chute, "Schenley's New Magnet Programs Outlined," *Press*, December 6, 1982, A-3; and Pittsburgh Public Schools, *Membership Report as of September 27, 1982* (Pittsburgh, 1982), 7.

36. Young, interview; and "Editorial: New Spirit of Schenley," *Triangle*, October 1979. Some discipline problems persisted. In 1981, Charles Stitt '84 told the *Post-Gazette*, "I really don't like Schenley that much. There's like four clowns in every class I have. I can't get nothing done"; see David Guo, "City's Housing Projects: A Place to Call Home," *P-G*, June 15, 1981, 7.

37. Young, interview.

38. Schenley High School, graduation program, June 1980.

39. Young, interview; and Diane Thompson, interview by author, June 30, 2014.

40. Thompson, interview.

41. "Editorial: All Eyes on Reizenstein," *P-G*, January 6, 1976, 6. In Thompson's sixth grade year, 1978–79, Reizenstein was 69.2 percent black and 30.8 percent "other"; see

Pittsburgh Public Schools, *Membership Report, 1979,* 10: David Nilsson, "How City School Panel Plans Racial Balance," *Press,* October 29, 1972, A-19; David Nilsson, "1,000 Seeking Entry at Reizenstein School," *Press,* January 11, 1975, 2; and D. Thompson, interview.

42. D. Thompson, interview; and Pittsburgh Public Schools, *Membership Report, 1979,* 10.

43. D. Thompson, interview.

44. *Pennsylvania Human Relations Commission v. Board of Public Education of the School District of Pittsburgh,* 444 A.2d 792, 795–97 (Cmwlth. Ct. 1982).

45. The merger proposal apparently entailed "closing South and combining it with Schenley"; see ibid.

46. Al Donalson, "5-District Merger Court's Solution for Gen. Braddock," *Press,* April 28, 1981, A-1; and Eleanor Chute, "Woodland Hills Aces Court Test," *P-G,* July 27, 2000, A-3.

47. *Pennsylvania Human Relations Commission v. Board of Public Education of the School District of Pittsburgh,* 444 A.2d 792, 793, 795 (Cmwlth. Ct. 1982).

48. Eleanor Chute, "For Fifth Year, City Schools' Dropout Rate Falls," *Press,* August 27, 1984, A2.

49. Wallace, interview.

50. Ibid.

51. Ibid.

52. Ibid.; and Barbara Gubanic, "Remedial Program Is Trimmed," *P-G,* July 22, 1982, 8.

53. Wallace, interview.

54. Young, interview.

55. Carol Dyas, interview by author, December 5, 2012; and Wallace, interview.

56. Wallace, interview.

57. Carr led South, South Hills, Westinghouse, and Peabody; see "Teachers Face Transfer, Layoff or Demotion by Board," *P-G,* June 27, 1980, 8; Caren Marcus, "City Schools Map Wide Reforms," *Press,* July 22, 1981, A-10; Eleanor Chute, "Board Names City School Principals," *Press,* July 17, 1986, B6; and "Board Appoints Principals for Three Schools," *P-G,* May 27, 1988, 8. Vincent Carr, e-mail to author, February 24, 2016.

58. Wallace, interview.

59. Dyas, interview, December 5, 2012.

60. Neretta (Troxell) Brobst, interview by author, January 28, 2013.

61. Sperandeo, interview; and Haley, interview.

62. Haley, interview; Eleanor Chute, "Schenley Teacher Center Staffed," *Press,* April 28, 1983, A-14.

63. Sperandeo, interview.

64. Young, interview.

65. Brobst, interview.

66. Sperandeo, interview; and Carol (Gift) Sperandeo, e-mail to author, February 24, 2015.

67. Haley, interview.

68. Alexander Duncan Campbell Peterson, *Schools Across Frontiers: The Story of the International Baccalaureate and the United World Colleges* (Peru, IL: Open Court, 2003), 9, 29, 85, 153–60, 181; Wallace, interview; Eleanor Chute, "Magnets Attract," *P-G,* January 14, 1984, B1; Jackie Perhach, "Letters to the Editor: Matching Students to Jobs," *P-G,* March 22, 1997, A-6; Jackie Perhach, "Letters: Schenley Proud," *Press,* December 3, 1988, B2; Gabriel Ireton, "Principal Joins Own Line at Magnet School," *P-G,* November 3, 1984, 4; and Table on Schenley Magnet Recruitment as of March 28, 1984.

69. Eleanor Chute, "Schenley Adds Magnet Courses," *Press,* September 15, 1982, A-2.

70. Brobst, interview.

71. Rutherford, "The 'Unraveling,'" 86.

72. Barbara Gubanic, "Schenley Magnet Proposal Criticized," *P-G,* September 30, 1982, 4; and Brobst, interview.

73. Rutherford, "The 'Unraveling,'" 86.

74. Eleanor Chute, "Schenley Adds Magnet Courses," *Press,* September 15, 1982, A-2; and Eleanor Chute, "City School Desegregation OK'd," *Press,* November 19, 1982, A-20.

75. Eleanor Chute, "City School Desegregation OK'd," *Press,* November 19, 1982, A-1. In December 1982, the PHRC agreed that Schenley would have until the fall of 1984 to meets its goals; see "Human Relations Panel Approves City School Plan," *Press,* December 21, 1982, A-8.

76. Eleanor Chute, "Magnets Attract," *P-G,* January 14, 1984, B1; and Mary Ellen Kirby, interview by author, March 27, 2013.

Chapter 8

The epigraph to this chapter is drawn from Cristina Rouvalis, "High Grades," *P-G,* April 16, 1988, 7.

1. Jason Brown, interview by author, July 24, 2014.

2. Dawn (Gust) Vero, e-mail to author, August 13, 2014.

3. Leah Wahrhaftig, interview by author, June 10, 2014; and Leah Wahrhaftig, e-mail to author, June 11, 2014.

4. Andrea Boykowyzc, interview by author, June 19, 2014.

5. Mary Ellen Kirby, e-mail to author, June 18, 2014.

6. Kirby, interview.

7. Brobst, interview.

8. Eleanor Chute, "She Works to Get Black-White Balance in City Schools," *Press*, September 16, 1985, B1; and Jackie Perhach, "Letters to the Editor: Matching Students to Jobs," *P-G*, March 22, 1997, A-6.

9. Young, interview.

10. Jane Perlez, "New York's Schools: Profiles of Chancellor Finalists," *New York Times*, December 28, 1987, B4; David Treadwell, "Urban Pittsburgh Schools at Head of Their Class," *Los Angeles Times*, September 22, 1990, accessed May 26, 2016, http://articles.latimes.com/1990-09-22/news/mn-633_1_school-districts; Keith Henderson, "New Life for Pittsburgh's Schenley High," *Christian Science Monitor*, January 13, 1986, accessed May 26, 2016, http://www.csmonitor.com/1986/0113/dpitt2.html; and Debra Hughes, "A Threatened Pittsburgh School Becomes a Center for Renewal," *Education Week*, December 1, 1982, accessed May 26, 2016, http://www.edweek.org/ew/articles/1982/12/01/02160026.h02.html.

11. AP, "Pittsburgh Teachers 'Rejuvenated,'" *Indiana (PA) Gazette*, May 29, 1984, 16.

12. Eleanor Chute, "City Teacher Center May Lure Suburbs," *Press*, October 18, 1984, B8.

13. Language proficiency and rankings refer to District-wide California Achievement Test (CAT) data; see Carole Patton Smith, "City Test Scores Show Schenley Turnaround," *P-G*, August 28, 1987, 4.

14. Schenley High School, graduation program, June 1980; and Normandie Fulson, "Principal's Message," *Triangle*, June, 1993. For more information on graduates' college placements, see Bill Mitchell, interview by author, February 29, 2016; Dan Donovan, "Showing Up," *Press*, September 11, 1989, A2; and Hope Kleman, "Top Ten Spartans," *Triangle*, June 1990.

15. Rachel Pottinger, e-mail to author, February 1, 2015.

16. "Schenley's Stars Earn Top Awards," *Triangle*, October 1987.

17. Eleanor Chute, "Bennett: Bar Contraceptives in Schools," *Press*, June 10, 1986, B5; and David Tinker, survey, July 30, 2014.

18. "Schenley Ranks Among the Elite," *Triangle*, December 1987.

19. Jason Adams, "Mrs. Jatkowski Receives Outstanding Honor," *Triangle*, November 1986.

20. Barbara Gubanic, "New Magnet Plan for Schenley High Disputed by Board," *P-G*, September 16, 1982, 4; and Eleanor Chute, "City Magnet School Solution Signup a 5-Day Vigil," *Press*, October 24, 1985, A2.

21. Tara Bradley-Steck (AP), "The 'Exclusive' Public Schools," *Journal-News* (Rockland County, NY), February 22, 1987, B7; and Carole Patton Smith, "First Magnet Lottery Held at Three Schools," *P-G*, October 23, 1987, 4.

22. Karla (White) Payne, e-mail to author, August 18, 2014; Tynesha (Hayes) Frazier, survey, January 27, 2015; Jeff Evans, survey, July 30, 2014; and Carl Vero, e-mail to author, September 5, 2014.

23. Schenley had 814 students when the Teacher Center opened in September 1983, and 1,265 students by September 1993; see Pittsburgh Public Schools, *Membership Report as of September 28, 1983* (Pittsburgh, 1983), 7; and Pittsburgh Public Schools, *Membership Report as of October 5, 1993* (Pittsburgh, 1993), 13.

24. Carol Dyas, interview by author, August 16, 2015.

25. Pittsburgh Public Schools, *Membership Report as of October 3, 2001* (Pittsburgh, 2001), 13; Pittsburgh Public Schools, *Membership Report, 1982*, 7; and Pittsburgh Public Schools, *Membership Report as of October 2, 1990* (Pittsburgh, 1990), 12.

26. *Enter to Learn, Go Forth to Serve: The Story of Schenley High School (1916–2011)* (Pittsburgh: City of Pittsburgh Housing Authority, Creative Arts Corner, 2013), film; *Pennsylvania Human Relations Commission v. Board of Public Education of the School District of Pittsburgh*, 444 A.2d 792, 795 (Cmwlth. Ct. 1982); and Jim Gallagher, "5 Schools to Start New Tots' Classes," *P-G*, July 18, 1985, 14.

27. Wallace, interview; and Susan Mannella, "Magnets: Parents Wait for Hours to Enroll Children in Special Schools," *P-G*, November 10, 1981, 5.

28. Eleanor Chute, "Officials to Seek 1989 Deadline to Desegregate Schenley High," *Press*, February 20, 1985, B5; and Barbara Gubanic, "School Cutback Plan May Halve 4-Mill Hike," *P-G*, December 9, 1982, 4.

29. Esther Wahrhaftig, interview by author, July 1, 2014.

30. Kirby, interview.

31. G. Ryin Gaines, e-mail to author, January 28, 2015.

32. E. Wahrhaftig, interview.

33. Allison Render and James Howard, "Schenley Welcomes New Teachers," *Triangle*, December 1984. Despite his credentials, Dilts was memorable for nurturing trepidatious math students; see Brown, interview.

34. Michael A. Fuoco, "Leonard Kubiak Sr.: Peabody Principal Cared for Students, Staff," *P-G*, April 11, 2013, C-3; and L. Wahrhaftig, interview. Kubiak won the Spectroscopy Society's science teaching award in 1984; see Manuel R. Miller and David Pensenstadler, *Keivin Burns Award for Excellence in Science Teaching, Final Report 2014* (Pittsburgh:

Spectroscopy Society of Pittsburgh, 2014). Andrea Boykowycz '89 called Kubiak a mix of "Christianity" and "pyramid-and-crystal astrology," "but by God you learned your chemistry in her class"; see Andrea Boykowycz, survey, July 31, 2014.

35. "McFarland Among 1992 Pa. Teacher Finalists," *Triangle*, December 1991; Jerry Sharpe, "Standing Out: Schenley Freshmen Win with Home Models," *Press*, May 11, 1992, A2; and "Congratulations State Coordinator," *Triangle*, March 1991.

36. Paul McKrell, text message to author, May 26, 2016; Dawn (Gust) Vero, survey, July 30, 2014; Krista Vitanza Borso, survey, January 27, 2015; Matt Rahuba, survey, August 14, 2014.

37. Boykowycz, survey; and Mitchell, interview.

38. Vero, survey; Elizabeth Haney, survey, July 31, 2014; Michelle Allersma, survey, July 21, 2014; Rebecca Hromiko, survey, August 14, 2014; and David Kirk, survey, July 31, 2014. Jason Brown '89, who scored a perfect seven on his art IB exam, credited the trio with his success (interview).

39. Alexandra McInnes, e-mail to author, April 30, 2015; Scott Connelly, survey, July 30, 2014; Joyce Stiffler, survey, July 30, 2014; Kathryn (Takacs) Whigham, survey, July 31, 2014; and Larry Smith, survey, July 31, 2014.

40. Arts Propel was a District-wide program, and Schenley was one of three schools specifically mentioned in *Newsweek*; see Farai Chideya, "Surely for the Spirit, but also for the Mind," *Newsweek*, December 2, 1991, 61; and Barbara Kantrowitz and Pat Wingert, "The Best Schools in the World," *Newsweek*, December 2, 1991, 50–52.

41. Donald Miller, "School Mural Draws on Students, Experts," *P-G*, April 23, 1984, 21.

42. Haley, interview.

43. Brobst, interview.

44. "[Dyas] was the glue of that school"; see Brown, interview.

45. Missy (Kaefer) Stokes, survey, July 30, 2014.

46. Samba Johnson, interview by author, October 23, 2014; Keshona (Turner) Beasley, survey, January 27, 2015; and Flojaune Griffin, survey, January 29, 2015.

47. Dyas, interview, December 5, 2012. "Spartan Spirit" was appropriated from "Funky Chicken," a children's camp standard; see Bo Shoemaker, *A History of Camp Cory* (Charleston, SC: History Press, 2011), 132.

48. Carole Patton Smith, "City Test Scores Show Schenley Turnaround," *P-G*, August 28, 1987, 4; and Carole Patton Smith,

"It's 'Cool to Be Smart' Now at Schenley High School," *P-G*, February 15, 1988, 1, 4.

49. Young, interview.

50. Mitchell, interview.

51. Brobst, interview.

52. Ibid.

53. Eleanor Chute, "Wallace Explains How Test Score Gap Can Be Closed More," *Press*, November 16, 1985, C3; and Robert Nicklos, memo to Mary Ellen Kirby, "Re: International Studies Lottery," December 14, 1995.

54. Carole Patton Smith, "It's 'Cool to Be Smart' Now at Schenley High School," *P-G*, February 15, 1988, 4.

55. Young, interview; and Haley, interview.

56. Haley, interview; and Nicole Allison, "Classics Enter Third Year," *Triangle*, October 1990.

57. "We started looping. . . . Everybody patterned off of Schenley. We never got the recognition that we should have"; see Haley, interview.

58. Lisa Lighty, "Senior Spartan Classics Story," essay collection, 1996.

59. Haley, interview.

60. Ibid.

61. R. Daniel Lavelle, interview by author, August 1, 2014; Griffin, survey; and Janine Jelks-Seale, interview by author, January 29, 2015.

62. Haley, interview; and Dyas, interview, December 5, 2012.

63. Lisa Lighty, "Senior Spartan Classics Story," essay collection, 1996.

64. Tom Podgorski, "Senior Farewell," essay collection, 1996. "It was more like a family because you built familiarity over a long time"; see Dyas, interview, December 5, 2012.

65. Haley, interview.

66. "Keep Program, Schenley Students Ask Board," *P-G*, April 19, 1994, C-4; and Haley, interview.

67. Rahuba, survey.

68. Dawn (Gust) Vero, e-mail to author, August 13, 2014.

69. Brown, interview.

70. Samba Johnson '91, who spent summers playing basketball at the Ozanam Center, said, "Everybody you came in contact with felt the same pride about Schenley" (interview).

71. Jack Higgins, interview by author, May 19, 2016.

72. Suber, interview.

73. "There was no crossover in the classrooms"; see Boykowycz, interview.

74. L. Wahrhaftig, interview.

75. Brown, interview. Andrea Boykowycz '89 described being treated better than other students, including tacit permission for organized cutting to study at Hillman Library or on the

floor outside the principal's office (interview). Michelle Allersma, e-mail to author, September 12, 2014.

76. Tracey Kroner, e-mail to author, September 24, 2014.

77. Young, interview.

78. Brown, interview.

79. Tina Calabro, "Reformed Schools," *In Pittsburgh*, June 21–June 27, 1989, 8.

80. Nonblack student council presidents were Diane Thompson '85, Heidi Abdelhady '88, and Kristen Winfield '92; see D. Thompson, interview; "Meet Student Government," *Triangle*, December 1987; and Dave Smith, "Meet Student Government Officers," *Triangle*, October 1990. The interracial homecoming king and queen were Ralph Stone '87 and Annette Chatman '87, respectively; see *Journal*, 1986, 59.

81. Xiaowei (Gao) Nguyen, survey, July 30, 2014.

82. E. Wahrhaftig, interview.

83. "Register of the Theodore A. Viehman Papers, 1910–1961," Finding Aid at the Wisconsin Historical Society, Library-Archives Division, accessed June 16, 2016, http://digicoll.library.wisc.edu/cgi/f/findaid/findaid-idx?c=wiarchives;view=reslist;subview=standard;didno=uw-whs-us0196an; "Mr. Chester Story Retires from Schenley Faculty," *Triangle*, June 6, 1947; and Mark Allen, "Tradition Continues," *Triangle*, May 1978. Class plays appeared to cease after *Headen for Eden* in 1951, as Principal Bernard J. McCormick felt operettas allowed more students to participate; see "Mr. McCormick Observes Tenth Anniversary," *Triangle*, May 23, 1956; and Marylynne Pitz, "Final Curtain Call," *P-G*, April 26, 2006, C-2. "Most of the kids that were in [*Five on the Black Hand Side*] were really corny," but the casting of the popular Denise Allen Bey '72 ensured that "all the cool kids went to see it"; see Watson, interview. Suber, interview; *Enter to Learn, Go Forth to Serve: The Story of Schenley High School* (Pittsburgh: City of Pittsburgh Housing Authority, Creative Arts Corner, 2013), film; Jeffrey Burton, e-mail to author, February 2, 2015; Diane R. Powell, "Babusci: Image Lift for Schenley H.S.," *New Pittsburgh Courier*, December 18, 1982, A-3; Christopher Rawson, "In the Wings," *P-G*, April 24, 2008, W-16; David Oresick, e-mail to author, May 27, 2016; Derek Steele, interview by author, September 2, 2014; Cooper Miller, interview by author, September 18, 2014; L. Wahrhaftig, interview; and G. Ryin Gaines, e-mail to author, January 28, 2015. For more information on Schenley's history at the Gene Kelly Awards, see appendix D. Teressa LaGamba, e-mail to author, September 16, 2014; Kelly McKrell, e-mail to author, February 1, 2015;

Greg Galuska, e-mail to author, October 29, 2014; and Casey McDermott, "Award Winning Kelly Critic Review: 'All Shook Up,' Schenley, April 24–May 3," *P-G*, May 5, 2008, accessed May 27, 2016, http://www.post-gazette.com/ae/high-school-musicals/2008/05/05/Award-winning-Kelly-Critic-review-All-Shook-Up-Schenley-April-24-May-3/stories/200805050243.

84. *Journal*, 1985, 93; Richard C. Wallace memo to Mary Ellen Kirby, "Re: Retention of White/Other Recruits for Schenley Magnets," August 29, 1984; and Linda Wu, "ESL—Schenley's Melting Pot," *Triangle*, December 1990.

85. Ly Hong, "My Parents Are My Heroes," *Triangle*, February 1990.

86. Sharice Smalls, "Learning to Cope in a Painted World," *Triangle*, December 1987.

87. "'Fame' Comes to Schenley High Program," *North Hills (PA) News Record*, August 8, 1986, 10; and Kristin (Hare) Hasty, e-mail to author, September 4, 2014.

88. Eva Trapp, interview by author, January 29, 2015.

89. Betsy Kline, "Ballet, Schenley High Cooperative Effort off to Energetic Start," *Press*, August 26, 1986, B5.

90. Richard Ward, "Student of the Month," *Triangle*, October 1986.

91. *Youth Summer Intensive 2013* (Denver: Denver Ballet Theatre Academy, 2013), brochure; Jerry Vondas, "Ballet's Schenley Program Opens Some Doors," *Press*, September 13, 1988, B7; Kathy Valin, "Dance Review: DeLeone, Ballet Go Together Like Peas in a Pod," *Cincinnati Enquirer*, May 3, 2004, D7; and Jack Anderson, "Happy Birthday, Miami City Ballet," *New York Times*, October 17, 1995, C13.

92. Jerry Vondas, "Ballet's Schenley Program Opens Some Doors," *Press*, September 13, 1988, B7.

93. National Register of Historic Places, Schenley High School, Pittsburgh, Allegheny County, PA, National Register #86002706.

94. Toni Brooks, "New Gym Opens in October," *Triangle*, October 1986; and William "Arnie" Powell, "New Gym Finally Underway," *Triangle*, October 1985.

95. Allersma, survey; and Jim Gallagher, "Schools Plan Face Lifts; to Borrow $38 Million," *P-G*, January 24, 1985, 7.

96. Lucas, interview; and Jason Barrows, "Sports Commentary," *Triangle*, December 1984.

97. Allersma, survey; and "Residents Protest New Schenley Gym," *P-G*, October 12, 1983, 8.

98. Lucas, interview.

99. Bill Zlatos, "Schenley, Soviet Pupils Will Link by Computer to Ponder the World," *Press*, January 7, 1991, D1. The *Triangle* described pupils "typing the messages onto a disk and then having [the teacher] transfer it into the E-mail system"; see Claudia Pierce, "Comrade, Can You Hear Me?" *Triangle*, April 1992.

100. Tonya Galloway, "Schenley Student Stars in Movie," *Triangle*, May 1985; and John Tiech, *Pittsburgh Film History: On Set in the Steel City* (Charleston, SC: The History Press, 2010), 50–51.

101. Peter Lieberman, "Taking Stock in Studies," *North Hills News Record*, November 24, 1992, A13; Suber, interview; and John Gold, "Fundraiser Hoops a Success," *Triangle*, May 1991.

102. Ann Carnahan, "Teen Plunges 3 Stories, Lands Safely," *Press*, May 1, 1985, B1; and Dyas, interview, December 5, 2012.

103. Mike Pellegrini, "City Schools Superintendent to Retire Early," *P-G*, February 1992, 1.

104. "One [teacher] in particular has told me she simply could not stand the administration [at the Teacher Center], and the whole thing was simply being pumped up because Wallace was determined that this should succeed. Schenley certainly seemed to get whatever was wanted. . . . If you were to ask if I felt that the time teachers spent at Schenley resulted in any great changes in approaches to teaching I would say that would be doubtful. Certainly in some cases there probably was some gain"; see Vincent Carr, e-mail to author, February 24, 2016. Neighborhood schools' administrators asked Wallace, "Why are you throwing all the best resources into the worst school?"; see Brobst, interview.

105. Susan (Forgrave) Monroe, e-mail to author, June 2, 2014; Brobst, interview; Richard Wertheimer, e-mail to author, April 24, 2015; Haley, interview; Howard Bullard, interview by author, February 4, 2015.

106. Bill Zlatos, "Closing the Gap," *Press*, November 12, 1990, B1, B4; and Bill Zlatos, "Wallace Wins National Education Award," *Press*, December 5, 1990, D4.

107. Pittsburgh Public Schools, *Membership Report as of October 6, 1992* (Pittsburgh, 1992), 6.

108. Wallace, interview.

109. Bill Zlatos, "Emotions High for Schenley Vote," *Pittsburgh Tribune-Review*, June 25, 2008, B1.

Chapter 9

1. "School Zone," *Seventeen*, September 1996, 197–202; and Sarah Franzen, "Jackson Urges Schenley Youth to Make Good Choices," *Triangle*, November 1995.

2. Pittsburgh Board of Public Education, *School Profiles: School Year 1997–1998* (Pittsburgh, 1998), 258–59. College acceptances included Harvard, Yale, Cornell, Dartmouth, MIT, the University of Chicago, Georgetown, and Carnegie Mellon, among others; see "College Acceptances," *Triangle*, May 1991; "What Are You Going to Do Now?" *Triangle*, June 1994. "Schenley's Senior Top Ten," *Triangle*, June 1996. Ryan Romano, "National Merit Scholars," *Triangle*, June 1991; "Awards • Accolades • Appreciations," *Triangle*, November 1995; Rhonda Miller, "Schenley Debaters Stroll to US Title," *P-G*, June 20, 2000, A-1; Neretta J. Troxell, "Letters to the Editor: A Public School Was First to Offer the IB Program," *P-G*, April 15, 1994, B2; and Vince Guerrieri, "USC Has High Hopes for 'International' Program," *Pittsburgh Tribune-Review*, September 6, 2001, SW1.

3. Lee Scott, interview by author, August 12, 2014.

4. Rachel Ombres, e-mail to author, February 16, 2015; Watson, interview; Ilisabeth Smith, "Noonan Is Drawn to Tennis," *P-G*, May 13, 1998, East-11; and Jessica Dugan Tones, Facebook message to author, June 15, 2016.

5. Carmen Bruce, interview by author, September 11, 2014.

6. Robert Nicklos, memo to Mary Ellen Kirby, "Re: International Studies Lottery," December 14, 1995.

7. 2001 Schenley graduate (name withheld by request), Facebook message to author, June 20, 2016.

8. Robert Nicklos, memo to Mary Ellen Kirby, "Re: International Studies Lottery," December 14, 1995; Pittsburgh Public Schools, *Membership Report as of October 2, 1991* (Pittsburgh, 1991), 12; and Nicole Wingard Williams, assistant Pittsburgh Public Schools solicitor, e-mail to author, February 3, 2015.

9. Nate Gerwig, e-mail to author, June 16, 2016.

10. In 1960, Schenley had a 50.6 percent to 49.4 percent black majority; see Pittsburgh Board of Public Education, *Quest for Racial Equality*, 12; and Pittsburgh Public Schools, *Membership Report as of October 5, 1994* (Pittsburgh, 1994), 13.

11. Parenthetical percentages indicate the group's peak in any single 1990s graduating class; see *Journal*, 1993, 6–17; *Journal*, 1999, 6–17; *Journal*, 1995, 6–17; and *Journal*, 1994, 6–17.

12. Pittsburgh Board of Public Education, *School Profiles, 1997–1998*, 258–59.

13. Nate Gerwig, e-mail to author, June 16, 2016.

14. James Porco, interview by author, July 29, 2014.

15. Cindy Dallas '98 was a black student who found it meaningful to see "bougie" black people; see Cindy Dallas, interview by author, July 15, 2015.

16. Ellen Franklin, survey, January 27, 2015; Johnson, interview; Ericka (Waters) Singleton, survey, July 30, 2014; and Rich Abbott, survey, July 30, 2014.

17. Lavelle, interview; Jesse Andrews, interview by author, August 13, 2014; and Melissa Donnelly, survey, January 27, 2015.

18. Jared Lubawski, e-mail to author, September 5, 2014; and Nate Gerwig, e-mail to author, June 16, 2016.

19. For more information on Schenley's performance in the state basketball playoffs, see appendix C. Colin Dunlap, "Schenley's 80-Game Win Streak Ends," *P-G*, January 7, 2009, D-1.

20. Steele, interview.

21. "That was like our language. . . . The literal translation [of nephs] was [swear on the dead homies]. It was a way we can remember them. It was paying homage. Even ones I grew up with, they're considered nephs now"; see Higgins, interview.

22. Mary Warnock, survey, July 21, 2014; Gabrielle Riswold, interview by author, July 30, 2014; and Sherri Massey, survey, July 30, 2014.

23. Bruce, interview. Former principal Howard Bullard taught at several high schools during his forty-year career and called Allderdice the District's most segregated of the schools. "I could walk in the cafeteria and tell you where any student was from by where they were sitting"; see Howard Bullard, interview by author, July 18, 2015.

24. Bruce, interview.

25. Miller, interview.

26. Laura (Sirbaugh) Ratica, e-mail to author, September 3, 2014; and Laura (Sirbaugh) Ratica, e-mail to author, September 5, 2014.

27. Protective teachers included Susan (Forgrave) Monroe, Neretta (Troxell) Brobst, Anthony Gemello, Kathy Olesak, Fred Lucas, Connie Weiss, and Norman Brown; see Leland Scruby, interview by author, January 31, 2015.

28. Pam Latimer, "Child Care and Parenting Programs," *Triangle*, March 1987; AP, "Teen Mothers Learn While Babies Are Tended," *Post-Crescent* (Appleton, WI), February 20, 1971, A1; and Beth Ann Lipera, "Child Care," *Triangle*, April–May 1994.

29. Rachel Ombres, e-mail to author, February 16, 2015.

30. Ali Alibeji, interview by author, September 8, 2014; Nate Gerwig, interview by author, August 18, 2014; and E. Wahrhaftig, interview.

31. *Commonwealth v. Wayne Cordell Mitchell*, 902 A.2d 430 (Pa. 2006); Lauran B. Webb, *Murder in Schenley Heights: The Day the Sugar Rolled Off of Sugar Top* ([Pittsburgh]: Lauran Webb Breakthrough Ministries, 2012), 66, 71–72; and "State & Local News Briefs," *P-G*, October 23, 2002, B-3.

32. Jonathan D. Silver, "Killing Suspect Seized; Witness Flees," *P-G*, May 17, 2002, C-1, C-2; and Donnelly, survey.

33. Susan (Baclawski) Jeffers, e-mail to author, September 4, 2014.

34. Jo Rifkin, "For Schenley Kids, a Holocaust Revelation," *Jewish Chronicle* (Pittsburgh), June 4, 1998, 1, 39; and Barak Naveh, interview by author, July 31, 2014.

35. Griffin, survey.

36. Naveh, interview.

37. Gary Rotstein, "Senator Finds Students Aren't Rapt by Social Security Issue," *P-G*, May 28, 1998, B-1, B-8.

38. Griffin, survey; and Njaimeh Njie, survey, July 31, 2014.

39. Alethea Granberg, "SAT Scoring System Recentered—Schenley Student Receives a 1600," *Triangle*, December 1995.

40. Susan (Baclawski) Jeffers, e-mail to author, September 4, 2014.

41. Melissa Gatto, e-mail to author, January 31, 2015.

42. Haji Muya, interview by author, October 23, 2014.

43. Ibid.; and Alexa Chu, "A Big Difference," *P-G*, September 2, 2008, B-1.

44. Alibeji, interview.

45. Abass Kamara, e-mail to author, May 27, 2016; and Ayo Adisa, e-mail to author, May 28, 2016.

46. Ayo Adisa, e-mail to author, May 28, 2016.

47. Lavelle, interview.

48. Riswold, interview.

49. Ibid.

50. Of those who left, "[s]ome of it had to do with PBT, and some of it had to do with Schenley"; see Trapp, interview.

51. Katie McGuire Gaines, e-mail to author, March 16, 2015.

52. "The past generation told us not to venture down to the lunchroom"; see Trapp, interview.

53. Ibid.

54. Ibid.

55. Laurence Arnold, "Where Were You When . . . ?," *Asbury Park (NJ) Press*, October 4, 1995, A6; and Jamel McKelvia, interview by author, August 19, 2014.

56. McKelvia, interview.

57. Laura (Sirbaugh) Ratica, e-mail to author, September 3, 2014.

58. Sara (Dawida) Novelly, e-mail to author, August 14, 2014.

59. Denise (Guthrie) Argote, survey, July 31, 2014.

60. Cyril H. Wecht, Mark Curriden, and Angela Powell, *Tales from the Morgue* (Amherst, NY: Prometheus Books, 2005), 97–130; Jim McKinnon and Tom O'Boyle, "Mystery Still Shrouds Fatal Arrest by Police," *P-G*, October 18, 1995, A-1, A-16; and Jan Ackerman, "DA Won't Appeal Gammage Ruling," *P-G*, July 31, 1998, A-1, A-17.

61. Mike Bucsko, "About 750 March to Protest the Verdict in John Vojtas Trial," *P-G*, November 23, 1996, A-1.

62. McKelvia, interview; and Griffin, survey. Wecht was elected class president each year from eighth grade until graduating in 1948; see Cyril Wecht, interview by author, September 21, 2016.

63. Lauren (Wilharm) Walker, survey, September 8, 2014; Eli Lopatin, survey, January 27, 2015; Justin Willis, survey, January 28, 2015; and Ken Kyle and Stephen Thompson, "The Roles of Morality Development and Personal Power in Mass School Shootings," in *School Violence and Primary Prevention*, ed. Thomas W. Miller (New York, Springer, 2008), 98–100.

64. Lorraine Adams and Dale Russakoff, "Dissecting Columbine's Cult of the Athlete," *Washington Post*, June 12, 1999, A1.

65. Megan Stanton, interview by author, November 15, 2014.

66. Lorraine Adams and Dale Russakoff, "Dissecting Columbine's Cult of the Athlete," *Washington Post*, June 12, 1999, A1; and Nate Gerwig, e-mail to author, June 16, 2016.

67. Griffin, survey; and Lauren (Wilharm) Walker, e-mail to author, October 16, 2014.

68. These rankings are based on 1981 California Achievement Test scores in readings and language; see Carole Patton Smith, "City Test Scores Show Schenley Turnaround," *P-G*, August 28, 1987, 4.

69. Brobst, interview; Haley, interview; and Wallace, interview.

70. Carrick ranked fifth of ten District high schools in the percentage of pupils proficient or advanced on the 2003 Pennsylvania System of School Assessment; see A+ Schools, *Second Annual Report to the Community on Public School Progress in Pittsburgh* (Pittsburgh, 2006), 46–56. Carrick's highest track had only twenty students per grade by 2002, and some such graduates did not apply to college; see Alexis (Orchowski) Tressler, interview by author, February 23, 2016. Brobst, interview.

71. Jerry Byrd, "Carrick Parents' Warning: Don't Bus Our Kids," *Press*, March 15, 1979, A-2; and Brobst, interview.

72. Roth lamented the lack of academic rigor, complaining, "I graduated with a 3.95 and never took a book home"; see Chris Roth, interview by author, February 24, 2016.

73. William G. Oresick, e-mail to author, April 29, 2016; Luke Meyers, interview by author, January 26, 2015; and A+ Schools, *Second Annual Report*, 52.

74. "My Predecessor at Peabody as principal [Leonard Kubiak] had written to [Superintendent] Wallace bemoaning the loss of students and its impact on Peabody"; see Vincent Carr, e-mail to author, February 24, 2016. In the late 1980s, Ebon Kennedy '90 transferred from Peabody to Schenley, even though the former was considered academically superior; see Calabro, "Reformed Schools," 8.

75. Vincent Carr, e-mail to author, February 24, 2016; and Mary Niederberger, "Stretching Skills," *Press*, September 18, 1989, B1.

76. Mike Pellegrini, "Principal to Assist 5 Afraid of School," *P-G*, May 7, 1992, 6; and Carmen J. Lee, "City Schools Move to Tighten Security," *P-G*, March 31, 1993, B-1.

77. Johnna A. Pro, "Neighborhoods Clash in School," *P-G*, September 9, 1993, B-1; Mike Pellegrini and Jim McKinnon, "Brain Hemorrhage Caused Youth's Death," *P-G*, October 2, 1991, 4; "Local News Briefs: Teen Loses Part of Ear," *Press*, October 4, 1991, B5; and Cindi Lash and Jim McKinnon, "Racial Brawl Erupts at Allderdice," *P-G*, February 19, 1994, A-1, A-3. "[T]here were always things like [the February 1994 fight] going on. The KKK graffiti from the Greenfield kids, race fights, anti-Jewish slurs. I don't think it seemed like a big deal, it was just what happened every once in a while"; see Eve (Singer) Kovsky, e-mail to author, May 30, 2016. AP, "Superintendent Calls Report 'Yellowed,'" *Indiana (PA) Gazette*, June 30, 1992, 7.

78. Mackenzie Carpenter, "Who Will Rule the Schools?" *P-G*, May 11, 1997, A-1, A-14; Carmen J. Lee, "School Budget Holds Tax Line," *P-G*, November 22, 1995, B-6; and "Pittsburgh Public Schools 1996 Proposed Redistricting Plan," *P-G*, March 13, 1996.

79. Carmen J. Lee, "Tax Rise Key Factor in School Election," *P-G*, May 20, 1993, B-1, B-4. For more information on the District's budget problems, see Carmen J. Lee, "Schools Grimace at Cutbacks," *P-G*, October 14, 1996, B-1, B-2; Mackenzie Carpenter, "Louise Brennen Steers Her Own Course," *P-G*, May 12, 1997, A-1, A-10; Carmen J. Lee, "Doubtful School Board OKs Budget," *P-G*, December 18, 1997, B-1; and Carmen J. Lee, "City Schools to

Spend $424 Million Next Year," *P-G*, November 17, 1999, B-1, B-7.

80. Frank Reeves, "Foes of Busing for Integration Present Their Case to Lawmakers," *P-G*, October 27, 1995, D-4.

81. Frank Reeves, "Murphy Urges End to School Busing," *P-G*, June 2, 1995, A-1, A-3. Other vocal busing opponents were state senator Jack Wagner, state representatives Frank Gigliotti and Harry Readshaw, and city councilman Joe Cusick, all of the South Hills; see Carmen J. Lee, "Supporters of School Redistricting Urge Board to Implement Its Plan," *P-G*, April 9, 1996, B-1, B-5.

82. "Around the Rivers," *P-G*, June 1, 1995, C-3; and Carmen J. Lee, "Busing Report Drawing Criticism," *P-G*, December 15, 1995, A-21.

83. Rutherford, "The 'Unraveling,'" 93.

84. "Pittsburgh Public Schools 1996 Proposed Redistricting Plan," *P-G*, March 13, 1996.

85. Mark S. Warnick, "Greatest Impact of Plan Could Be on Brashear," *P-G*, February 29, 1996, A-1, A-12; and Carmen J. Lee, "Reinventing the City Schools," *P-G*, February 29, 1996, A-1, A-12.

86. Bill Scheer, "Pittsburgh Actions Defend Desegregation," *The Militant*, May 27, 1996, accessed May 28, 2016, http://www.themilitant.com/1996/6021/6021_27.html.

87. Rutherford, "The 'Unraveling,'" 101–2.

88. Pittsburgh Public Schools, *Membership Report as of October 1, 1996* (Pittsburgh, 1996), 12.

89. Rutherford, "The 'Unraveling,'" 104–5.

90. Carmen J. Lee, "Ridge Signs Neighborhood Schools Bill," *P-G*, July 13, 1996, B-1, B-2.

91. Eleanor Chute, "Walking in Circles," *P-G*, May 16, 2004, A-1.

92. Rutherford, "The 'Unraveling,'" 102.

93. Eleanor Chute, "School Redistricting Is Work in Progress," *P-G*, June 9, 1998, D-2.

94. Pittsburgh Public Schools, *Membership Report, 1992*, 4; Rutherford, "The 'Unraveling,'" 117; and Eleanor Chute, "Many Schools, Fewer Pupils," *P-G*, October 23, 2003, C-2.

95. Richard Wertheimer, "The Pittsburgh School Board," *The Principal's Office* (blog), February 27, 2015, accessed May 28, 2016, http://k12success.blogspot.com/2015/02/the-pittsburgh-school-board.html; and Eleanor Chute, "New Chief of Schools Inspires Optimism," *P-G*, February 25, 2000, B-1.

96. Helen Faison, a black woman and longtime District administrator, was interim superintendent from 1999 to 2000; see Eleanor Chute, "New Chief of Schools Inspires Optimism," *P-G*, February 25, 2000, B-1. Carmen J. Lee, "Schools Propose a 23.3% Tax Hike," *P-G*, November 14, 2000, A-1, A-3.

97. Carmen J. Lee, "Schools Propose a 23.3% Tax Hike," *P-G*, November 14, 2000, A-1, A-3.

98. Carmen J. Lee, "School Budget to Raise Taxes," *P-G*, December 21, 2000, A-1, A-23; and Jean Fink, "Letters to the Editor: School Board Members Represent the People and Should Have Significant Input," *P-G*, March 13, 2001, A-10.

99. Timothy McNulty, "Murphy Calls School Closings 'Unsettling,'" *P-G*, November 22, 2000, D-5; and Timothy McNulty and Carmen J. Lee, "City Neared Insolvency as Schools Built Surplus," *P-G*, September 24, 2003, A-11.

100. Carmen J. Lee, "Three Winners Plan to Reverse School Closings," *P-G*, November 7, 2001, A-11; Carmen J. Lee, "City School Board Trims, Passes New Budget," *P-G*, December 20, 2001, C-19; and Carmen J. Lee, "School Board Gets a Scolding," *P-G*, June 19, 2002, B-1, B-7.

101. Stephanie Strom, "Private Groups in Pittsburgh Halt Millions in School Aid," *New York Times*, July 16, 2002, A8.

102. Eleanor Chute, "City School Test Scores on Rise," *P-G*, October 4, 2002, B-1, B-2; Maggi Newhouse, "Test Scores Show Mixed Results," *Pittsburgh Tribune-Review*, August 25, 2004, A1; Elsie Hillman and William Trueheart, "Letters to the Editor: John Thompson Deserves Our Thanks for His Dedication," *P-G*, December 11, 2004, A-10; Carmen J. Lee, "School Officials Rank Top Concerns," *P-G*, March 6, 2000, B-1, B-6; and Timothy McNulty and Carmen J. Lee, "City Neared Insolvency as Schools Built Surplus," *P-G*, September 24, 2003, A-1, A-11.

103. Carmen J. Lee, "Hopes Rise for School Board Harmony," *P-G*, May 22, 2003, A-1, A-5; Amy McConnell Schaarsmith, "City Schools Dismissing Thompson," *P-G*, December 11, 2014, A-1, A-6; and Patrick Dowd, interview by author, March 14, 2016.

104. Amy McConnell Schaarsmith, "Board Opens Exit Door for City Superintendent," *P-G*, July 1, 2014, A-1, A-6.

105. Amy McConnell Schaarsmith, "School Chief Buyout OK'd," *P-G*, January 27, 2005, A-8; and Dowd, interview.

106. Amy McConnell Schaarsmith, "Board OKs Roosevelt," *P-G*, July 28, 2005, A-1.

107. Eleanor Chute, "Excess School Capacity 'a Luxury,'" *P-G*, May 27, 2005, A-1, A-11.

Chapter 10

1. Amy McConnell Schaarsmith, "Board OKs Roosevelt," *P-G*, July 28, 2005, A-1.

2. Tim Grant, "Roosevelt's Bottom Line: 'Student Achievement,'" *P-G*, August 6, 2005, A-1, A-6; and AP, "City District's Choice for Superintendent Illustrates Trend," *Beaver County (PA) Times*, August 1, 2005, A-8.

3. Amy McConnell Schaarsmith, "Board OKs Roosevelt," *P-G*, July 28, 2005, A-1, A-11; and Bill Peduto, interview by author, January 26, 2015.

4. Joe Smydo, "20 Schools to Close," *P-G*, November 10, 2005, A-1, A-8.

5. Joe Smydo, "School Closing Plan Revised," *P-G*, February 10, 2006, A-1, A-8; David Treadwell, "Urban Pittsburgh Schools at Head of Their Class," *Los Angeles Times*, September 22, 1990, accessed May 26, 2016, http://articles.latimes.com/1990–09–22/news/mn-633_1_school-districts; Keith Henderson, "New Life for Pittsburgh's Schenley High," *Christian Science Monitor*, January 13, 1986, accessed May 26, 2016, http://www.csmonitor.com/1986/0113/dpitt2.html; Barbara Kantrowitz and Pat Wingert, "The Best Schools in the World," *Newsweek*, December 2, 1991, 50–52; and Eleanor Chute, "Excess School Capacity 'a Luxury,'" *P-G*, May 27, 2005, A-11.

6. Joe Smydo, "20 Schools to Close," *P-G*, November 10, 2005, A-8.

7. Larkin Page-Jacobs, "Asbestos and the End of Schenley High," *WESA.FM*, June 13, 2012, accessed May 29, 2016, http://wesa.fm/post/asbestos-and-end-schenley-high#stream/0; and Tony LaRussa, "Officials to Re-Evaluate Schenley Status," *Pittsburgh Tribune-Review*, December 10, 2005, B6.

8. Joe Smydo, "Could Schenley Survive the Ax?" *P-G*, December 10, 2005, A-1, A-5; Joe Smydo, "Roosevelt Details Why Schenley May Close," *P-G*, November 20, 2007, A-1, A-7; and Tony LaRussa, "Officials to Re-Evaluate Schenley Status," *Pittsburgh Tribune-Review*, December 10, 2005, B1.

9. Schenley High School Task Force, *Summary Report* (Pittsburgh: June 23, 2006).

10. Joe Smydo, "Partial Schenley Renewal Costs Less," *P-G*, January 12, 2006, B-1; and Joe Smydo, "School Closing Plan Revised," *P-G*, February 10, 2006, A-1, A-8.

11. Schenley High School Task Force, *Summary Report*; Astorino, *Schenley High School Evaluation Study, January 31, 2006* (Pittsburgh, 2006).

12. Tony LaRussa, "Officials to Re-Evaluate Schenley Status," *Pittsburgh Tribune-Review*, December 10, 2005, B1; and Lisa Fischetti, interview by author, November 3, 2014.

13. Joe Smydo, "Ceiling Collapse at Schenley High Clouds Building's Future," *P-G*, July 11, 2007, B-3.

14. Howard Bullard, executive director of secondary schools, open letter to Schenley High parents, August 24, 2007; Dennis L. Astorino to Mark Roosevelt, "Re: Plaster Failure Investigation, Schenley High School, Pittsburgh, Pennsylvania," October 19, 2007; and Joe Smydo, "Roosevelt Details Why Schenley May Close," *P-G*, November 20, 2007, A-7.

15. L. Brad Shotwell and Vincent E. Sagan, Wiss, Janney, Elstner Associates, Inc., report to Dino Perischetti, Astorino, "Re: Plaster Failure Investigation, Schenley High School, Pittsburgh, Pennsylvania," October 12, 2007; Dennis L. Astorino, report to Mark Roosevelt, "Re: Plaster Failure Investigation, Schenley High School, Pittsburgh, Pennsylvania," October 19, 2007; Thomas L. Blank and Ryan M. Pierce, L. Robert Kimball & Associates, report to Mark Roosevelt, "Re: Plaster Failure—Schenley High School," November 16, 2007; and Pittsburgh Board of Education, "Pittsburgh Schenley High School: Summary of Recent Plaster Related Events," [November 2007].

16. Dennis L. Astorino, report to Mark Roosevelt, "Re: Plaster Failure Investigation, Schenley High School, Pittsburgh, Pennsylvania," October 19, 2007.

17. Pittsburgh Public Schools, "District Announces Year Two Plans of Exce1.9–12, The Plan for High School Excellence," press release, October 31, 2007.

18. Chris Young, "Class Dismissed," *Pittsburgh City Paper*, January 31, 2008, accessed May 29, 2016, http://www.pghcitypaper.com/pittsburgh/class-dismissed/Content?oid=1339688; and Rebecca Nuttall, "Classroom Experiment," *Pittsburgh City Paper*, August 8, 2014, accessed May 29, 2016, http://www.pghcitypaper.com/pittsburgh/classroom-experiment/Content?oid=1769910.

19. James Hill, e-mail to author, March 24, 2015; and Pittsburgh Public Schools, "District Announces Year Two Plans of Exce1.9–12, The Plan for High School Excellence," press release, October 31, 2007.

20. Joe Smydo, "Roosevelt Details Why Schenley May Close," *P-G*, November 20, 2007, A-7; Kathy Fine, e-mail to Jenny Lakin, March 19, 2008; and Bobby Kerlik, "Aggressive Support Vowed to Save Schenley," *Pittsburgh Tribune-Review*, November 11, 2007, C3.

21. Joe Smydo, "Schenley's Supporters Band Together," *P-G*, November 28, 2007, A-1;

Teressa LaGamba, e-mail to author, September 16, 2014; "Local & State: 100 Parents, Alumni Discuss Schenley High Closing," *P-G*, November 11, 2007, B-4; Eleanor Chute, "Schenley High School Supporters Plot Strategy," *P-G*, November 18, 2007, B-2; and Jill Weiss, e-mail to Bill Peduto, December 5, 2007.

22. Joe Smydo, "Schenley Backers Loud, Clear," *P-G*, November 9, 2007, A-1, A-8; and Mark Roosevelt, interview by author, October 31, 2014.

23. Mark Roosevelt, interview by author, November 14, 2014.

24. Jill Weiss, e-mail to Bill Peduto, December 5, 2007; and Annette Werner, e-mail to author, January 27, 2015.

25. Jennifer Baron, "$113M, 495,000 SF Mixed-Use Bakery Square Project Progresses in East Liberty," *Pop City*, October 3, 2007, accessed May 29, 2016, //www.popcitymedia .com/devnews/pittsburghdvlp1003.aspx.

26. Annette Werner, e-mail to author, March 21, 2015.

27. Peduto, interview; Joe Smydo, "Schenley Proposal Called 'Irresponsible,'" *P-G*, June 13, 2008, B-1, B-2; and Michael A. Fuoco, "Old County Jail Reborn with New Look and Mission," *P-G*, October 10, 2000, B-1.

28. Joe Smydo, "Schenley Proposal Called 'Irresponsible,'" *P-G*, June 13, 2008, B-2; and Peduto, interview.

29. Dowd and Romaniello supported closing Schenley in 2005 and renewed that position in 2007; see Dowd, interview; Joe Smydo, "School Closing Plan Revised," *P-G*, February 10, 2006, A-8; and Bill Zlatos, "Plan to Shut School Revived," *Pittsburgh Tribune-Review*, November 1, 2007, B6. McCrea "always followed" Colaizzi and Isler, who reliably voted with Roosevelt initiatives, and although Fink "was sympathetic to Schenley," some felt she had an understanding with the superintendent. "[He] didn't mess with her district, and in return, she supported his initiatives," see Annette Werner, e-mail to author, March 20, 2015. "Allegheny County Schools," *P-G*, November 7, 2007, A-13.

30. Chris Young, "Controversial Pittsburgh Public School Board Member Mark Brentley Facing Three Challengers in Upcoming Primary," *Pittsburgh City Paper*, April 7, 2011, accessed May 29, 2016, http://www.pghcitypaper.com/ pittsburgh/controversial-pittsburgh-public-school-board-member-mark-brentley-facing-three-challengers-in-upcoming-primary/ Content?oid=1385314.

31. Annette Werner, e-mail to author, March 21, 2015; Sumpter, interview; and Pittsburgh Board of Education, *Transcript of Proceedings, Pittsburgh Board of Education Legislative Meeting, November 14, 2007* (Pittsburgh, 2007), 33–35, 67–68.

32. Pittsburgh Board of Education, *Transcript of Proceedings, Pittsburgh Board of Education Legislative Meeting, February 27, 2008* (Pittsburgh, 2008), 34–38; Kathy Fine, interview by author, August 3, 2014; Annette Werner, e-mail to author, March 20, 2015; and Annette Werner, e-mail to author, March 22, 2015.

33. Eleanor Chute, "City Schools Spent $23 Million on Now-Closed Buildings," *P-G*, February 24, 2013, A-3.

34. Pittsburgh Board of Education, *Transcript, Board of Education Meeting, February 27, 2008*, 34.

35. Chris Young, "Roosevelt Asks to Delay School District Restructuring," *Pittsburgh City Paper*, January 31, 2008, accessed May 29, 2016, http://www.pghcitypaper.com/ pittsburgh/roosevelt-asks-to-delay-school-district-restructuring/Content?oid=1339689.

36. Pittsburgh Board of Public Education, *Meeting Agenda, February 27, 2008* (Pittsburgh, 2008), 554–55.

37. Pittsburgh Board of Education, *Transcript, Board of Education Meeting, February 27, 2008*, 14–16.

38. Ibid., 60–62.

39. Ibid., 43, 58–61.

40. Ibid., 34–38, 60–62.

41. Roosevelt, interview, October 31, 2014; and Fischetti, interview.

42. The team, while never explicitly defined, had grown to approximately twelve members; see Jill Weiss, e-mail to Ernie Hogan, Annette Werner, Brenda Smith, David Brewton, Susan Kalisz, Linda Metrupolis, Laurie Klatscher, Vivian Loftness, Rob Pfaffmann, Tim Stevens, and Bill Lafe, April 11, 2008.

43. Fine, interview.

44. Roosevelt, interview, November 14, 2014; Albert L. Filoni, MacLachlan, Cornelius & Filoni, Inc., contract estimate to Paul Gill, "What's Next for Schenley?" May 15, 2008; and Joe Smydo, "Schenley May Close in June," *P-G*, May 20, 2008, A-1.

45. Pittsburgh Board of Public Education, *Meeting Agenda, June 25, 2008* (Pittsburgh, 2008), 1710-12.

46. Mark Rauterkaus, "I Knew It Would Be a 5–4 Vote—But There Were Switches," *Mark Rauterkaus & Running Mates Ponder Current Events*, June 25, 2008, accessed May 29, 2016, http://rauterkus.blogspot .com/2008/06/i-knew-it-would-be-5-4-vote -but-there.html; Annette Werner, e-mail to author, March 20, 2015; and Annette Werner, e-mail to author, October 16, 2014.

47. Pittsburgh Board of Education, *Transcript of Proceedings, Pittsburgh Board of Education Legislative Meeting, June 25, 2008* (Pittsburgh, 2008), 118–20; and Annette Werner, e-mail to author, March 22, 2015.

48. Pittsburgh Board of Education, *Meeting Agenda, June 25, 2008*, 1711; and Pittsburgh Board of Education, *Transcript, Board of Education Meeting, June 25, 2008*, 11–13.

49. Pittsburgh Board of Education, *Transcript, Board of Education Meeting, June 25, 2008*, 118–20.

50. Ibid., 37–39.

51. Ibid., 32.

52. Ibid., 118–20.

53. Ibid., 117.

54. Annette Werner, e-mail to Linda Lane, March 25, 2011.

55. Joe Smydo, "Arnet Quits City School Board," *P-G*, June 27, 2009, B-1; and Karamagi Rujumba, "Roosevelt's Departure Challenges City Schools," *P-G*, October 7, 2010, A-1.

56. Bill Donahue, "Back in the Ol' Hippie Hothouse," *New York Times Magazine*, September 18, 2011, MM58; and AP, "Board Rejects Plan to Keep Antioch College Open," *Akron Beacon Journal*, May 10, 2008, B4.

57. Roosevelt, interview, November 14, 2014.

58. Larkin Page-Jacobs, "Asbestos and the End of Schenley High," *WESA.FM*, June 13, 2012, accessed May 29, 2016, http://wesa.fm/post/asbestos-and-end-schenley-high#stream/0.

59. L. Robert Kimball & Associates, *Asbestos and Hazardous Materials Inspections of the Schenley High School, 4101 Bigelow Boulevard, Pittsburgh, Pennsylvania, Prepared for Facilities Division, Pittsburgh Public Schools, August 2009* (Pittsburgh, 2009), 2; and AmyJo Brown, "Asbestos at Schenley High May Have Been Less Prevalent Than Believed," *Pittsburgh City Paper*, July 25, 2012, accessed May 29, 2016, http://www.pghcitypaper.com/pittsburgh/asbestos-at-schenley-high-may-have-been-less-prevalent-than-believed/Content?oid=1546892.

60. L. Robert Kimball & Associates, *Asbestos and Hazardous Materials, Schenley High, August 2009*, 4.

61. AmyJo Brown, "Asbestos at Schenley High May Have Been Less Prevalent Than Believed," *Pittsburgh City Paper*, July 25, 2012, accessed May 29, 2016, http://www.pghcitypaper.com/pittsburgh/asbestos-at-schenley-high-may-have-been-less-prevalent-than-believed/Content?oid=1546892.

62. Annette Werner, e-mail to Jill Weiss, December 4, 2009.

63. Barbara Daly Danko, "Letters to the Editor: Schenley Asbestos," *P-G*, October 5, 2012, A14.

64. Randall Taylor letter to Pittsburgh Board of Pittsburgh Education, [August 3, 2012].

65. Fischetti, interview.

66. AmyJo Brown, "Asbestos at Schenley High May Have Been Less Prevalent Than Believed," *Pittsburgh City Paper*, July 25, 2012, accessed May 29, 2016, http://www.pghcitypaper.com/pittsburgh/asbestos-at-schenley-high-may-have-been-less-prevalent-than-believed/Content?oid=1546892.

67. Bill Zlatos, "Schenley High Going up for Sale Again," *Pittsburgh Tribune-Review*, September 27, 2012, B3.

68. "School Board to Get Latest Estimates on Schenley Work," *P-G*, January 24, 2013, B-6; and Eleanor Chute, "Controversy Swirls Around Schenley High Sale," *P-G*, February 16, 2013, A-12.

69. Eleanor Chute, "School Panel Backs Plans for Schenley Apartments," *P-G*, February 7, 2013, A-1, A-12; and AmyJo Brown, "Most Likely to Succeed?" *Pittsburgh City Paper*, February 13, 2013, accessed May 29, 2016, http://www.pghcitypaper.com/pittsburgh/most-likely-to-succeed-facing-an-uphill-battle-a-group-of-schenley-grads-want-to-keep-the-building-full-of-students/Content?oid=1618064.

70. PMC Property Group, *PMC/Schenley HSB Associates, L. P./Submission in Response to Request for Proposals for the Sale and Re-Use of Schenley High School, 4101 Bigelow Boulevard, Pittsburgh, PA 15213 Issued on October 8, 2012* (Pittsburgh, 2013), submitted response; Andy Warhol School of Visual and Performing Arts, *AWSVPA* (January 2013), submitted response; Ralph A. Falbo, Inc., *Ralph A. Falbo Inc. and Beacon Communities Development, LLC Response to Request for Proposals for the Sale and Re-use of Schenley High School* (Pittsburgh: January 18, 2013), submitted response; and Kossman Development Company, *Proposal for the Sale and Re-Use of Schenley High School* (Pittsburgh, 2013), submitted response.

71. Eleanor Chute, "Schenley Sold to Developer," *P-G*, February 28, 2013, B-1, B-3.

72. Anya Sostek, "The Last Class of Schenley Represents Bittersweet Chapter in Proud History," *P-G*, May 29, 2011, A-9.

73. Rebecca Nuttall, "Classroom Experiment," *Pittsburgh City Paper*, August 8, 2014, accessed May 29, 2016, http://www.pghcitypaper.com/pittsburgh/classroom-experiment/Content?oid=1769910. It is difficult to compare outcomes for Spartan Classics Academy and University Prep students

because standardized testing data were not broken down by track. However, 2006 data from Schenley's economically disadvantaged students are comparable to University Prep scores in 2015; see Pennsylvania Department of Education, "The 2006 PSSA Mathematics and Readings Disaggregated (Subgroup) Performance Level Results, Grades 3–8 and 11 School Level," [2006], 322, accessed June 15, 2016, http://www.education.pa.gov/Documents/Data%20and%20Statistics/PSSA%20and%20AYP%20Results/2005%202006%20PSSA%20AYP/2005%2006%20School%20Level%20Math%20and%20Reading%20PSSA%20Results%20by%20Subgroups.pdf; and A+ Schools, *2015 Report to the Community on Public School Progress in Pittsburgh* (Pittsburgh, 2015), 80–81.

74. A+ Schools, *2015 Report to the Community*, 82–83.

75. Mike White, "Lack of Sportsmanship in 99-Point Victory," *P-G*, January 21, 2011, S-5. For more information on asbestos plaster at the Peabody and Schenley buildings, see L. Robert Kimball & Associates, *Asbestos and Hazardous Materials, Schenley High*, August 2009, 2–4; AGX, Inc., *AHERA Three-Year Re-Inspection, Pittsburgh Obama 6–12* (Pittsburgh, 2012), 5–11; and Annette Werner, e-mail to author, June 13, 2016.

76. Eleanor Chute, "City Schools Spent $23 Million on Now-Closed Buildings," *P-G*, February 24, 2013, A-3.

77. In 2006, Schenley was 26.9 percent white, with 49.9 percent of students eligible for free or reduced-cost lunches. Nine years later, University Prep was 4 percent white and 88 percent economically disadvantaged, while Obama Academy was 18 percent white and 68 percent economically disadvantaged; see A+ Schools, *Second Annual Report*, 55; and A+ Schools, *2015 Report to the Community*, 80, 82.

78. A+ Schools, *2015 Report to the Community*, 80, 82; and Nicole Wingard Williams, assistant Pittsburgh Public Schools solicitor, e-mail to author, February 3, 2015.

79. "Editorial: Stable Schools," *P-G*, October 31, 2011, A-16.

80. Population fell 1.44 percent during that period, while enrollment plunged 13.23 percent; see Joe Smydo, "Enrollment at City Schools Falls 4 Percent," *P-G*, October 9, 2007, B-1; Eleanor Chute, "Pittsburgh City Schools' Enrollment Still Falling," *P-G*, October 29, 2013, B-1; Steve Levin, "Pittsburgh Population Drops, Still in Top 25 Percent," *P-G*, July 10, 2008, B-1; and Gary Rotstein, "Census Estimate Shows City Population Ebbing," *P-G*, May 21, 2015, B-1.

81. Roosevelt, interview, October 31, 2014.

82. Edward Alexei, e-mail to author, May 3, 2016.

83. Joe Smydo, "Schenley May Close in June," *P-G*, May 20, 2008, A-1. Concord's addition was not complete until 2011. The four buildings impacted by Schenley's dissolution were Reizenstein, Milliones, Peabody, and Frick. Although no Schenley program was reassigned to Frick, its transition to a science and technology magnet would not have been feasible without closing Schenley; see Eleanor Chute, "City Schools Spent $23 Million on Now-Closed Buildings," *P-G*, February 24, 2013, A-3.

84. Fischetti, interview.

85. Schenley High School Task Force, *Summary Report*; J. Greer Hayden, HHSDR Architects/Engineers, contract estimate to Vidyadhar S. Patil and Daryl Saunders, "Re: Schenley High School, HHSDR #3289," September 7, 2005.

86. Albert L. Filoni, MacLachlan, Cornelius & Filoni, Inc., contract estimate to Paul Gill, "What's Next for Schenley?" May 15, 2008; and HHSDR Architects/Engineers, *Renovation Cost Estimate, Schenley Facility, February 12, 2013* (Pittsburg, 2013).

87. Schenley High School Task Force, *Summary Report*; Vivian Loftness, interview by author, February 2, 2015.

88. Peduto, interview.

89. Annette Werner, e-mail to author, April 22, 2015; Joe Smydo, "Schenley Group Questions Asbestos Work at Other Schools," *P-G*, January 12, 2009, A-1, A-3; L. Robert Kimball & Associates, *Suspect Asbestos Bulk Sampling Form, Robert Lee Vann Elementary School, June–July 2008* (2008); L. Robert Kimball & Associates, *Suspect Asbestos Bulk Sampling Form, Woolslair K-5, April 9–10, 2009* (2009); and L. Robert Kimball & Associates, *Suspect Asbestos Bulk Sampling Form, Miller African Centered Academy, January 26–27, 2009* (2009).

90. Tony LaRussa, "Officials to Re-Evaluate Schenley Status," *Pittsburgh Tribune-Review*, December 10, 2005, B1; Joe Smydo, "UPMC, CMU: No Plan to Buy Schenley," *P-G*, December 2, 2007, B-1; and Bill Zlatos, "Historic Schenley High Has Value on Market," *Pittsburgh Tribune-Review*, November 2, 2007, B3.

91. Joe Smydo, "Schenley Backers Loud, Clear," *P-G*, November 9, 2007, A-8.

92. Vivian Loftness, e-mail to author, May 2, 2016; Vivian Loftness, "The Next Page: Schenley High School: A 'Green Building' Ahead of Its Time," *P-G*, June 15, 2008, G-6; Loftness, interview; and Albert L. Filoni, MacLachlan, Cornelius & Filoni, Inc., contract

estimate to Paul Gill, "What's Next for Schenley?" May 15, 2008.

93. Chris Young, "Making the Grade," *Pittsburgh City Paper*, August 30, 2007, accessed May 30, 2016, http://www.pghci typaper.com/pittsburgh/making-the-grade/Content?oid=1338973; and Karamagi Rujumba, "Roosevelt's Departure Challenges City Schools," *P-G*, October 7, 2010, A-11.

94. Eleanor Chute, "Promise Program Gets a Reality Lesson," *P-G*, July 26, 2015, B-1.

95. Carey Harris, interview by author, April 26, 2016; and Karamagi Rujumba, "Roosevelt's Departure Challenges City Schools," *P-G*, October 7, 2010, A-11.

96. Roosevelt, interview, October 31, 2014; and Roosevelt, interview, November 14, 2014.

97. Mark Roosevelt, interview by Elizabeth Seamans, *Mark Roosevelt in Uncharted Waters*, camera roll 2, 2008, transcript, 1–2, 4.

98. Roosevelt, interview, October 31, 2014.

99. Chris Young, "Class Dismissed," *Pittsburgh City Paper*, January 31, 2008, accessed May 29, 2016, http://www.pghci typaper.com/pittsburgh/class-dismissed/Content?oid=1339688.

100. Tina Calabro, interview by author, January 14, 2015; and Tina Calabro, e-mail to author, May 2, 2016.

101. Fischetti, interview.

102. Haley, interview.

103. Roosevelt, interview, November 14, 2014; Mark Roosevelt, interview by Elizabeth Seamans, *Mark Roosevelt: In Uncharted Waters*, camera roll 2, 2008, transcript, 4–6; and Roosevelt, interview, October 31, 2014.

104. Elizabeth Seamans, interview by author, October 15, 2014.

105. Roosevelt, interview, October 31, 2014.

106. Suber, interview.

107. Bullard, interview, February 4, 2015.

108. Roosevelt, interview, October 31, 2014; Roosevelt, interview, November 14, 2014; and Karamagi Rujumba, "Roosevelt's Departure Challenges City Schools," *P-G*, October 7, 2010, A-1.

Chapter 11

1. Joe Smydo, "Schenley's Supporters Band Together," *P-G*, November 28, 2007, A-1, A-7.

2. Joe Smydo, "A Plea for Schenley," *P-G*, November 14, 2007, B-1.

3. Bullard, interview, February 4, 2015.

4. Joe Smydo, "A Plea for Schenley," *P-G*, November 14, 2007, B-5.

5. Teressa LaGamba, e-mail to author, September 16, 2014.

6. Greg Galuska, e-mail to author, November 10, 2014.

7. Greg Galuska, e-mail to author, October 29, 2014.

8. Bill Zlatos, "Last Bell at Schenley?" *Pittsburgh Tribune-Review*, June 11, 2008, B7.

9. Joe Smydo, "Schenley Spirit Will Live On," *P-G*, June 11, 2008, A-10.

10. Bill Zlatos, "Last Bell at Schenley?" *Pittsburgh Tribune-Review*, June 11, 2008, B1, B7.

11. Michele Feingold, e-mail to author, June 25, 2008; *Enter to Learn, Go Forth to Serve: The Story of Schenley High School (1916–2011)* (Pittsburgh: City of Pittsburgh Housing Authority, Creative Arts Corner, 2013), film; and "Reader Forum," *P-G*, June 11, 2008.

12. April Weitzel, survey, August 13, 2014; and Bill Zlatos, "Last Bell at Schenley?" *Pittsburgh Tribune-Review*, June 11, 2008, B1.

13. Bill Zlatos, "New Surroundings, Same Spartan Pride," *Pittsburgh Tribune-Review*, August 29, 2008, B1; and Sally Kalson, "Any School Should Be Proud of Reizenstein," *P-G*, November 16, 2005, A-2.

14. Teressa LaGamba, e-mail to author, September 16, 2014.

15. Joe Smydo, "Miffed Schenley Students 'Making Do' with New Digs," *P-G*, January 3, 2009, A-1.

16. James Hill, interview by author, January 8, 2015; James Hill, e-mail to author, September 5, 2014; Joe Smydo, "Ex-Schenley Students Try Reizenstein on for Size," *P-G*, August 29, 2008, A-2; and Donald Miller, "Reizenstein Celebrates Arrival of 'Celebration' Sculpture," *P-G*, May 26, 1990, 12.

17. Bill Zlatos, "New Surroundings, Same Spartan Pride," *Pittsburgh Tribune-Review*, August 29, 2008, B6.

18. Joe Smydo, "Ex-Schenley Students Try Reizenstein on for Size," *P-G*, August 29, 2008, A-1, A-2.

19. Joe Smydo, "Miffed Schenley Students 'Making Do' with New Digs," *P-G*, January 3, 2009, A-3.

20. Jeff Dugan, interview by author, September 8, 2014.

21. Nicole Wingard Williams, assistant solicitor to Pittsburgh Public Board of Education, e-mail to author, February 3, 2015; and Erik Rauterkaus, "End of an Era—Schenley Prepares to Close Its Doors Forever," *The Eagle* (Obama Academy), June 3, 2011, accessed May 31, 2016, http://www.obamaeagle.org/news/2011/06/03/end-of-an-era-schenley-pre pares-to-close-its-doors-forever/.

22. Kate Luce Angell, "Keeping the Spirit Alive!," *P-G*, April 27, 2011, C-3.

23. John Grupp, "Schenley Sports Will Live On," *Pittsburgh Tribune-Review*, June 28, 2008, C3; and Lewis Thompson, interview by author, March 17, 2016.

24. James Hill, e-mail to author, September 8, 2014.

25. Muya, interview.

26. James Hill, e-mail to author, September 5, 2014.

27. Joe Smydo, "City Schools Spotlight Magnet Programs," *P-G*, November 1, 2008, A-11.

28. Anya Sostek, "The Last Class of Schenley Represents Bittersweet Chapter in Proud History," *P-G*, May 29, 2011, A-9.

29. James Hill, e-mail to author, September 5, 2014; and Joe Smydo, "Miffed Schenley Students 'Making Do' with New Digs," *P-G*, January 3, 2009, A-3.

30. Anya Sostek, "The Last Class of Schenley Represents Bittersweet Chapter in Proud History," *P-G*, May 29, 2011, A-9.

31. Erin McMahon, survey, January 29, 2015; and Erin McMahon, e-mail to author, February 1, 2015.

32. Natalie Sorce, survey, January 27, 2015; and Naveh, interview.

33. A+ Schools, *2010 Report to the Community on Public School Progress in Pittsburgh* (Pittsburgh, 2010), 109.

34. Hannah Guy, survey, January 28, 2015; and Teressa LaGamba, survey, July 31, 2014.

35. Pittsburgh Public Schools, "2006 Schenley High School International Baccalaureate Diploma Recipients Honored Today," press release, December 22, 2006; and Anya Sostek, "The Last Class of Schenley Represents Bittersweet Chapter in Proud History," *P-G*, May 29, 2011, A-1.

36. Teresita Kolenchak, "Facaros Named to Oakmont Council," *P-G*, September 22, 2009, accessed May 31, 2016, http://old.post-gazette.com/pg/09265/999885-100.stm?cmpid=latest.xml; and Erik Rauterkaus, "End of an Era II—Mrs. Facaros Remembers," *The Eagle* (Obama Academy), June 3, 2011, accessed May 31, 2016, http://www.obamaeagle.org/news/2011/06/03/end-of-an-era-ii-mrs-facaros-remembers/.

37. Anya Sostek, "The Last Class of Schenley Represents Bittersweet Chapter in Proud History," *P-G*, May 29, 2011, A-1.

38. For more information on Iasella, see Sorce, survey; and "Mario Iasella," LinkedIn, accessed June 15, 2016, https://www.linkedin.com/in/mario-iasella-98b2096. For more information on Ehman, see Guy, survey; Njie, survey; Christina Brown, survey, July 31, 2014; and Janielle Pratt, survey, January 27, 2015.

39. "Reader Forum," *P-G*, June 11, 2008, accessed May 20, 2016; Guy, survey; and Sorce, survey.

40. Pittsburgh Public Schools, "Pittsburgh Schenley to Celebrate Class of 2008 International Baccalaureate Diploma Recipients," press release, December 19, 2008; and Pittsburgh Public Schools, "Pittsburgh Schenley to Celebrate Class of 2010 International Baccalaureate Diploma Recipients," press release, December 22, 2010.

41. "City: University Partnership School to Bear Mrs. Milliones' Name," *P-G*, January 15, 2009, B-6; and Rebecca Nuttall, "Classroom Experiment," *Pittsburgh City Paper*, August 8, 2014, accessed May 29, 2016, http://www.pghcitypaper.com/pittsburgh/classroom-experiment/Content?oid=1769910.

42. Rebecca Nuttall, "Classroom Experiment," *Pittsburgh City Paper*, August 8, 2014, accessed May 29, 2016, http://www.pghcitypaper.com/pittsburgh/classroom-experiment/Content?oid=1769910.

43. A+ Schools, *2014 Report to the Community on Public School Progress in Pittsburgh* (Pittsburgh, 2014), 78–99.

44. Ibid., 82–83; and A+ Schools, *2015 Report to the Community*, 80–81.

45. Molly Born, "Pittsburgh Milliones School Suffering Safety 'Crisis,' Group Says," *P-G*, March 1, 2016, accessed May 31, 2016, http://www.post-gazette.com/news/education/2016/03/01/Pittsburgh-Milliones-school-suffering-safety-crisis-group-says/stories/201602290191; and Alexander Genova, "'Ma She's Bleeding Everywhere': Thirty Pittsburgh Schoolgirls Arrested After a Small Tiff Turned into a Vicious Brawl with Several Hospitalized," *Daily Mail* (London), February 29, 2016, accessed February 29, 2016, http://www.dailymail.co.uk/news/article-3469814/Thirty-Pittsburgh-schoolgirls-arrested-small-tiff-boy-turned-bloody-brawl-hospitalized.html.

46. Bob Allen, "Charges Expected After 30-Girl Fight at University Prep," *CBS Pittsburgh*, February 29, 2016, accessed May 31, 2016, http://pittsburgh.cbslocal.com/2016/02/29/university-prep-on-lockdown-after-large-fight-in-hallway/.

47. Samson X. Horne, "Hill District Clergy, Community Outraged over School Brawl at University Prep," *New Pittsburgh Courier*, March 2, 2016, accessed May 31, 2016, http://newpittsburghcourieronline.com/2016/03/02/hill-district-clergy-community-outraged-over-school-brawl-at-university-prep/.

48. Chris Horne, interview by author, April 26, 2016.

49. Joe Smydo, "Accredited IB School to Open at Reizenstein," *P-G*, August 4, 2009, B-1; and L. Thompson, interview.

50. Pittsburgh Board of Education, *Meeting Agenda, December 15, 2009* (Pittsburgh, 2009), 89; and Marissa Rosenbaum, "Obama Academy Opens in Pittsburgh," *Duquesne (University) Duke*, April 29, 2010, 7.

51. Pittsburgh Board of Education, *Transcript of Proceedings, Pittsburgh Board of Education Legislative Meeting, December 15, 2009* (Pittsburgh, 2009), 28–31, 36–38, 41–43.

52. Marissa Rosenbaum, "Obama Academy Opens in Pittsburgh," *Duquesne (University) Duke*, April 29, 2010, 7; Hannah Green, interview by author, November 17, 2015; and L. Thompson, interview.

53. Roosevelt, interview, November 14, 2014; Fischetti, interview; and Sumpter, interview. For more information about Walters's interest in a distinct entity, see H. Green, interview; James Hill, interview by author, October 27, 2015; L. Thompson, interview; and Josh Green, interview by author, November 14, 2015.

54. H. Green, interview.

55. L. Thompson, interview.

56. A+ Schools, *2015 Report to the Community*, 76–97. Proficiency refers to the percentage of students who scored proficient or advanced on 2015 Keystone exams; see Pennsylvania Department of Education, "2015 Keystone Exam School Level Data," [2015], Microsoft Excel document, accessed May 31, 2016, www.education.pa.gov/_layouts/download.aspxopen_in_new.

57. Harris, interview.

58. Obama Academy phased in lower grades as Schenley was phased out, and did not reach its full 6–12 grade configuration until the 2011–12 school year; see Joe Smydo, "Accredited IB School to Open at Reizenstein," *P-G*, August 4, 2009, B-8. Sharon Eberson, "Kelly Awards Announced for Area High School Musicals," *P-G*, May 26, 2013, A-11; Marylynne Pitz, "Teen Talent Hailed with Kelly Awards," *P-G*, May 25, 2014, A-13; "High-Schoolers Honored at Annual Gene Kelly Awards," *Pittsburgh Tribune-Review*, May 31, 2015, C3; Sharon Eberson, "Obama Academy Actress Captures Third Kelly Award," *P-G*, May 29, 2016, B-1; and Pete Vitti, e-mail to author, March 17, 2016.

59. Pete Vitti, e-mail to author, March 17, 2016; A+ Schools, *2015 Report to the Community*, 77, 83; and Pete Vitti, e-mail to author, April 18, 2016.

Conclusion

1. "Schenley & Peabody High Schools Graduate Last Classes," *CBS Pittsburgh*, June 13, 2011, accessed June 5, 2016, http://pittsburgh.cbslocal.com/2011/06/13/schenley-peabody-high-schools-graduate-last-classes/.

2. Nevenka Kurjakovic, interview by author, April 28, 2015.

3. Rule, "Modern Secondary School," 16–20; Gary Orfield et al., *Brown at 60: Great Progress, a Long Retreat and an Uncertain Future* (Los Angeles: Civil Rights Project/Proyecto Derechos Civiles, 2014), 39–49.

4. Obama, Perry, University Prep, and Westinghouse are all at least 73 percent black, with at least 68 percent of students categorized as "economically disadvantaged"; see A+ Schools, *2015 Report to the Community*, 76–97.

5. Diane Thompson, e-mail to author, May 1, 2016; Mitchell, interview; and D. Thompson, interview.

Appendix A

1. Andrew R. Dodge and Betty K. Koed, eds., *Biographical Directory of the United States Congress, 1774–2005: The Continental Congress, September 5, 1774, to October 21, 1788, and the Congress of the United States from the First Through the One Hundred Eighth Congresses, March 4, 1789, to January 3, 1989, Inclusive* (Washington, DC: US Congress, 2005), 608.

2. "Obituary News: Alexander Cooper, 81, Ex-Judge, GOP Chief," *P-G*, September 4, 1972, 46.

3. New York Times News Service, "The Man Who Broke Japan's Code," *St. Louis Post-Dispatch*, November 10, 1969, 3D.

4. "Lowell's Plan for One Game a Year Rapped," *Brooklyn Daily Eagle*, January 7, 1930, 2; "Frank Glick Will Coach Lehigh Football Eleven," *Wilmington (DE) Morning News*, August 23, 1921, 7; and "Tea Table Topics," *Evening News* (Harrisburg, PA), March 26, 1945, 4.

5. Richard N. Swett and Colleen M. Thornton, *Leadership By Design: Creating an Architecture of Trust* (Atlanta: Greenway Communications, 2005), 130.

6. "Former Commissioner Dr. McClelland Dies," *Press*, January 9, 1978, A-1, A-4.

7. "Pittsburgh Soldier Wins Many War Decorations," *Post*, June 15, 1919, sec. 2, 4.

8. Fleming, *History of Pittsburgh*, 4: 314.

9. "'First Lady of Pittsburgh' Dies," *Press*, October 22, 1952, 28.

10. "A. L. Schultz, District Manager of the American Bridge Company, Pittsburgh District." *The Successful American* 3–4 (January 1901–December 1901): 270.

11. "Sara Soffel, Jurist, Dies at 89," *Press*, October 7, 1976, 16; and "Obituary News: Sara

Soffel, 89, County Ex-Judge," *P-G*, October 7, 1976, 24.

12. "Some of the Leading Practicing Attorneys of the Greater City," *Post*, June 9, 1905; and "Impressive Rites Mark Passing of Atty. Stanton," *Courier*, March 26, 1932, sec. 1, 1, 4.

13. Eliza Smith Brown et al., *African American Historic Sites Survey of Allegheny County* (Harrisburg, PA: Pennsylvania Historical and Museum Commission, 1994), 134.

14. "Pulitzer Prizes in Journalism Announced," *Altoona (PA) Tribune*, May 16, 1923, 11; Hadley, "Central High," *Pittsburgh History*, 74–75; "All Schools to Open Soon," *Press*, 1; and Willa Cather, *Collected Stories* (New York: Vintage Books, 1992), 170.

15. Christopher J. Walsh, *Who's #1?: 100-Plus Years of Controversial National Champions in College Football* (Lanham, MD: Taylor Trade Publishing, 2007), 275; and "Charley Gelbert and the Kids," *Post*, October 19, 1899, 6.

16. "Thompson Sixth Ex-Pitt Gridder Tapped by Hall," *Daily Courier* (Connellsville, PA), May 6, 1971, 6; Alex Scassa Sr., "Col. Joe Thompson Entering Hall of Fame," *Beaver County (PA) Times*, February 3, 1970, B-3, B-4; and see appendix C.

Appendix B

1. Steve Levin, "Solomon Abrams: Educator at Hebrew Institute with Passionate Love of Learning," *P-G*, November 17, 2005, D-6.

2. Amaris Elliott-Engel, "Allen Promotes Mentoring to Diversify Bench," *Legal Intelligencer* (Philadelphia), February 29, 2008, accessed June 16, 2016, http://www .thelegalintelligencer.com/id=900005504618/ Allen-Promotes-Mentoring-to-Diversify-Bench.

3. Andrews admitted that some characters were inspired by actual people (interview), and many alumni believed that Mr. McCarthy, the charismatic, yet sensitive history teacher, was reminiscent of Schenley's Barak Naveh; see Jasmine Kurjakovic, interview by author, June 16, 2015. "For one month last summer, Schenley High School was once again a high school"; see Anya Sostek, "*Me & Earl* Premiers Today at Sundance Film Festival," *P-G*, January 25, 2015, E-1; and "*Me and Earl and the Dying Girl* Sweeps," *Great Falls (MT) Tribune*, February 2, 2015, C-3.

4. Lenore Brundage, "Baer Paintings Move Into High Fashion World," *Press*, February 19, 1961, sec. 4, 2.

5. "Balfour Appointed Member of State Recreation Board," *Press*, September 30, 1953, 9.

6. Fred A. Bernstein, "Derrick Bell, Pioneering Law Professor and Civil Rights Advocate, Dies at 80," *New York Times*,

October 7, 2011, A18; David Remnick, *The Bridge: The Life and Rise of Barack Obama* (New York: Alfred A. Knopf, 2010), 211–214; and *Journal*, 1948.

7. Scott Mervis, "Getting to the Root of Success," *P-G*, October 20, 1996, F-3.

8. "DeJuan Blair," *Basketball-Reference.com*, accessed June 2, 2016, http://www.bas ketball-reference.com/players/b/blairdeo1 .html.

9. "Braemer Appointed to New Bank Office Here," *Evening Standard* (Uniontown, PA), January 2, 1957, 1.

10. Marylynne Pitz, "Lawyer Byrd Brown Dies; Giant in Civil Rights Struggle," *P-G*, May 4, 2001, A-12; and Alvin Rosensweet, "Marland Critics Still Critical," *P-G*, June 7, 1968, 9.

11. Frank Rich, "Theater: New Works by Young Playwrights," *New York Times*, May 11, 1984, C3; and Jerry Vondas, "Young Playwright Joins KD's Kids' Drive," *Press*, April 3, 1986, D12.

12. Bob Greene (AP), "Larry Brown Feels MVP Means Recognition," *The Bee* (Danville, VA), January 8, 1973, 11-A.

13. Nate Guidry, "Ray Brown, Acclaimed Jazz Bassist from City, Dies," *P-G*, July 4, 2002, A-1, A-11; and Douglas Martin, "Ray Brown, Master Jazz Bassist, Dies at 75," *New York Times*, July 4, 2002, B6.

14. Dan Fitzpatrick, "Jack Buncher: Developer Who Built Real Estate Empire," *P-G*, December 5, 2001, B-6.

15. Scott Mervis, "Obituary: Nick Cenci / Launched Careers of Lou Christie and The Vogues," *P-G*, June 16, 2014, accessed June 2, 2016, http://www.post-gazette.com/news/ obituaries/2014/06/17/Nick-Cenci-Record -exec-broke-careers-of-Lou-Christie-and-The -Vogues/stories/201406170033.

16. "Horticulturist Frank Curto Dies at 72," *Press*, February 24, 1971, 71.

17. Paul Zeise, "Hardwood to Hollywood," *P-G*, April 13, 2009, C-1, C-2; and "Cynthia Dallas," *IMDb.com*, accessed June 2, 2016, http://www.imdb.com/name/ nm2728768/?ref_=fn_al_nm_1.

18. AP, "Marc Daniels, 77, Dies; Directed 'I Love Lucy,'" *New York Times*, April 29, 1989, 10.

19. David Devine, *Tucson: A History of the Old Pueblo from the 1854 Gadsden Purchase* (Jefferson, NC: McFarland, 2015), 124; and J. E. Alexander, "Ex-Pittsburgher Mayor of Tucson," *P-G*, January 25, 1963, 13.

20. Michael Beaven, "Walsh Jesuit Will Host Boy's All-Star Game," *Akron Beacon Journal*, March 21, 2012, C-4.

21. Lee C. Lawyer, Charles C. Bates, and Robert B. Rice, *Geophysics in the Affairs of Mankind: A Personalized History of Exploration*

Geophysics (Tulsa, OK: Society of Exploration Geophysicists, 2001), 278.

22. Johnna A. Pro, "Kenny Durrett: Basketball Star Who Went On to Coach in Wilkinsburg," *P-G*, January 8, 2001, B-4; and "Ken Durrett," *Basketball-Reference.com*, accessed June 2, 2016, http://www.basketball-reference.com/players/d/durreke01.html.

23. Falk attended Schenley briefly, ultimately graduating from Phillips Exeter; see Leon Falk Jr., interview by Minnie Sussman and Corinne Krause, June 14, 1974, National Council of Jewish Women (NCJW), Pittsburgh Section Papers, University of Pittsburgh. David Guo and Carmen J. Lee, "Philanthropist Leon Falk Jr. Dies," *P-G*, June 10, 1988, 20; and Mary Niederberger, "Pitt, Falk School Due to Discuss Dorm Plans," *Press*, December 5, 1989, B-1.

24. "Gainsford Pilots WVU Swimmers," *Press*, May 10, 1955, 31.

25. Nestor L. Osorio, "Getting, Ivan A. (1912–2003)," in *Home Front Heroes: A Biographical Dictionary of Americans During Wartime*, vol. 2, *G–N*, ed. Benjamin F. Shearer (Westport, CT: Greenwood Press, 2007), 337–39; Jacob Neufeld, ed., *Reflections on Research and Development in the United States Air Force: An Interview with General Bernard A. Schriever, and Generals Samuel C. Phillips, Robert T. Marsh, and James H. Doolittle, and Dr. Ivan A. Getting* (Washington, DC: Center for Air Force History, 1993), 14–15; and William G. Lytle Jr., "Schenley High Youth Wins in State Edison Contest," *Press*, June 25, 1929, 1.

26. Chuck Otterson, "Fifties (55s?) Back in Series," *Palm Beach (FL) Post*, May 6, 1990, 2C; "American Tennis Players and Swimmers Capture All Events," *Cincinnati Enquirer*, July 21, 1924, 10; and AP, "Paul Wyatt, Harry Glancy Named on Olympic Team," *P-G*, June 25, 1928, 14.

27. Stuart Lavietes, "Burt Glinn, 82, Chronicler of Cold War in Pictures," *New York Times*, April 12, 2008, A17.

28. Glenn Fowler, "Dr. William Hammon Dies at 85; A Pioneer in Fight Against Polio," *New York Times*, September 23, 1989, 6; and Charles R. Rinaldo Jr., "Passive Immunization Against Poliomyelitis: The Hammon Gamma Globulin Field Trials, 1951–1953," *American Journal of Public Health* 95, no. 5 (May 2005): 790–99.

29. Nate Guidry, "City Jazz Icon Walt Harper Dies," *P-G*, October 26, 2006, A-11.

30. Bruce D. Patterson, "A Celebration of Philip Hershkovitz, Emeritus Curator of Mammals," *Field Museum of Natural History Bulletin* 59, no. 1 (January 1988): 24–29.

31. Hines left Schenley in the early 1920s to join Lois Deppe and His Serenaders; see

Alyn Shipton, *A New History of Jazz* (London: Continuum, 2001), 183. Jon Pareles, "Earl Hines, 77, Father of Modern Jazz Piano, Dies," *New York Times*, April 24, 1983, 32; and Robert Palmer, "Fatha Hines Stomping and Chomping On at 75," *New York Times*, August 28, 1981, C5.

32. "Judge Kaufman Dies At 53," *Press*, March 10, 1958, 1.

33. *Maryland Football 1996: Getting the Word Out* (College Park, MD: University of Maryland, 1996): 35.

34. Ray Fittipaldo, "Maurice Lucas: 'Enforcer' a Presence on Court," *P-G*, November 2, 2010, A-1, A-5; and Bill Brenner, "The Best of the ABA Bunch," *Indianapolis Star*, July 18, 1997, C-1.

35. Lauren Heinz, "John McSorley Jr.: Land Developer Remembered as Loving Father, Fine Athlete," *P-G*, May 17, 1996, A-18; and "Extra Referee for Hockey Tilt," *P-G*, March 22, 1935, 20.

36. AP, "Ex-Duquesne Basketball Coach Donald 'Dudey' Moore Dies at 74," *Press*, April 10, 1984, B6.

37. "Joe Moore: Heralded as 'Football's Greatest Line Coach,'" *P-G*, July 5, 2003, A-10.

38. Christopher McCarrick and Tim Ziaukas, "Still Scary After All These Years: Mr. Yuk Nears 40," *Western Pennsylvania History* 92, no. 3 (Fall 2009): 21–28.

39. Harry Tkach, "Robert Mosley: Opera Singer Who Grew Up in Oakland," *P-G*, May 6, 2002, B-7.

40. Ivan Oransky, "Obituary: Charles Frederick Mosteller," *The Lancet* 368, no. 9541 (September 26, 2006): 1062.

41. "Senator Honored by Colleagues," *Press*, March 15, 1972, 10; "Stan Noszka NBL Stats," *Basketball-Reference.com*, accessed June 3, 2016, http://www.basketball-reference.com/nbl/players/n/noszksto1n.html; and "Stan Noszka," *Basketball-Reference.com*, accessed June 3, 2016, http://www.basketball-reference.com/players/n/noszksto1.html.

42. "Bill Nunn," *IMDb.com*, accessed June 3, 2016, http://www.imdb.com/name/nm0638056/?ref_=fn_al_nm_1; *Journal* (1970): 32; and Tony Norman, "Character Roles Suit 'Henry's' Bill Nunn," *P-G*, July 12, 1991, 23.

43. Bill Heltzel, "Joseph M. O'Toole: Ex-Pirates Official Who Made His Mark Behind the Scenes," *P-G*, April 12, 1997, B-3; and "The Men Who've Called the Shots," *P-G*, April 5, 2015, E-5.

44. Dave Matter, "Notebook: Wilson Returns for MU," *St. Louis Post-Dispatch*, September 22, 2013, C9.

45. Cecil F. Poole, "Civil Rights, Law, and the Federal Courts: The Life of Cecil Poole, 1914–1997," oral history by Carole Hicke, 1993,

Regional Oral History Office, The Bancroft Library, University of California, Berkeley, vi–vii, 13–14.

46. Phil Jackman (*Baltimore Sun*), "King, Axthelm Miscast," *News Journal* (Wilmington, DE), April 13, 1986, F6C; Ron Cook, "Cooperstown: Prince Had 'Em All the Way," *Press*, August 4, 1986, C-1, C-3; Win Fanning, "On the Air: A Long Chat with Bob Prince," *P-G*, July 26, 1972, 33; Thelma Lovette Morris, e-mail to author, February 1, 2015; Jim O'Brien, *We Had 'Em All the Way: Bob Prince and His Pittsburgh Pirates* (Pittsburgh: James P. O'Brien Publishing, 1998), 102; Earl Kohnfelder, "Prince Lauded as Broadcaster, Human Being," *Press*, June 11, 1985, A-1, A-6; and AP, "Penguins Hire Bob Prince," *Kane (PA) Republican*, August 20, 1976, 5.

47. Chuck Otterson, "Former Tropics Coach Rakow Dies at 65," *Palm Beach (FL) Post*, August 28, 2000, 5C.

48. "Vivian Reed," *Internet Broadway Database*, accessed June 3, 2016, https://www.ibdb.com/Person/View/57369; Christopher Rawson, "Stage Preview: Diva Defines 'Bubbling Brown Sugar,'" *P-G*, January 27, 2005, B-1, B-5; "Student Gallery: Vivian Reed," *Triangle*, April 1962; "Vivian Reed (II)," *IMDb.com*, accessed June 3, 2016, http://www.imdb.com/name/nm0715744/?ref_=fn_al_nm_1; and "Vivian Reed Is Finally Getting that Big Break," *Courier*, November 16, 1968, 13.

49. Lori Shontz, "Still a Lofty Spirit," *P-G*, February 11, 2001, A-1, A-19; and Patricia Lowry, "Dahlen K. Ritchey: Architect Who Designed Civic Arena, Mellon Square," *P-G*, January 15, 2002, A-13.

50. Andrew McGill, "Robinson Unleashes a Barrage of Bills in County Council," *P-G*, November 6, 2013, A-7.

51. Melissa Fay Greene, *The Temple Bombing* (Boston: Addison-Wesley, 1996), 7–8, 380–83, 415–23.

52. "Bruno Gets Hall Call," *P-G*, February 5, 2013, D-6; Ed Blank, "TV's Wrestling Stars Get a Stranglehold on Movie and Ad Roles," *Press*, March 23, 1988, D6; Sammartino, Michelucci, and McCollough, *Bruno Sammartino*, 18–23; and Nicklos, interview. Joni Perri remembers seeing Sammartino force a smaller boy to shine his shoes; see Joni Perri, e-mail to author, March 30, 2014.

53. Wendeline O. Wright, "Life Lessons," *P-G*, February 1, 2015, D-5.

54. Sharon Voas, "Clifford Shull, Physics Pioneer," *P-G*, December 5, 1994, A-9; and *Journal*, February 1933, 35.

55. UP, "Gear Shift, Endurance Boost Sowell," *Pampa (TX) Daily News*, February 22, 1956, 7; and Jim O'Brien, "Courtney, Sowell Had Chariots, Too," *Press*, April 22, 1982, C-2.

56. Phil Axelrod, "Ted Stepien: Controversial Owner of Cleveland Cavaliers," *P-G*, September 12, 2007, A-11; Larry Pantages, "Stepien: Racial Remarks Were Taken Out of Context," *Akron Beacon Journal*, March 17, 1981, D4; and Fred P. Alger, "Stepien Leads City High School Scorers with 179 Points," *P-G*, March 16, 1943, 16.

57. Patricia Sabatini, "Benjamin Tatar: Actor Was Jackie Gleason's Aide, Lived with Ava Gardner," *P-G*, December 2, 2012, D-5; and "Ben Tatar," *IMDb.com*, accessed June 4, 2016, http://www.imdb.com/name/nm0851063/?ref_=fn_al_nm_1.

58. Martha Jo Black and Chuck Schoffner, *Joe Black: More Than a Dodger* (Chicago: Academy Chicago Publishers, 2015), 189–190; Canadian Press, "Hall of Fame," *Brandon (Manitoba, Canada) Sun*, August 30, 1975, 8; and Bernard E. Garnett, "Management Refutes Black Athletes' Claims of Professional Segregation," *Sedalia (MO) Democrat*, August 14, 1970, 9.

59. "Obituaries: Oliver Edmonds Turner M.D.," *P-G*, May 20, 2005, E-7; "Turner Elected by Health Group," *Evening News* (Harrisburg, PA), November 1, 1947, 1; Dolores Frederick, "New Test Developed Here for Diabetes," *Press*, September 19, 1976, B-9; UP, "Duff Enters Hospital for Treatment, Rest," *Shamokin (PA) News-Dispatch*, May 11, 1949, 11; and Chet Wade, "Gelet Was Rooney's Friend, Confidant as Well as His Physician," *P-G*, August 26, 1988, 19.

60. In 1950, Turrentine left Schenley to play music full-time; see Martin Weil, "Jazzman Stanley Turrentine Dies at 66," *Washington Post*, September 13, 2000, accessed June 4, 2016, https://www.washingtonpost.com/archive/local/2000/09/13/jazzman-stanley-turrentine-dies-at-66/f9d30be5-0a63-4bb6-9a45-d36cfca1811d/; and George Benson and Alan Goldsher, *Benson: The Autobiography* (Boston: Da Capo Press, 2014), 54, 4.

61. Bockris, *Warhol*, 151–57, 53–54; Shaffer, interview; and Kavaler, interview.

62. Win Fanning, "On the Air: War End Special Set Tuesday," *P-G*, January 25, 1973, 29.

63. AP, "Judge Swears in Son to Post on Bench," *Beaver County (PA) Times*, July 11, 1993, A8.

64. *Colgate Football Media Guide* (Hamilton, NY: Colgate University, 2008), 113. For more information about Kerr's tenure at Central, see Florent Gibson, "Peabody Draws with Central in Scholastic Title Battle," *Post*, November 23, 1913, Sporting 1; "Pittsburgh High Wins School Championship," *Post*, March 20, 1909, 9; and "Andy Kerr's Athletes Win Princeton Meet," *GT*, June 4, 1911, sec. 3,

4. "Who's Who in Sports: Coach 'Andy' Kerr," *Palo Alto Daily* (Stanford University), June 5, 1924, 2; George Moorhead, "Mr. Kerr's Team," *Triangle*, March 31, 1922; *Pitt Football Media Guide* (Pittsburgh: University of Pittsburgh, 2015), 138; AP, "Glenn Warner Takes Job at Stanford," *GT*, February 2, 1922, 9; and John Kekis (AP), "Colgate Powerhouse of '32 Wasn't Asked to the Party," *Galveston (TX) Daily News*, December 13, 1987, 4-C.

Appendixes C–E

These appendixes draw from sources too numerous to cite with specificity, but include the *Journal*, the *Triangle*, as well as dozens of newspapers, books, and alumni interviews. The Dr. Roger B. Saylor Football Records Collection at Penn State University Libraries was particularly helpful in chronicling Schenley's football history in appendix C. Further, William D. McCoy's *History of Pittsburgh Public Schools to 1942*, vol. 1 (Pittsburgh. 1959) and historical G. M. Hopkins maps at http://peoplemaps .esri.com/pittsburgh/ were integral to appendix E.

Selected Bibliography

Newspapers and Yearbooks

Advocate-Messenger (Danville, KY)
Akron Beacon Journal
Altoona (PA) Tribune
Asbury Park (NJ) Press
Beaver County (PA) Times
The Bee (Danville, VA)
The Blade (Toledo, OH)
Brandon (Manitoba, Canada) Sun
Brooklyn Daily Eagle
Cincinnati Enquirer
Cleveland Gazette
Cumberland (MD) News
Daily Courier (Connellsville, PA)
Daily Democrat (Huntington, IN)
Daily Mail (London)
Daily Notes (Canonsburg, PA)
Daily Pittsburgh Gazette
Daily Post (Pittsburgh)
Daily Republican (Monongahela, PA)
The Derrick (Oil City, PA)
Duquesne Duke (Duquesne University)
The Eagle (Obama Academy)
Education Week
Evening News (Harrisburg, PA)
Evening Standard (Uniontown, PA)
Galveston (TX) Daily News
Gazette Times (Pittsburgh)
Great Falls (MT) Tribune
Harrisburg (PA) Telegraph
High School Journal (Pittsburgh Central
    High School)
Indiana (PA) Gazette
Indianapolis Star
In Pittsburgh
Jewish Chronicle (Pittsburgh)
Jewish Criterion (Pittsburgh)
The Journal (Schenley High School)
Journal-News (Rockland County, NY)
Kane (PA) Republican
Legal Intelligencer (Philadelphia)
Los Angeles Times
Milwaukee Journal Sentinel
Morning News (Wilmington, DE)
New Castle (PA) News

New Pittsburgh Courier News-Herald
    (Franklin, PA)
New York Times
North Hills (PA) News Record
Palm Beach (FL) Post
Palo Alto Daily (Stanford University)
Pampa (TX) Daily News
The Pantagraph (Bloomington, IL)
Pittsburgh City Paper
Pittsburgh Commercial
Pittsburgh Commercial Gazette
Pittsburgh Courier
Pittsburgh Daily Post
Pittsburgh Gazette
Pittsburgh Gazette Times
Pittsburgh Post
Pittsburgh Post-Gazette
Pittsburgh Post-Gazette and Sun-Telegraph
Pittsburgh Press
Pittsburgh Sun
Pittsburgh Tribune-Review
Post-Crescent (Appleton, WI)
Reading (PA) Times
The Record-Argus (Greenville, PA)
The Schenleyan (Schenley Standard Evening
    High School)
Sedalia (MO) Democrat
Shamokin (PA) News-Dispatch
St. Louis Post-Dispatch
The Triangle (Schenley High School)
Washington (DC) Herald
Washington Post
Wilmington (DE) Morning News

Other Sources

Alberts, Robert C. Pitt: The Story of the
    University of Pittsburgh, 1787–1987.
    Pittsburgh: University of Pittsburgh
    Press, 1986.
"A. L. Schultz, District Manager of the
    American Bridge Company,
    Pittsburgh District." The Successful
    American 3–4 (January 1901–
    December 1901): 270–71.

Altenbaugh, Richard J. *The American People and Their Education: A Social History.* Upper Saddle River, NJ: Merrill/Prentice Hall, 2003.

Alumni Association of the Pittsburgh High School. *Alumni Register: Pittsburgh High School.* Crafton, PA: Cramer Printing & Publishing, 1905.

The American Architect 111, no. 2146 (February 7, 1917).

Baldwin, Leland D. *Pittsburgh: The Story of a City, 1950–1865.* Pittsburgh: University of Pittsburgh Press, 1937.

Bauman, John F., and Edward K. Muller. *Before Renaissance: Planning in Pittsburgh, 1889–1943.* Pittsburgh: University of Pittsburgh Press, 2006.

Benson, George, and Alan Goldsher. *Benson: The Autobiography.* Boston: Da Capo Press, 2014.

Bernstein, Steven. "Pittsburgh's Benevolent Tyrant: Christopher Lyman Magee." *Western Pennsylvania History* 86, no. 2 (Summer 2003): 34–40.

Bigham, John. *Class Book: The Class of 1880, Pittsburgh Central High School, Academical Department.* Pittsburgh, 1905.

Black, Martha Jo, and Chuck Schoffner. *Joe Black: More than a Dodger.* Chicago: Academy Chicago Publishers, 2015.

Bockris, Victor. *Warhol: The Biography.* New York: Da Capo Press, 2003.

Bodnar, John E., Roger Simon, and Michael P. Weber. *Lives of Their Own: Blacks, Italians, and Poles in Pittsburgh, 1900–1960.* Urbana: University of Illinois Press, 1982.

Brown, Eliza Smith, Daniel Holland, Laurence A. Glasco, Ronald C. Carlisle, Arthur B. Fox, and Diane C. DeNardo. *African American Historic Sites Survey of Allegheny County.* Harrisburg, PA: Pennsylvania Historical and Museum Commission, 1994.

Buni, Andrew. *Robert L. Vann of the "Pittsburgh Courier": Politics and Black Journalism.* Pittsburgh: University of Pittsburgh Press, 1974.

Bush, Perry. "A Neighborhood, a Hollow, and the Bloomfield Bridge: The Relationship Between Community and Infrastructure." *Pittsburgh History* 74, no. 4 (Winter 1991): 160–72.

Caley, Percy B. "Historical, Social and Economic Background of Schenley High School." In *Schenley High School: Prepared for an Evaluation by the Commission on Secondary Schools March 13–16, 1950.* Pittsburgh: Schenley High School, 1950.

Cather, Willa. *Collected Stories.* New York: Vintage Books, 1992.

Chideya, Farai. "Surely for the Spirit, but also for the Mind." *Newsweek,* December 2, 1991.

Colcord, D. H. "Electrical Equipment in a Pittsburgh High School." *The American City* 20 (January–June 1919): 579–85.

———. "Electric Motor Drive in the Schenley High School in Pittsburgh." *Electrical Review* 74 (January 4, 1919–June 28, 1919): 331–35.

DeMarco, Marcella. "Magnet Programs in the Pittsburgh Schools: Development to Implementation, 1977 through 1982." PhD diss., University of Pittsburgh, 1983.

DeVault, Ileen A. *Sons and Daughters of Labor: Class and Clerical Work in Turn-of-the-Century Pittsburgh.* Ithaca, NY: Cornell University Press, 1990.

Devine, David. *Tucson: A History of the Old Pueblo from the 1854 Gadsden Purchase.* Jefferson, NC: McFarland, 2015.

Dodge, Andrew R., and Betty K. Koed, eds. *Biographical Directory of the United States Congress, 1774–2005: The Continental Congress, September 5, 1774, to October 21, 1788, and the Congress of the United States from the First Through the One Hundred Eighth Congresses, March 4, 1789, to January 3, 1989, Inclusive.* Washington, DC: US Congress, 2005.

Donahue, Bill. "Back in the Ol' Hippie Hothouse." *New York Times Magazine*, September 18, 2011.

Donovan, John J. *School Architecture: Principles and Practices*. New York: Macmillan, 1921.

Dougherty, Jack. "Northern Desegregation and the Racial Politics of Magnet Schools in Milwaukee, Wisconsin." In *With All Deliberate Speed: Implementing "Brown v. Board of Education,"* edited by Brian J. Daugherity and Charles C. Bolton, 217–30. Fayetteville: University of Arkansas Press, 2008.

"Economy in Stone Construction." *Stone* 42 (January–December 1921): 251–52.

Enter to Learn, Go Forth to Serve: The Story of Schenley High School (1916–2011). City of Pittsburgh Housing Authority, Creative Arts Corner. 2013. Film.

Feldman, Jacob. *The Jewish Experience in Western Pennsylvania: A History, 1755–1945*. Pittsburgh: Historical Society of Western Pennsylvania, 1986.

Fleming, George Thornton. *History of Pittsburgh and Environs*. Vol. 2. New York: American Historical Society, 1922.

———. *History of Pittsburgh and Environs*. Vol. 4. New York: American Historical Society, 1922.

———. *My High School Days: Including a Brief History of the Pittsburgh Central High School from 1855 to 1871 and Addenda*. Pittsburgh: Press of Wm. G. Johnston, 1904.

Frommer, Myrna Katz, and Harvey Frommer. *Growing Up Jewish in America: An Oral History*. Lincoln: University of Nebraska Press, 1995.

Gerwig, George W. "Fifty Years in Pittsburgh Schools." *Western Pennsylvania Historical Magazine* 25, no. 3–4 (September–December 1942): 149–55.

Glasco, Laurence. "Double Burden: The Black Experience in Pittsburgh." In *African Americans in Pennsylvania: Shifting Perspectives*, edited by Joe William Trotter Jr. and Eric Ledell Smith, 405–42. University Park and Harrisburg: Pennsylvania State University Press and Pennsylvania Historical Museum Commission, 1997.

Goldin, Claudia. "America's Graduation from High School: The Evolution and Spread of Secondary Schooling in the Twentieth Century." *Journal of Economic History* 58, no. 2 (June 1998): 345–74.

Goldman, M. R. "Hill District of Pittsburgh, as I Knew It." *Western Pennsylvania Historical Magazine* 51, no. 3 (July 1968): 279–95.

Greene, Melissa Fay. *The Temple Bombing*. Boston: Addison-Wesley, 1996.

Hadley, S. Trevor. "Central High School: Pittsburgh's First." *Pittsburgh History* 73, no. 2 (Summer 1990): 70–76.

Hamilton, Heppie Wilkins. *The Old Central High School (P.C.H.S.): Reminiscences of the Class of 1859 with an Introduction and Addenda*. Pittsburgh: Dean Pupils Association, 1915.

Harper, Colter. "'The Crossroads of the World': A Social and Cultural History of Jazz in Pittsburgh's Hill District, 1920–1970." PhD diss., University of Pittsburgh, 2011.

Herrnstein, Richard J., and Charles Murray. *The Bell Curve: Intelligence and Class Structure in American Life*. New York: Free Press, 1994.

Hill, Ralph Lemuel. "A View of the Hill: A Study of Experiences and Attitudes in the Hill District of Pittsburgh, Pennsylvania from 1900 to 1973." PhD diss., University of Pittsburgh, 1973.

Hoppe, Arthur. "Curriculum Developments." *Education Leadership* 18, no. 6 (March 1961): 391–99.

Howard, Clara E. "Organizing a New High School Library." *Bulletin of the American Library Association* 11 (January–November 1917): 176–79.

Hylton, J. Gordon. "Before the Redskins Were the Redskins: The Use of Native American Team Names in the

Formative Era of American Sports, 1857–1933." *North Dakota Law Review* 86, no. 4 (2010): 879–903.

Kantrowitz, Barbara, and Pat Wingert. "The Best Schools in the World." *Newsweek*, December 2, 1991.

Keebler, Alina Laó, *The History and Architecture of the Henry Clay Frick School*. Pittsburgh: Frick ISA, 1996.

Killikelly, Sarah Hutchins. *The History of Pittsburgh: Its Rise and Progress*. Pittsburgh: B. C. & Gordon Montgomery, 1906.

Kirby, Mary Ellen. Schenley magnet recruitment data table. [March 28, 1984.]

Kyle, Ken, and Stephen Thompson. "The Roles of Morality Development and Personal Power in Mass School Shootings." In *School Violence and Primary Prevention*, edited by Thomas W. Miller, 94–123. New York: Springer, 2008.

Lawyer, Lee C., Charles C. Bates, and Robert B. Rice. *Geophysics in the Affairs of Mankind: A Personalized History of Exploration Geophysics*. Tulsa, OK: Society of Exploration Geophysicists, 2001.

Linfield, H. S. "Statistics of Jews." *American Jewish Yearbook* 29 (1927–28): 227–81.

Lonich, David W. "Metropolitanism and the Genesis of Municipal Anxiety in Allegheny County." *Pittsburgh History* 76, no. 2 (Summer 1993): 79–88.

McCarrick, Christopher, and Tim Ziaukas. "Still Scary After All These Years: Mr. Yuk Nears 40." *Western Pennsylvania History* 92, no. 3 (Fall 2009): 18–31.

McCoy, William D. *The Establishment and Development of the Pittsburgh Central High School: Prepared in Commemoration of the One Hundredth Anniversary of the First Graduating Class 1859–1959*. Pittsburgh: Pittsburgh Public Schools, 1959. Pittsburgh Public Schools Records, Detre Library & Archives, Heinz History Center.

———. *History of Pittsburgh Public Schools to 1942*. Vol. 1. Pittsburgh, 1959.

———. *History of Pittsburgh Public Schools to 1942*. Vols. 5–6. Pittsburgh, 1959.

Moron, Alonzo G. "Distribution of the Negro Population in Pittsburgh, 1910–1930." MA thesis, University of Pittsburgh, 1933.

Neufeld, Jacob, ed. *Reflections on Research and Development in the United States Air Force: An Interview with General Bernard A. Schriever, and Generals Samuel C. Phillips, Robert T. Marsh, and James H. Doolittle, and Dr. Ivan A. Getting*. Washington, DC: Center for Air Force History, 1993.

North, Lila Ver Planck. "Pittsburgh Schools." In *The Pittsburgh District: Civic Frontage*, edited by Paul Underwood Kellogg, 217–305. New York: Russell Sage Foundation Publications, 1914.

O'Brien, Jim. *We Had 'Em All the Way: Bob Prince and His Pittsburgh Pirates*. Pittsburgh: James P. O'Brien Publishing, 1998.

Oransky, Ivan. "Obituary: Charles Frederick Mosteller." *The Lancet* 368, no. 9541 (September 26, 2006): 1062.

Oresick, Jake. "What's in a Namesake?: Mary Schenley." *Western Pennsylvania History* 98, no. 3 (Fall 2015): 22–35.

Osorio, Nestor L. "Getting, Ivan A. (1912–2003)." In *Home Front Heroes: A Biographical Dictionary of Americans During Wartime*, vol. 2, G–N, edited by Benjamin F. Shearer, 337–39. Westport, CT: Greenwood Press, 2007.

Ossian, Lisa L. *The Forgotten Generation: American Children and World War II*. Columbia: University of Missouri Press, 2011.

Parnes, Herbert S. *A Prof's Life: It's More than Teaching*. Lincoln, NE: iUniverse, 2001.

Patterson, Bruce D. "A Celebration of Philip Hershkovitz, Emeritus Curator of Mammals." *Field Museum of Natural History Bulletin* 59, no. 1 (January 1988): 24–29.

Peterson, Alexander Duncan Campbell. *Schools Across Frontiers: The Story of* the International Baccalaureate and the United World Colleges. Peru, IL: Open Court, 2003.

Pine, Kurt. "The Jews in the Hill District of Pittsburgh, 1910–1940: A Study of Trends." MA thesis, University of Pittsburgh, 1943.

Price, Edward J. Jr. "School Segregation in Nineteenth-Century Pennsylvania." Pennsylvania History 43, no. 2 (April 1976): 121–37.

Proctor, Ralph Jr. "Racial Discrimination Against Black Teachers and Black Professionals in the Pittsburgh Public School System, 1834–1973." PhD diss., University of Pittsburgh, 1979.

———. Voices from the Firing Line: A Personal Account of the Pittsburgh Civil Rights Movement. Pittsburgh: Introspec Press, 2013.

"Proposed Academic and Schenley District High School Building." The Builder 28, no. 11 (March 1911): 16–38.

"Recent School Buildings in Pittsburgh, Pa." American School Board Journal 53, no. 6 (December 1916): 32–40.

Remnick, David. The Bridge: The Life and Rise of Barack Obama. New York: Alfred A. Knopf, 2010.

Ribowsky, Mark. The Power and the Darkness: The Life of Josh Gibson in the Shadows of the Game. New York: Simon & Schuster, 1996.

Rinaldo, Charles R. Jr. "Passive Immunization Against Poliomyelitis: The Hammon Gamma Globulin Field Trials, 1951–1953." American Journal of Public Health 95, no. 5 (May 2005): 790–99.

Rule, James N. "The Place of the Modern Secondary School in a Democracy." In Third Yearbook of the National Association of Secondary Principals, 14–23. Pittsburgh, 1920.

Rutherford, William Dodge. "The 'Unraveling': Resistance to Desegregation in the Pittsburgh Public Schools, 1971–1998." BA thesis, Tufts University, 2014.

Sammartino, Bruno, Bob Michelucci, and Paul McCollough. Bruno Sammartino: An Autobiography of Wrestling's Living Legend. Pittsburgh: Imagine, 1990.

Sauvain, Edward. Report on a Questionnaire Submitted to the Principal of the Pittsburgh Public School by the Survey Commission, Schenley High School. Pittsburgh: Schenley High School, 1927. William R. Oliver Special Collections Room, Carnegie Library of Pittsburgh.

Schenley High School. The History of Schenley High School. Pittsburgh: Schenley High School, [1963]. William R. Oliver Special Collections Room, Carnegie Library of Pittsburgh.

Sewald, Jeff. "What Do I Know?: Sala Udin." Pittsburgh Quarterly, Fall 2013.

Shipton, Alyn. A New History of Jazz. London: Continuum, 2001.

Shoemaker, Bo. A History of Camp Cory. Charleston, SC: History Press, 2011.

Shull, Clifford G. "Biography of Clifford G. Shull." In Nobel Lectures in Physics, 1991–1995, ed. Gosta Ekspong, 141–45. Singapore: World Scientific, 1997.

Smith, Scott, and Steven Manaker. "Pittsburgh's African-American Neighborhoods, 1900–1920." Pittsburgh History 78, no. 4 (Winter 1995–96): 158–62.

Steiner, Lilian McKibbin. "'Sugar Top' and the 'Cobblestone Jungle': Urban Redevelopment in Pittsburgh's Hill District, 1955–1959." Thesis, Haverford College, 2010.

Stern, Malcolm H. "Early Jews of Fall River, Massachusetts." Rhode Island Jewish Historical Notes 5, no. 2 (November 1968): 145–46.

Swett, Richard N., and Colleen M. Thornton. Leadership By Design: Creating an Architecture of Trust. Atlanta: Greenway Communications, 2005.

Tager, Jack. Boston Riots: Three Centuries of Violence. Boston: Northeastern University Press, 2001.

Tiech, John. *Pittsburgh Film History: On Set in the Steel City*. Charleston, SC: The History Press, 2010.

Trotter, Joe W., and Jared N. Day. *Race and Renaissance: African Americans in Pittsburgh Since World War II*. Pittsburgh: University of Pittsburgh Press, 2010.

US Bureau of the Census. *Fourteenth Census of the United States 1920*. Vol. 1, *Population, Number and Distribution of Inhabitants*. Washington, DC: Government Printing Office, 1921.

US National Education Association, Commission on the Reorganization of Secondary Education. "Cardinal Principles of Secondary Education." *US Bureau of Education Bulletin*, no. 35 (1918): 7–32.

Van Trump, James D. "The Church of the Ascension, Pittsburgh: A Brief Chronicle of Its Seventy-Five Years." *Western Pennsylvania Historical Magazine* 48, no. 1 (January 1965): 1–18.

Walsh, Christopher J. *Who's #1?: 100-Plus Years of Controversial National Champions in College Football*. Lanham, MD: Taylor Trade Publishing, 2007.

Webb, Lauran B. *Murder in Schenley Heights: The Day the Sugar Rolled Off of Sugar Top*. [Pittsburgh]: Lauran Webb Breakthrough Ministries, 2012.

Weber, Michael P. *Don't Call Me Boss: David L. Lawrence, Pittsburgh's Renaissance Mayor*. Pittsburgh: University of Pittsburgh Press, 1988.

Wecht, Cyril H., Mark Curriden, and Angela Powell. *Tales from the Morgue*. Amherst, NY: Prometheus Books, 2005.

Windsor, P. L. "University of Illinois Library School." *Library Journal* 44 (January–December 1919): 410.

Index

Typeset by
REGINA STARACE

Printed and bound by
THOMSON-SHORE

Composed in
CHARTER AND SCALA SANS

Printed on
NATURES BOOK